# Joshua·Ezra
# Nehemiah·Esther

# Joshua · Ezra
# Nehemiah · Esther

## H.A. IRONSIDE

LOIZEAUX BROTHERS
*Neptune, New Jersey*

FIRST EDITION, JOSHUA 1950
FIRST EDITION, EZRA 1913
FIRST EDITION, NEHEMIAH 1914
FIRST EDITION, ESTHER 1905

COMBINED EDITION, 1983

ISBN 0-87213-396-6

PRINTED IN THE UNITED STATES OF AMERICA

10 9 8 7 6 5 4

# CONTENTS

## *JOSHUA*

# CONTENTS

## *EZRA*

# CONTENTS

## *NEHEMIAH*

# CONTENTS

## *ESTHER*

# Joshua

# The Divinely Appointed Leader

Now after the death of Moses the servant of the Lord it came to pass, that the Lord spake unto Joshua the son of Nun, Moses' minister, saying, Moses My servant is dead; now therefore arise, go over this Jordan, thou, and all this people, unto the land which I do give to them, even to the children of Israel. Every place that the sole of your foot shall tread upon, that have I given unto you, as I said unto Moses. From the wilderness and this Lebanon even unto the great river, the river Euphrates, all the land of the Hittites, and unto the great sea toward the going down of the sun, shall be your coast. There shall not any man be able to stand before thee all the days of thy life: as I was with Moses, so I will be with thee: I will not fail thee, nor forsake thee. Be strong and of a good courage: for unto this people shalt thou divide for an inheritance the land, which I sware unto their fathers to give them. Only be thou strong and very courageous, that thou mayest observe to do according to all the law, which Moses my servant commanded thee: turn not from it to the right hand or to the left, that thou mayest prosper whithersoever thou goest. This book of the law shall not depart out of thy mouth; but thou shalt meditate therein day and night, that thou mayest observe to do according to all that is written therein: for then thou shalt make thy way prosperous, and then thou shalt have good success. Have not I commanded thee? Be strong and of a good courage; be not afraid, neither be thou dismayed: for the Lord thy God is with thee whithersoever thou goest. Joshua 1:1-9.

THE book of Joshua is distinctly the book of the inheritance and links very intimately with the Epistle to the Ephesians in the New Testament. We have the manifestation of divine life in the book of Genesis; redemption in the book of Exodus; then the entrance into the holiest and the believer's sanctification typically set forth in Leviticus; the people of God under trial and testing in Numbers; and the government of God in Deuteronomy. Then we naturally move right on to the book of Joshua, in which we have the people of the Lord entering upon their inheritance.

In 1 Corinthians 10:11 we read that these things happened unto them for our types. So we are warranted to think of the land of Canaan as a type of the present blessings that are ours in Christ and to see in the wars of Israel a picture of the Christian's conflict. Israel's inheritance was of an earthly character. We might say they were blessed with all temporal blessings in earthly places in the land of Canaan. We, according to the Epistle to the Ephesians, are blessed with all spiritual blessings in heavenly places in Christ.

As we open this book we are introduced to the divinely appointed leader who is to guide the people into their inheritance. It is very significant that the name "Joshua" is the same as the name that our blessed Lord bore here on earth. *Jesus* is the anglicized Greek form of *Joshua.* The word *Joshua* means "Jehovah the Saviour," and we may see in this Joshua of the Old Testament, a type of the Jesus of the New Testament. Moses, the lawgiver, led the people to the very border of the land but was not permitted to lead them into it. Joshua took up where Moses left off. The Apostle Paul tells us that the law was Israel's child leader till Christ, but when Christ came they were no longer under the child leader. So we have in type the dispensation of the law passing away and the new dispensation of grace beginning. Of course, the people were actually under the law during all the days of Joshua and the Old Testament, and during the time of our Lord's earthly ministry. It was not until the Lord's Resurrection that believers were delivered from the law. Joshua typifies the risen One leading us on into the privileges of the new creation.

We read first of the death of Moses. "Now after the death of Moses the servant of the Lord it came to pass, that the Lord spake unto Joshua the son of Nun, Moses' minister." This was when Israel was encamped east of the Jordan in the land of Moab. The Jordan was the eastern border of that part of the land separating Palestine from Moab. At God's command

Moses went up to the top of Mount Nebo and viewed
the land and there died. The Lord Himself, we are
told, buried him and no one knows where his sepul-
cher is to this day. Moses was so anxious to go into
the land. He pleaded with the Lord to permit it, but
he had failed at the water of Meribah, and God told
him he could not enter Canaan. Moses prayed earnestly to be allowed to go in. Finally, God said,
"Speak to Me no more about this matter." But He
told him he could view the land from the top of Mount
Nebo. Moses got into the land eventually when on the
Mount of Transfiguration he and Elijah appeared
with the Lord Jesus, and they were speaking of those
things which should shortly be accomplished at Jerusalem—the work of the Cross which our Saviour was
just about to consummate.

When Moses died God put Joshua in his place. He
was to lead the people into their inheritance. The
Lord had promised the land to them long before; He
gave it to them by title. Now He says very definitely,
"Moses My servant is dead; now therefore arise, go
over this Jordan, thou, and all this people, unto the
land which I do give to them, even to the children of
Israel. Every place that the sole of your foot shall tread
upon, that have I given unto you, as I said unto
Moses."

It is one thing to have title to an inheritance,
but it is quite another thing to make it one's own
practically. We who are saved are blessed with all
spiritual blessings in heavenly places in Christ, but

how much of our inheritance have we actually appropriated? How much do you really enjoy of that which is yours in Christ? Many of us live in doubt, trouble, and perplexity most of the time. We fail to enter into and enjoy that which God has given us in His Son.

I have often likened this to a library. People sometimes come into my little study and look about. I have a few books which I have accumulated in the course of fifty years, perhaps some three thousand or more, and some people who are not used to doing much reading think that I have quite a collection. There are not nearly as many as there would be if a lot of my friends would return borrowed books. Sir Walter Scott once called those people, "Good bookkeepers."

But some folks look around and ask, "Do all these books belong to you?"

I say, "Yes; they are all mine." And I wish some other people could say the same thing about all the books they have!

The next question they ask is, "Have you read them all?"

I reply that I have read all that are worth reading. Sometimes I just get started and find that the book is worthless, so I do not finish it.

Well, the next question will be, "Do you know all that is in them?"

And I have to say, "No; I certainly do not. This little head of mine is much too small to contain all that is in these books."

Now our possessions in Christ are like that. The

entire library is mine, but I do not really possess it. God has given us an inheritance, but we do not appropriate all that is ours.

Notice the extent of Israel's inheritance. "From the wilderness and this Lebanon even unto the great river, the river Euphrates, all the land of the Hittites, and unto the great sea toward the going down of the sun, shall be your coast." That took in the land from Euphrates down to the border of the land of Egypt, and the Mediterranean Sea, and then from the desert of Arabia on the south to Damascus on the north. God gave all this to Israel; and for a very brief time during Solomon's reign they possessed most of it, but they have never actually possessed for themselves all the land to which they were entitled. Some day they will. We are told in one of the Minor Prophets (Obadiah 17) that the house of Israel shall possess their possessions. Oh, I wish that we as Christians might possess our possessions, and so enjoy the riches of our inheritance!

Just what do you mean by that, you ask? I mean, God has given us His Word. In this Word He has put before us our inheritance. He would have us study His Word, make it our own; enter into everything that it reveals. If we did this we would be able always to live a victorious life in Christ; we would really enjoy our inheritance in Him. Instead of dillydallying with the things of this poor world we would find something so much better in Him. A young man, after his conversion, was asked by some former friends of his to go to a movie. "No," he replied, "thanks, but I have no time; all my time is filled with the things of Christ." That is what it means to be delivered from the things of the world.

"There shall not any man be able to stand before thee all the days of thy life: as I was with Moses, so I will be with thee: I will not fail thee, nor forsake thee." God said, "You will not have to turn back; I'll drive out your foe before you." Alas, alas, they did not believe God's Word, and again and again the enemy reigned over them because of their own disobedience.

Now we wrestle not with flesh and blood; we are not engaged in a conflict with other nations. But our foes are spiritual, and the same God who fought for the people of Israel is the One who will give victory while we obey Him. We sing sometimes

> *Trust and obey, for there's no other way*
> *To be happy in Jesus,*
> *But to trust and obey.*

In the next verse we have a word of encouragement. "Be strong and of good courage: for unto this people shalt thou divide for an inheritance the land, which I sware unto their fathers to give them." We may take these words home to our hearts today when we are fearful of our spiritual foes.

"Only be thou strong and very courageous, that thou mayest observe to do according to all the law, which Moses My servant commanded thee: turn not from it to the right hand or to the left, that thou mayest prosper whithersoever thou goest." Victory depended on their adherence to the Word of God, and it is just as true today. We have so much more of God's Word than they had. They had only the five books of Moses and possibly the book of Job, which may have been written at that time. This is all the Bible they had, and God said, "Take this Word and walk in obedience to it, and you won't need to fear any foe; I'll ever be with you."

Now we have the whole Bible, and God calls upon us to search this Word; let it be the man of our counsel, the food of our souls, and the sword with which we face the enemy. God promises that if you will be strong and of a good courage and walk in obedience to His Word you will never need to dread the conflict; you will never need to fear; you will be able, at all times, to say with the Apostle Paul, "Thanks be to God, which giveth us the victory through our Lord Jesus Christ" (1 Cor. 15:57).

If you do not have victory through Christ Jesus, I can tell you why. It is because you are neglecting reading and obeying your Bible. Read your Bible as you ought to and obey it, and you will be able to live a life of victory. John Bunyan had written in the front of his Bible, on the flyleaf, "This Book will keep you from sin or sin will keep you from this Book." We have the Scriptures to read, and we are to walk in obedience to the Word as it is opened to us by the Holy Spirit.

Young people, if you want to know what will make your life prosperous, get God's own recipe for good success. "This book of the law shall not depart out of thy mouth; but thou shalt meditate therein day and night, that thou mayest observe to do according to all that is written therein: for then thou shalt make thy way prosperous, and then thou shalt have good success." There you have it. Do you want your life to be prosperous? Do you want a successful career? Then take God's Word, read it, and obey it, and God promises those two things.

"Have not I commanded thee? Be strong and of a good courage; be not afraid, neither be thou dismayed: for the Lord thy God is with thee whithersoever thou goest." There seemed good reason why they should be afraid—unused to warfare as they were, facing seven nations with walled cities and armies, nations that had been constantly quarreling with each other down through the centuries, and the people of Israel were to go against these nations and take possession of their land. They might well tremble if they thought only of their own power and their own ability. But as they walked in obedience to the Word of the Lord He promised to deal with the enemies and to empower Israel to overcome them. Although we belong to a different dispensation we may take these words as an exhortation delivered to us personally, and as we read them and walk in obedience, we can count on God for victory.

Joshua was commanded not only to read but to meditate on the law of God. It is by meditation that we really make the Word our own. To read attentively is like eating the Word. Meditation answers to digestion of the truth. Mere intellectual acquaintance with the letter of Scripture avails little. It is as we weigh carefully what God has revealed that we obtain from it that spiritual power that enables us to rise above our difficulties and triumph by grace over all our foes. Thus we grow in grace and in the knowledge of our Lord Jesus Christ.

We become weak and are easily overcome when we neglect this important spiritual exercise, for the Word fed upon alone gives strength.

# Preparation for the Inheritance

## JOSHUA 1:10-18

Then Joshua commanded the officers of the people, saying, Pass through the host, and command the people, saying, Prepare you victuals; for within three days ye shall pass over this Jordan, to go in to possess the land, which the Lord your God giveth you to possess it. And to the Reubenites, and to the Gadites, and to half the tribe of Manasseh, spake Joshua, saying, Remember the word which Moses the servant of the Lord commanded you, saying, The Lord your God hath given you rest, and hath given you this land. Your wives, your little ones, and your cattle, shall remain in the land which Moses gave you on this side Jordan; but ye shall pass before your brethren armed, all the mighty men of valour, and help them; until the Lord have given your brethren rest, as He hath given you, and they also have possessed the land which the Lord your God giveth them: then ye shall return unto the land of your possession, and enjoy it, which Moses the Lord's servant gave you on this side Jordan toward the sunrising. And they answered Joshua, saying, All that thou commandest us we will do, and whithersoever thou sendest

us, we will go. According as we hearkened unto
Moses in all things, so will we hearken unto thee:
only the Lord thy God be with thee, as He was with
Moses. Whosoever he be that doth rebel against
thy commandment, and will not hearken unto thy
words in all that thou commandest him, he shall
be put to death: only be strong and of a good courage. Joshua 1: 10-18.

ISRAEL had a long period of wandering in the wilderness. They were forty years making their way
to the land of Canaan, and yet it could have been
made in eleven days. But God led them about by way
of the wilderness lest they should be discouraged if
they immediately came in contact with their enemies.
They journeyed during the first two years from Egypt
to Kadesh-Barnea, which was on the southwestern
edge of the land, and from it they might have gone
right up into their inheritance and taken possession of
it. But you remember that at the request of the people,
the Lord permitted Moses to send out spies in order
to find out whether God was as good as His word!
He had told them exactly what kind of land it was—
a land flowing with milk and honey; but the people
requested Moses to send spies to see what it was actually like, and he selected twelve men who went
throughout all Palestine investigating. When they
returned, ten of them reported that the land was
everything God had said it was. "But," they added,
"we never will be able to overcome the nations that
dwell there. They are stronger than we; their cities
are walled up to heaven; and there we saw the giants:

and we were in their sight as grasshoppers, and so we were in our own sight. We are not able to go against them." Only two of the men encouraged the people. They were Joshua and Caleb. They said, "Let us go up at once and possess the land; for we are well able to overcome the foes." But the people would not believe them. So the Lord turned them back and they were destined to wander in the wilderness for thirty-eight years because they did not believe God. They refused to do as He had directed them. But He did not forsake them; He watched over them and protected them during all the years of their wilderness wanderings.

The people at last were encamped on the east of the Jordan, looking over toward Jericho. Then the word of God came to Joshua, saying, "Pass through the host, and command the people, saying, Prepare you victuals; for within three days ye shall pass over this Jordan, to go in to possess the land, which the Lord your God giveth you to possess it."

This land is typical of what we have in Christ. God "hath blessed us with all spiritual blessings in heavenly places in Christ." Yet we can possess our inheritance only as we recognize our death and resurrection with our Lord Jesus Christ. God had told Israel long before when in Egypt that they were to go three days' journey into the wilderness, which speaks of death and resurrection. Now the people of Israel were to go over Jordan in three days.

I wonder how far you and I have entered into our possessions in Christ. Many of us have come to Him

as poor, needy sinners, and have trusted Him as our
Saviour, but are we now identified with Him in His
death, burial, and Resurrection? In God's reckoning
every believer has been raised again with Christ. You
remember what the Apostle Paul said, "God forbid
that I should glory, save in the cross of our Lord
Jesus Christ, by whom the world is crucified unto me,
and I unto the world" (Gal. 6:14). It is only as we
take this place of identification with Christ practically that we enter into and enjoy our present inheritance in Him. It is the Word of God that brings
these truths before us. Do we meditate upon the
Word? Do we appropriate its precious truths? Do
we feed our souls upon the blessed realities therein revealed? We would not think of going without our
regular meals from day to day, but how many of us
go without spiritual food! We cannot depend on another ministering to us; we must study the Word for
ourselves. One who does not give time daily to meditation on the Word and to waiting on God in prayer
will never be a strong Christian; he will never lay
hold of that which the Lord intends him to enjoy as
he is linked up with a risen Christ.

Well, Joshua here commands the people to prepare
victuals for a three days' journey. They are to pass
over Jordan right against Jericho. But first we notice
that there is a particular group to whom he gives a
special message. This group was made up of two and
a half tribes—the Reubenites, Gadites, and half the
tribe of Manasseh. Why did Joshua address himself
to these tribes particularly? Well, for this reason:

You remember how Israel under Moses overcame their foes on the east side of the Jordan, and the men of Reuben, Gad, and half the tribe of Manasseh came to Moses, and they said, "This is a wonderful land, a great land for cattle, marvelous pastures here on the east side of Jordan, and we have cattle; therefore, we have come to ask if we might not have our inheritance here in this land instead of going over the Jordan. May we not settle here where we can find suitable accommodation?" Moses was very angry with them, and said, "Your brethren have to pass over the Jordan and they have to meet the seven nations, mightier and greater than they are; they have to overcome the enemies before they can have their inheritance and enjoy the land, yet you would settle down on the east side of Jordan in rest and freedom." But the tribes said, "No, we don't want to do that. We are willing to send our warriors over the Jordan to fight with the rest, but when at last they have obtained their land and have discomfited their foes, then our warriors will return to this side of Jordan. Meantime, we will arrange to make our wives and children comfortable in the cities on the east side, and we will make proper preparation for the care of our cattle, etc." Finally, Moses agreed to this. Sometimes God allows His people to take second best if they are not willing to take His best. Too many Christians today have been saved by grace but are content to settle down, as it were, on the east of Jordan. They have trusted Christ; they have heard the voice of God when He said, "When I see the blood I will pass over you," and

they have come to the verge of Jordan, but they have
missed many blessings because they have stopped on
the east side. In other words, they are world-border-
ing Christians. These two and a half tribes settled in
the land just bordering Canaan, and they were exposed to the nations of the east, to Assyria, Babylon,
and the other countries roundabout. They were the
first to be attacked by the enemies outside the land,
who came down upon Israel in later times.

Let us ask our own hearts, "What kind of a Christian am I—out-and-out for God, or am I dwelling on
the border of the world?" God made a dry way
through Jordan for His people, and He has made a
dry way through death for us today. We died with
Christ at Calvary when He died in our place. There
we were crucified with Him. Is this a reality to our
souls? When Christians come to me and ask if there
is any harm in this and that, something that pertains
to the east side of Jordan, something in which the
world indulges, I say, "Why don't you ask if there
would be any harm in going to a prayer meeting?"

"Oh," they answer, "Anybody knows there is no
harm in going to a prayer meeting." Well, that is the
answer. They would not think of asking the question
if there was not a doubt in their minds. It is things
like that of which the apostle speaks when he says that
he that doubteth is condemned if he does the thing
concerning which he is in doubt.

As to something of which you stand in doubt, you
may be sure it will never help you spiritually; it will
never help to make Christ more precious to you; it

will never make you love His Word more; it will never enable you to triumph over sin. A great many of these things may not be wicked but are just bordering on the edge of the world, as it were. Like these two and a half tribes, you are settling down on the east side of Jordan. You have not gone through death, burial, and resurrection with Christ experimentally. Some have made a profession of this in Christian baptism, but are not living it out from day to day. In this ordinance we confess that we have died to the world, to sin, and to the law, and that we now are to live unto God as those who are alive from the dead. May our profession and our lives agree that the Lord Jesus may be magnified in us!

After Joshua's address to the two and a half tribes who were to cross over the river to aid their brethren in taking possession of the inheritance, proceedings went on apace for the actual entering into that land which belonged already to Israel by divine gift, but which they were responsible to make their own practically. To do this required faith in God and spiritual energy for they were to find every inch of ground contested by bitter and powerful foes. But this but gave an opportunity to prove the faithfulness of the God who had delivered them from Egypt and was now leading them on.

# Give Me a True Token

JOSHUA 2

Now therefore, I pray you, swear unto me by the Lord, since I have shewed you kindness, that ye will also shew kindness unto my father's house, and give me a true token. Joshua 2: 12.

By faith the harlot Rahab perished not with them that believed not, when she had received the spies with peace. Hebrews 11: 31.

Likewise also was not Rahab the harlot justified by works, when she had received the messengers, and had sent them out another way? James 2: 25.

ISRAEL'S crossing the Jordan River speaks to us of our death with Christ. Joshua sent spies over to Jericho to find out the exact state of affairs, and we are told that these spies entered the city and came to a harlot's house, whose name was Rahab, and they lodged there.

A good many have questioned the immoral character of this woman Rahab and have pointed out that the word translated "harlot" does not necessarily mean an immoral woman but might mean simply a woman keeping a place of public entertainment, that is, an innkeeper; but the New Testament leaves us in no doubt as to Rahab's real character. She was like so many of her sinful sisters in that heathen land—a woman who had departed from the path of chastity and was living a wicked, unclean life. Yet God in His infinite mercy sent His messengers to this woman's house and brought not only deliverance to her own soul but to those also of her household. What a great salvation!

Christ Jesus came into the world to save sinners, not good people, not people who fancy they are good enough for God as they are, but those who are ready to take their place as lost sinners needing a Saviour.

A woman went to Charles Wesley, the great hymn writer, and said to him, "Mr. Wesley, I have come to ask you to pray for me, for I am a great sinner."

Mr. Wesley answered, "Indeed, you certainly are a great sinner, and I will be glad to pray for you."

The lady exclaimed, "Who has been talking about me to you? I am just as good as anyone else in this community!"

So many people have this attitude when they go before God. God is saving sinners—those who will confess and forsake their sins.

The spies came to Rahab's house and she received them. She hid them because she knew that the authorities would soon be seeking them. In fact, it was not long until they came to her house. We read,

**The king of Jericho sent unto Rahab, saying, Bring forth the men that are come to thee, which are entered into thine house: for they be come to**

**search out all the country. And the woman took the
two men, and hid them, and said thus, There came
men unto me, but I wist not whence they were:
And it came to pass about the time of shutting of
the gate, when it was dark, that the men went out:
whither the men went I wot not: pursue after them
quickly; for ye shall overtake them.**

Now Rahab did something that manifested the
new attitude that she had taken toward the God of
Israel. She was an idolater; she had been worshiping
idols all through the years, but she had heard of the
wonderful power of Jehovah, as had all her people.
They had heard of how God had delivered Israel out
of Egypt, and of the drying up of the Red Sea, and
the way He sustained this multitude throughout their
journeying in the wilderness. And Rahab's soul was
strangely moved. There was something about the
stories which she heard that appealed to her heart,
and she felt it was a divine providence that she had
the representatives of the God of Israel in her house.
She did what she could to protect them. She took
them to the top of her house and hid them with the
stalks of flax.

Rahab did not tell the truth in regard to the spies;
and one might ask, "Does God commend this woman
for her lying?" No, not at all, but remember her
background. She had never heard the word of the
law of God, "Thou shalt not bear false witness." She
was brought up in a system that made no distinction
between truth and lying. She was a poor, heathen
woman who sought to know the true God by taking

the wrong method in order to shield His messengers. Of course, it was wrong for her to lie, but God saw her heart, overruled the blunder she was making to protect His servants, and eventually revealed Himself to her.

"But she had brought them up to the roof of the house, and hid them with the stalks of flax, which she had laid in order upon the roof." In the Epistle of James we are told that "Rahab the harlot was justified by works, when she had received the messengers, and had sent them out another way. For as the body without the spirit is dead, so faith without works is dead also" (2:25, 26). When she hid the spies she showed the real faith that was in her heart. Her faith was manifested by her works in hiding them and sending them away safely. Whenever there is genuine faith in God it will always be accompanied by good works. We are not saved by works. Let no one make a mistake as to that. Scripture is absolutely clear that we are saved by grace alone through faith, and that not of ourselves; it is the gift of God. "Faith cometh by hearing, and hearing by the Word of God." "Not of works, lest any man should boast." But on the other hand, where there is genuine faith, where people really believe God, where they truly receive His testimony, their faith will be manifested by their works, and that is what the Apostle James stresses.

**And before they were laid down, she came up unto them upon the roof; and she said unto the**

**men, I know that the Lord hath given you the land, and that your terror is fallen upon us, and that all the inhabitants of the land faint because of you.**

All the people had heard about the God of Israel, and they were filled with terror, but they had no desire to know Him. In this Rahab was different from the rest. She wanted to acquaint herself with the God of Israel, and she grasped this wonderful opportunity that had come to her in order that He might be made known to her.

She continued to say,

**We have heard how the Lord dried up the water of the Red Sea for you, when ye came out of Egypt; and what ye did unto the two kings of the Amorites, that were on the other side Jordan, Sihon, and Og, whom ye utterly destroyed. And as soon as we had heard these things, our hearts did melt, neither did there remain any more courage in any man, because of you: for the Lord your God, He is God in heaven above, and in earth beneath.**

A wonderful confession, "The Lord your God, He is God in heaven above, and in earth beneath"! By faith Rahab the harlot made this confession. She had committed her soul to this true and living God. We are told in Romans 10:9, 10, "If thou shalt confess with thy mouth the Lord Jesus, and shalt believe in thine heart that God hath raised Him from the dead, thou shalt be saved. For with the heart man believeth unto righteousness; and with the mouth confession is made unto salvation." Do not make any mistake.

There is no merit in the confession. You are not saved by *confessing* Christ; you are saved by *trusting* Christ. You confess Him because you are saved. God is calling upon all who are still in their sins to put their trust in the Lord Jesus Christ, to turn to Him and then confess Him as their Saviour and Lord. He says, "Whosover therefore shall confess Me before men, him will I confess also before My Father which is in heaven" (Matt. 10:32). I am sure there are people who have trusted Christ but do not say anything about it to other folk, but I know that they are not triumphant and happy. Victorious Christians are those who delight to confess the name of Jesus.

Rahab had no difficulty about confessing her faith in the one true and living God. But she wanted assurance of future security, so before these men left she said to them,

**Now therefore, I pray you, swear unto me by the Lord, since I have shewed you kindness, that ye will also shew kindness unto my father's house, and *give me a true token*.**

Is that what your heart is saying? Are you crying, "Oh give me a true token; give me definite, positive assurance that God has really saved me"? Well, thank God, He gives such a true token in His Word. Rahab was concerned not only for herself, but for her household as well. And when people really know the Lord then they are concerned about the salvation of others —those whom they love, their own household. She continued,

**And that ye will save alive my father, and my mother, and my brethren, and my sisters, and all that they have, and deliver our lives from death.**

In this Rahab showed a remarkable understanding of the desires of the God of Israel, for all through Scripture we see it is the purpose of God, His desire and will to save His people in families, in households. If He shows mercy to one person in a household it is an indication that He wants to save every member of that family. You remember what He said of Abraham, "Shall I hide from Abraham that thing which I do?" (He was speaking of the judgment of Sodom and Gomorrah.) "For I know him, that he will command his children and his household after him" (Gen. 18: 17, 19). Oh, Christian fathers and mothers, what about your attitude toward your households? Have you recognized your responsibility? Are you acting for God in the home to command your children after you? I know we live in a day of self-expression when we are taught that we should not quell the natural desires of our children, and most of us have given way to this teaching. As a result we have unconverted children in our homes, whose ways are the expression of their vile, wicked, corrupt natures. Scripture says, "Foolishness is bound in the heart of a child; but the rod of correction shall drive it far from him" (Prov. 22: 15).

Mrs. William Booth, wife of the first general in the Salvation Army, who reared a large family of eight children, claimed every one of them for God before they were born. She used to say, "I refuse to bring any child into the world to be damned in hell at last." She claimed every one of her children for God. In their early days some of those children thought their mother was rather stern and hard because she would not allow them to go into the things of the world like other children, but the day came when every one of them thanked their mother for standing between them and the world, and all grew up to preach Christ and seek to bring others to Him.

A tremendous responsibility rests on parents in these matters. Too many parents say, "I will let my child go just so far in the ways of the world, and I hope eventually he will come to God," only to learn that later on he does not desire to know God at all. Your child may rebel against your correction, but he will thank you for it later on when he has come to know the Lord. Your child may look upon you as old-fashioned, but when at last he has turned to Christ for salvation then he will indeed thank you for ever having sought to lead him in the way of righteousness.

Rahab was a poor woman who had gone down into the depth of sin, but now had turned to God, and her heart cried out for the deliverance of her loved ones. So she pleaded for her household.

**The men answered her, Our life for yours, if ye utter not this our business. And it shall be, when the Lord hath given us the land, that we will deal kindly and truly with thee.**

In the New Testament we read of the Philippian jailor who came, thinking only of himself. He cried out, "Sirs, what must I do to be saved?" Apparently his family was gathered about him. Paul said, "Believe on the Lord Jesus Christ, and thou shalt be saved, and thy house" (Acts 16 : 30, 31). That night there was great rejoicing in that house. The whole household was brought to faith in Christ and they confessed His name in baptism.

If you are the only saved member in your household, lay hold of God and in faith cry to Him for salvation for the other members of your family. Live Christ before them and look to God to bring them all to Himself. In this we may closely emulate the faith of Rahab.

**Then she let them down by a cord through the window: for her house was upon the town wall, and she dwelt upon the wall.**

I could not help but wonder, a few years ago, whether I was looking over Rahab's house. I went to see the ruins of the very Jericho destroyed under Joshua. That ruined city was uncovered a few years ago and they found that the walls had fallen outward. As I looked at a ruined house I wondered if it might be that of Rahab, from the window of which she had let down the spies.

She bade them:

**Get you to the mountain, lest the pursuers meet you; and hide yourselves there three days, until**

the pursuers be returned: and afterward may ye go
your way. And the men said unto her, We will be
blameless of this thine oath which thou hast made
us to swear. Behold, when we come into the land,
thou shalt bind this line of scarlet thread in the
window which thou didst let us down by: and thou
shalt bring thy father, and thy mother, and thy
brethren, and all thy father's household, home unto
thee. And it shall be, that whosoever shall go out
of the doors of thy house into the street, his blood
shall be upon his head, and we will be guiltless:
and whosoever shall be with thee in the house, his
blood shall be on our head, if any hand be upon him.
And if thou utter this our business, then we will
be quit of thine oath which thou hast made us to
swear.

What a beautiful picture of God's salvation!

They gave her a scarlet cord. I take it that it was
the very cord with which they had been let down.
She was to bind the scarlet cord in the window so
that anyone could see it. The people of the land beholding it would not have any idea what it was for,
no more perhaps than an ordinary ornament. In His
Word God has given to us a scarlet line and saves
all who are in the house that is thus marked off from
the rest of the world.

Rahab was commanded to get her father, mother,
brethren, her friends and relatives, and bring them
into the house. They were all protected by the scarlet
cord and they would be safe in the day when the
judgment should fall upon Jericho. They were sheltered by the red cord in the window.

All who are in Christ are sheltered by His precious blood. That is the true token, for the Father looks upon that. Christ has died for me; therefore my soul is safe.

**And it shall be, that whosoever shall go out of the doors of thy house into the street, his blood shall be upon his head, and we will be guiltless: and whosoever shall be with thee in the house, his blood shall be on our head, if any hand be upon him.**

In other words, they said, "Rahab, we will be your surety, and you and all in your house will be saved if protected by the scarlet cord." Christ is the surety for all who put their trust in His precious blood. But if Rahab or anyone else in the house left the protection of the scarlet cord, it was at their own risk.

Dear friends, if you refuse to trust the Lord Jesus Christ, if you refuse to find shelter beneath His precious blood, in the day when God arises to shake terribly the earth and all the things that men have trusted in go to pieces, you will be left a poor, lost, ruined soul, and your blood will be on your own head because you despised the sacrifice offered by our Lord Jesus Christ.

**And she said, According unto your words, so be it. And she sent them away, and they departed: and she bound the scarlet line in the window.**

Later when the armies of Israel began crossing the Jordan and the people of Jericho were on the wall, their hearts trembled as they saw the great army coming, and when later on the priests bearing the ark marched around Jericho, blowing their trumpets, people watched and no doubt thought it was some strange enchantment, and they were filled with terror. Rahab would look out the window and would say to herself, "Our city will never be able to stand against the God of Israel." But she could say, "There is the scarlet cord in the window and I am secure." And all who will put their trust in Christ are secure through His precious blood. Such can well afford to sing:

> *Under Thy wings, my God, I rest*
> *Under Thy shadow safely lie;*
> *By Thy own strength in peace possessed,*
> *While dread evils pass me by.*

It is the will of God that all who believe on the Lord Jesus Christ should have this definite assurance, knowing that they are eternally secure because of the atoning blood of the Lamb.

The truth of this runs like a scarlet line all though Scripture, from Abel's lamb slain at the gate of Eden to the Lamb on the throne in the heavenly city, where all the redeemed join in the new song of redemption by His blood. If we would sing that song in heaven let us be sure we learn it here on earth.

# Crossing the Jordan

## JOSHUA 3

And Joshua rose early in the morning; and they removed from Shittim, and came to Jordan, he and all the children of Israel, and lodged there before they passed over. And it came to pass after three days, that the officers went through the host; and they commanded the people, saying, When ye see the ark of the covenant of the Lord your God, and the priests the Levites bearing it, then ye shall remove from your place, and go after it. Yet there shall be a space between you and it, about two thousand cubits by measure; come not near unto it, that ye may know the way by which ye must go: for ye have not passed this way heretofore. And Joshua said unto the people, Sanctify yourselves: for tomorrow the Lord will do wonders among you. And Joshua spake unto the priests, saying, Take up the ark of the covenant, and pass over before the people. And they took up the ark of the covenant, and went before the people. Joshua 3: 1-6.

THE time had come for which Israel had waited so long: they were about to enter the land of promise, the inheritance which God had vouchsafed to them. Had there been the energy of faith they might have gone up into that land from Kadesh-Barnea, the place of opportunity, thirty-eight years before. But because of their unbelief God had turned them back and made them wander in the wilderness until all that unbelieving generation had died. Now their children were encamped in the plains of Moab, looking toward the land, but with the river Jordan rolling between them and their promised possessions.

Jordan speaks of death, with judgment following. It is the dark river flowing down to the Dead Sea. To plunge into it would have meant the drowning of all the host of Israel. But God was about to make a dry way through that mystic river as He had done forty years before through the Red Sea. We read that Israel went down into the sea and came up out of Jordan. The two coalesce, for both speak of death. The Dead Sea says Christ's death is our death. We have died with Him. The Jordan says they who die with Him live in Him, henceforth to walk in newness of life. Thank God, our Lord Jesus Christ has died for us, and those who have put their trust in Him will never come into judgment, but are passed out of death into life. God sees us linked up with the Lord Jesus Christ in His death and Resurrection.

We read in the sixth chapter of Romans, "Know ye not, that so many of us as were baptized into Jesus Christ were baptized into His death? Therefore we are buried with Him by baptism into death: that like as Christ was raised up from the dead by the glory of the Father, even so we also should walk in newness of life" (6: 3, 4).

These verses we have before us are typical of this precious truth. Israel looked over to the other side of Jordan to the land God had promised them, which typifies our present inheritance in Christ, the privileges which are enjoyed by all believers who actually enter into the truth of their union with Christ in His death and Resurrection.

Canaan typifies not merely heaven after we die (as in 1 Peter 1) but the heavenly experiences which are ours to enjoy while still in our mortal bodies here on earth. It is this the apostle had in view when he exclaimed, "I am crucified with Christ; nevertheless, I live; yet not I, but Christ liveth in me; and the life that I now live in the flesh I live by the faith of the Son of God, who loved me and gave Himself for me" (Gal. 2:20).

The priests bearing the ark of the covenant were to go forward first. That ark typified our Lord Jesus Christ, the meeting-place between God and man. The wood of the ark spoke of His perfect humanity; the gold, of the glory of His deity. He must go down into death first to make a dry way for His people. By dying and rising again He has "abolished death and brought life and immortality to light through the Gospel."

In the fourth verse of Joshua 3 we read that there was to be a space maintained between the ark and the people of about two thousand cubits, which would be approximately half a mile according to our method of computation. This was to teach due reverence for the ark of God. It had to lead the way. Alone the priests were to go down into the river and then the waters would be rolled back. Christ entered into death alone. No one could participate in the work of propitiation.

> *Alone He bare the cross;*
> *Alone its grief sustained.*

We can imagine with what interest and suppressed excitement the people watched that ark, as, borne on the shoulders of the priests, it was carried down to the river. It passed on before the people, who were to share in the safety and blessing it was to ensure, but who could do nothing themselves to stem the Jordan's flow.

God's command to the priests was, "When ye are come to the brink of the water of Jordan ye shall stand still in Jordan." What a test of faith this must have been! But it was God's Word and must be acted upon. Only thus could the way be opened for Israel to go dry-shod into Canaan, and only through the death of Christ could a way be opened for us to enter into the rest that remains for the people of God.

Notice verses 11 to 13 :

**Behold the ark of the covenant of the Lord of all the earth passeth over before you into Jordan. Now therefore take you twelve men out of the tribes of Israel, out of every tribe a man. And it shall come to pass, as soon as the soles of the feet of the priests that bear the ark of the Lord, the Lord of all the earth, shall rest in the waters of Jordan, that the waters of Jordan shall be cut off from the waters**

**that come down from above; and they shall stand upon an heap.**

To the natural way of thinking, this might have seemed impossible, but God had given His Word and that Word never fails. The twelve men referred to were selected for a specific purpose, of which we shall read later on.

Now notice carefully verses 14 to 17:

**And it came to pass, when the people removed from their tents, to pass over Jordan, and the priests bearing the ark of the covenant before the people; And as they that bare the ark were come unto Jordan, and the feet of the priests that bare the ark were dipped in the brim of the water, (for Jordan overfloweth all his banks all the time of harvest,) That the waters which came down from above stood and rose up upon an heap very far from the city Adam, that is beside Zaretan: and those that came down toward the sea of the plain, even the salt sea, failed, and were cut off; and the people passed over right against Jericho. And the priests that bare the ark of the covenant of the Lord stood firm on dry ground in the midst of Jordan, and all the Israelites passed over on dry ground, until all the people were passed clean over Jordan.**

The people of Israel were standing there in absolute silence, reverently looking on as the ark of the covenant went down to the river Jordan. It pictures Christ going down into the dark water of death. The moment the priests' feet rested in Jordan, the waters were dried up—the waters that had already reached the point of overflowing went down to the salt sea, and the water which came down from above rolled very far back from the city Adam.

Now, I do not know where the city Adam was. It says, "The city Adam, that is beside Zaretan." You will see that those who make the maps have indicated a city called Adam near the source of the Jordan, but they put a question mark after the name because they are not sure where the city of Adam was located. That is not important, however; but I will tell you what is important: that when our Lord Jesus Christ died on the Cross the waters of judgment were rolled very far back—back to the first man, Adam. Adam's sins were taken into account when Jesus died on the Cross, as well as the sins of all his race. We are told in Romans 3:23-26: "For all have sinned, and come short of the glory of God; Being justified freely by His grace through the redemption that is in Christ Jesus: Whom God hath set forth to be a propitiation through faith in His blood, to declare His righteousness for the remission of sins that are past, through the forbearance of God: To declare, I say, at this time His righteousness: that He might be just, and the justifier of him which believeth in Jesus."

That expression, "sins that are past," refers not to our past offences, but to the sins of those who lived before the Cross. All down through the ages God had been, if I may so say, saving men on credit. The actual work of propitiation or atonement had not yet been accomplished. But in view of it, God remitted the sins of all who turned to Him in repentance and faith, and when Jesus died on the Cross all these sins were settled for, as well as those of all who at any time since would receive the Lord Jesus by faith. So now God can be just and the justifier of all who believe.

The ark remained in the bed of the Jordan "until all the people had clean passed over." So Christ in His death made complete propitiation for all men everywhere, that all may be saved, if they will. God saw all who would ever believe passing through to blessing when His blessed Son died in our stead.

As we realize our identification with Him in that death, we enter into the life of joy and high privilege which is the happy portion of all who believe.

Israel did nothing to merit this deliverance. It was God who wrought in grace on their behalf. So in the work of the Cross, all has been done that needed to be done in order that sinners might be saved. Christ is Himself the Ark and He went down into death that a way might be opened for us to enter into the blessing of redemption. It is ours to believe God and so to receive the effect of Christ's work.

# The Stones of Witness

And it came to pass, when all the people were clean passed over Jordan, that the Lord spake unto Joshua, saying, Take you twelve men out of the people, out of every tribe a man, And command ye them, saying, Take you hence out of the midst of Jordan, out of the place where the priests' feet stood firm, twelve stones, and ye shall carry them over with you, and leave them in the lodging place, where ye shall lodge this night. Then Joshua called the twelve men, whom he had prepared of the children of Israel, out of every tribe a man: and Joshua said unto them, Pass over before the ark of the Lord your God into the midst of Jordan, and take you up every man of you a stone upon his shoulder, according unto the number of the tribes of the children of Israel: that this may be a sign among you, that when your children ask their fathers in time to come, saying, What mean ye by these stones? Then ye shall answer them, That the waters of Jordan were cut off before the ark of the covenant of the Lord; when it passed over Jordan, the waters of Jordan were cut off: and these stones shall be for a memorial unto the children of Israel for ever. And the children of Israel did so as Joshua com-

manded, and took up twelve stones out of the midst
of Jordan, as the Lord spake unto Joshua, according to the number of the tribes of the children of
Israel, and carried them over with them unto the
place where they lodged, and laid them down there.
And Joshua set up twelve stones in the midst of
Jordan, in the place where the feet of the priests
which bare the ark of the covenant stood: and they
are there unto this day. Joshua 4: 1-9.

IT HAS been remarked that the Old Testament is
God's picture book. It teaches by type and illustration. We are told in 1 Corinthians 10:11 that
"All these things happened unto them for our ensamples: and they are written for our admonition,
upon whom the ends of the ages have come." There
are a great many people who recognize the fact that
some things written in the Old Testament were typical, but they hesitate to acknowledge that this is true
of all. We need to learn the lesson of these words.
Some will tell you that the books of the Old Testament, the so-called historical books, are largely made
up of Hebrew myths and legends, and we cannot at-
tach any credibility to them, but the Holy Spirit
says, "All these things happened." Therefore, he who
believes God accepts these various experiences of
Israel as actual history. In the second place, there
are certain typical lessons which we learn from them.
"All these things happened unto them for types."

We have seen in the previous chapter how the ark
going down into the waters of Jordan typified our
Lord Jesus Christ going down into the waters of

death when He could say, "Deep calleth unto deep at the noise of Thy waterspouts: all Thy waves and Thy billows are gone over Me" (Psalm 42:7). By His death on the Cross He has annulled him that had the power of death, that is the devil. Through Him the fear of death is gone, and Christians can say, "God forbid that I should glory, save in the Cross of our Lord Jesus Christ, by whom the world is crucified unto me, and I unto the world" (Gal. 6:14).

The believer is identified with the Lord Jesus in His death, burial, and Resurrection. This comes out very clearly, very beautifully in the present chapter. We are told that when the people were clean passed over Jordan, the Lord gave another command to Joshua. The priests bearing the ark of the covenant still stood in the river bed, but the people had passed over, when God said to Joshua,

**Take you twelve men out of the people, out of every tribe a man, and command ye them, saying, Take you hence out of the midst of Jordan, out of the place where the priests' feet stood firm, twelve stones, and ye shall carry them over with you, and leave them in the lodging place, where ye shall lodge this night.**

The twelve stones were to be a memorial of Israel's deliverance. They were to take up these stones from the river bed and carry them to the other side, and they were to be piled up as a monument that generations to come might look upon them and remember how God delivered His people.

> Then Joshua called the twelve men, whom he had prepared of the children of Israel, out of every tribe a man: and Joshua said unto them, Pass over before the ark of the Lord your God into the midst of Jordan, and take you up every man of you a stone upon his shoulder, according unto the number of the tribes of the children of Israel: that this may be a sign among you, that when your children ask their fathers in time to come, saying, What mean ye by these stones? Then ye shall answer them, That the waters of Jordan were cut off before the ark of the covenant of the Lord; when it passed over Jordan, the waters of Jordan were cut off: and these stones shall be for a memorial unto the children of Israel for ever.

God wanted to preserve this as a testimony. May I say that similarly the two ordinances given to Christian people were intended by God to emphasize these truths. Take the ordinance of baptism, Christian baptism which is set forth as a memorial. "As many of you as have been baptized unto Christ, were baptized unto His death." When a believer is baptized he is bearing testimony to the fact that Christ has died and that he takes his place in identification with Him in His death. God sees every believer dead, buried, and risen with Christ. I hesitate to participate in baptizing anyone if he does not really understand this. Baptism is not a means of salvation; baptism can only wash away the filth of the flesh, but in baptism a person is bearing witness to his death, burial, and resurrection from the dead through Jesus Christ. The intelligent person being baptized says, "I deserve to die, but Christ died in my stead; therefore His death is my death, and I take my place now in identification with Him. I have died with Him; died to all that He died to as a Man. I have died to the world, to sin in the flesh; I have died to the law; I now stand on altogether different ground before God."

The other ordinance is that of the Lord's Supper. As we gather about His table to partake of the broken bread and of the cup which represent the body and the precious blood of Christ, we remember that Christ died for us, and that He is living, and is coming again to take us to be forever with Himself. When your children ask you, "What mean ye by these ordinances?" we should be prepared to say, "Our Saviour died, and we died with Him; He arose in triumph, and we have been quickened together with Him. Now we are dead to that to which He died, and are called upon to live unto God." We have this set forth in the twelve stones taken out of the midst of Jordan—our resurrection with Christ.

But there was more than that. We read in verse 9,

**Joshua set up twelve stones in the midst of Jordan, in the place where the feet of the priests which bare the ark of the covenant stood: and they are there unto this day. For the priests which bare the ark stood in the midst of Jordan, until every thing was finished that the Lord commanded Joshua.**

How that should remind us of that word that the Saviour uttered ere He departed to the Father! I say that "word" for in our translation we have three words, "It is finished," but in the Greek there is only one word. What Jesus cried was *tetelestai*—"completed," "finished," "consummated"—the work of redemption was finished for all those who put their trust in Him.

The twelve stones were set up in the midst of Jordan, and when the priests, bearing the ark, came up out of the river the waters came down from above and covered up those twelve stones. The Word says, "They are there unto this day." You may take that as meaning until the book of Joshua was written, but I think we dare go even further and declare, "They are there unto *this* day." There is a lesson for us in this. We can see the infinite grace of God. Christ died for us and now we are dead to the world and all its sin.

That is what the twelve stones in the midst of the Jordan tell us. They say, "I have died with Christ; I no longer belong to the world that crucified Him; I no longer come under its judgment but under grace." That does not mean that we can be careless in our behavior. As believers we should be more careful than ever as to our conduct. That is what the apostle stresses when he says, "Sin shall not have dominion over you: for ye are not under the law, but under grace" (Rom. 6: 14). Again he says, "Reckon ye also yourselves to be dead indeed unto sin, but alive unto God through Jesus Christ our Lord" (Rom. 6: 11).

Those twelve stones on the other side in the land of

Canaan speak of resurrection with Christ. "If ye then be risen with Christ, seek those things which are above, where Christ sitteth on the right hand of God" (Col. 3:1). May I try to make this very personal?

Have you taken your place in baptism as professedly in association with our Lord Jesus Christ in His death? Are you living it out? Let me ask you, some of you dear young people who have confessed your faith in Christ in baptism, what does that mean to you? Do you recognize the fact that God now claims you as His own? You should walk absolutely apart from the world and all its toys and idols. That is what God desires for you. When you talk to some people about coming out from the world they will say that they cannot see any harm in this thing and in that thing, and yet their own lives manifest their harmfulness. They are useless Christians; they do not count for God.

I remember a young woman whom I met when I was in Texas. She was a Christian; there was no question about that. She confessed her faith in baptism, but there was one form of worldly amusement that she enjoyed very much and that was dancing. Someone challenged her, telling her that she could not witness for Christ on a ballroom floor. She replied, "I think I am as free to witness there for Christ as anywhere else."

The person who challenged her said, "If what you say is true, I cannot tell you not to go."

One night she was dancing with a young man, and as she did so she said to herself, "I ought to witness for Christ here." So she said to her dancing partner, "I want to ask you a question."

"All right," he replied, "what is it?"

She inquired, "Do you know the Lord Jesus Christ as Saviour?"

He answered, "No, do you?"

"Yes," she replied, "I do indeed."

The young man exclaimed, "Then what on earth are you doing here?" Though a mere worldling he realized that there are certain standards that Christians should seek to live up to, and this woman wasn't living up to them. She said to me, "That was the last dance I ever attended. To think I had to be rebuked like that by an unsaved young man!"

Those twelve stones in the midst of Jordan, how they ought to speak to our hearts of the grace of Christ and of what He endured for us. Have you taken your place with Him so that you can say from the heart, "God forbid that I should glory, save in the cross of our Lord Jesus Christ, by whom the world is crucified unto me, and I unto the world"?

But you say, "That means giving up so many things." Yes, but you get so much more in their place.

Those twelve stones on the other side of Jordan speak of Christ in resurrection—the blessedness, the happiness, the gladness of heart that comes to the one who is consciously identified with the risen Christ.

You will not care for the poor, trivial things of this world if your heart is taken up with Him.

And it came to pass, when all the people were clean passed over, that the ark of the Lord passed over, and the priests, in the presence of the people. And the children of Reuben, and the children of Gad, and half the tribe of Manasseh, passed over armed before the children of Israel, as Moses spake unto them: about forty thousand prepared for war passed over before the Lord unto battle, to the plains of Jericho. On that day the Lord magnified Joshua in the sight of all Israel; and they feared him, as they feared Moses, all the days of his life. And the Lord spake unto Joshua, saying, Command the priests that bear the ark of the testimony, that they come up out of Jordan. Joshua therefore commanded the priests, saying, Come ye up out of Jordan.

Typically, it speaks of Christ coming up out of death in resurrection life after He had completed the work of our redemption.

And it came to pass, when the priests that bare the ark of the covenant of the Lord were come up out of the midst of Jordan, and the soles of the priests' feet were lifted up unto the dry land, that the waters of Jordan returned unto their place, and flowed over all his banks, as they did before.

Notice just an added word here, "And the people came up out of the Jordan, on the tenth day of the first month, and encamped in Gilgal." That was their first camping place in Canaan, and there are many precious lessons connected with Gilgal which we shall

notice when we come to it in our next chapter. Those
twelve stones which they took out of the Jordan
were set up in Gilgal.

**And he spake unto the children of Israel, saying,
When your children shall ask their fathers in time
to come, saying, What mean these stones? Then
ye shall let your children know, saying, Israel
came over this Jordan on dry land. For the Lord
your God dried up the waters of Jordan from before you, until ye were passed over, as the Lord
your God did to the Red Sea, which He dried up
from before us, until we were gone over: that all
the people of the earth might know the hand of the
Lord, that it is mighty: that ye might fear the
Lord your God for ever.**

It is precious indeed when one enters into the reality of all this. The hymn writer has expressed it beautifully in the following verses:

> *Jesus died and we died with Him,*
>   *Buried in His grave we lay;*
> *One with Him in resurrection,*
>   *Soon with Him in heaven's bright day.*
> *Death and judgment are behind us,*
>   *Grace and glory are before;*
> *All the billows rolled o'er Jesus,*
>   *There exhausted all their power.*

# Lessons from Gilgal

JOSHUA 5

THIS chapter brings before us three oustanding subjects, all of which are of great importance in connection with our taking possession of the inheritance which God has given us in Christ. These may be indicated by three suggestive terms: Sharp Knives, Old Corn, and The Captain of Jehovah's Host.

The first of these topics comes before us in verses 1 to 9:

And it came to pass, when all the kings of the Amorites, which were on the side of Jordan westward, and all the kings of the Canaanites, which were by the sea, heard that the Lord had dried up the waters of Jordan from before the children of Israel, until we were passed over, that their heart melted, neither was there spirit in them any more, because of the children of Israel. At that time the Lord said unto Joshua, Make thee sharp knives, and circumcise again the children of Israel the second time. And Joshua made him sharp knives, and circumcised the children of Israel at the hill of the foreskins. And this is the cause why Joshua did circumcise; All the people that came out of Egypt, that were males, even all the men of war, died in the wilderness by the way, after they came out of Egypt. Now all the people that came out were circumcised: but all the people that were born in the wilderness by the way as they came forth out of Egypt, them they had not circumcised. For the children of Israel walked forty years in the wilderness, till all the people that were men of war, which came out of Egypt, were consumed, because they obeyed not the voice of the Lord: unto whom the Lord sware that He would not show them the land, which the Lord sware unto their fathers that He would give us, a land that floweth with milk and honey. And their children, whom He raised up in their stead, them Joshua circumcised: for they were uncircumcised, because they had not circumcised them by the way. And it came to pass, when they had done circumcising all the people, that they abode in their places in the camp, till they were whole. And the Lord said unto Joshua, This day have I rolled away the reproach of Egypt from off you. Wherefore the name of place is called Gilgal unto this day.

Israel had crossed the Jordan. They were now encamped between the river and the city of Jericho, whose high walls loomed before them. At the command of Joshua they were to go up against not only this city, but all the cities and nations that occupied the land of Canaan. In the strength of Jehovah, as they relied upon Him, they would be able to overcome these mighty foes—foes which speak to us of those wicked spirits in heavenly places who would seek to keep us from our enjoyment of our privileges in Christ.

But before attacking the enemy God called upon His people to use sharp knives upon their own flesh. The sharp knife speaks of self-judgment. Before a believer is fit to enter into combat with his spiritual enemies he needs to use this knife of self-judgment, which is the Word of God, in living power upon his own heart and life.

The rite of circumcision of old was designed by God to mark off His people from the nations around. It was a sign of separation, and it typified death to the flesh. The ancient rite is spoken of in Ephesians 2: 11, as "Circumcision made by hands." This, for the Christian, is no longer obligatory. It characterized Judaism and the Apostle Paul points out in the Epistle to the Galatians that everyone who goes back to that system, which God has now set aside, and depends upon the rite of circumcision to give him favor with God has fallen from grace; that is, he has left the high ground of salvation by grace alone and descended to the low level of attempted salvation by human merit. In place of the ancient sign, we read in Romans 2: 29 of the circumcision which is of the heart; that is, the putting away from the heart of every impure and unclean lust, ambition, or tendency.

In the Epistle to the Colossians, believers are said to be circumcized with the circumcision of Christ; that is, His death upon the Cross is counted by God as their death, and this has put an end to their old relationship as men in the flesh doing their own will in opposition to the will of God. This is to be made practical by the use of the sharp knife of self-judgment.

In Colossians 3 we read: "Mortify therefore your members which are upon the earth; fornification, uncleanness, inordinate affection, evil concupiscence, and covetousness, which is idolatry, for which things' sake the wrath of God cometh on the children of disobedience: in the which ye also walked sometime, when ye lived in them." The sins mentioned here are all such as every right-minded person recognizes as vile and abominable. The child of God is to deal unsparingly with any tendency toward these things which he finds in himself. He is to recognize himself dead indeed unto sin, but alive unto God through Christ Jesus our Lord.

But there are other sins which we are not inclined to think of as so obnoxious as those mentioned above and yet sins which are great hindrances to testimony for Christ. Of these we read in Colossians 3 : 8 to 11 : "But now ye also put off all these: anger, wrath, malice, blasphemy, filthy communication out of your mouth. Lie not one to another, seeing that ye have put off the old man with his deeds; And have put on the new man, which is renewed in knowledge after the image of him that created him: Where there is neither Greek nor Jew, circumcision or uncircumcision, Barbarian, Scythian, bond nor free: but Christ is all and in all." Many a servant of Christ has nullified his testimony by bad temper and a harsh attitude toward those who do not agree with him. This is as truly of the flesh as fornication or adultery, and against it one needs to use the sharp knife.

The reason Joshua was told to command the people of Israel to carry out the ordinance of circumcision at this time was because none of those born in the wilderness had been circumcised; therefore the reproach of Egypt was still upon them: they did not bear in their bodies the sign of separation unto God. But when His Word had been submitted to, the reproach of Egypt was rolled away. The camp where they were abiding at this time was then designated Gilgal, which means *rolling* and it speaks therefore of the place of self-judgment. They went forward afterward from this camp to battle and returned there when the conflict was over. So the soldier of Christ should ever encamp at the place of self-judgment and from there go forth in the power of the Spirit to meet his foes, returning thereto when the victory has been won; or if perchance he has met with defeat, going back to Gilgal to judge himself before God.

The second subject that comes before us is Old Corn, and of this we read in Joshua 5 : 10-12 :

And the children of Israel encamped in Gilgal, and kept the passover on the fourteenth day of the month at even in the plains of Jericho. And they did eat of the old corn of the land on the morrow after the passover, unleavened cakes, and parched corn in the selfsame day. And the manna ceased on the morrow after they had eaten of the old corn of the land; neither had the children of Israel manna any more; but they did eat of the fruit of the land of Canaan that year.

It is most interesting to note the deep significance of three different kinds of food upon which the people of Israel fed. When they kept the passover, which speaks of Christ's death for us upon the Cross, they ate the flesh of the lamb roast with fire. Like the priests in the sanctuary they ate "those things wherewith the atonement was made." For us this speaks of feasting our souls upon the work of our blessed Lord on Calvary. This is expressed beautifully in a well known hymn:

> *To Calvary, Lord, in spirit now*
> *Our weary souls repair,*
> *To feast upon Thy dying love*
> *And taste its sweetness there.*

As we meditate upon what the Lord Jesus went through for us in that hour when the judgment of God fell upon Him in order that our sins might forever be put away, we are eating in spirit of the lamb roast with fire.

As Israel journeyed through the wilderness, which speaks of this present evil world, through which God's people are now passing as strangers and pilgrims, the food that sustained them was the manna from heaven. This manna, as our blessed Lord shows us in John 6, was a type of Himself as the humbled One, who trod the path of faith in this world: our great example of devotion to the Father. He said, "Moses gave you not that bread from heaven. The bread of God is He that came down from heaven to give His life for the world." As we dwell upon the lowly path of our Saviour through this scene, we are feeding upon the manna.

Note the place where the manna was found. Morning by morning it came from heaven to earth. It was not upon the high trees or on the mountains where the people would have to climb to obtain it; nor was it down in the deep ravines where they would have to descend and search for it. It lay all about them upon the ground, on the dew, which is a type of the Holy Spirit. The manna occupied so low a place that every Israelite, when he stepped out of his tent door in the morning, had to do one of two things: he either had to gather it or trample on it. And this is exactly the place which our Lord Jesus has taken in His infinite love and grace. We may well pause and ask ourselves the question: Are we trampling on His loving-kindness or have we received Him as our blessed, adorable Saviour?

The manna then was food for the wilderness, but when the people crossed over Jordan and entered into their inheritance, which speaks of our place as associated with the risen Christ in heaven, the manna ceased, and they began to feed upon the old corn of the land. Jesus said, long years afterward: "Except a corn of wheat fall into the ground and die, it abideth alone, but if it die it shall bear much fruit." Christ Himself was the corn of wheat who fell into the ground in death; now He has come forth in resurrection: the old corn of the land speaks of Him as the Risen One. Therefore we who have received Him by faith are bidden to set our affections on things above, where Christ sitteth at the right hand of God. As we are occupied with Him in the heavenlies, we will receive new strength to enable us to appropriate and enjoy our present portion as a heavenly people.

The third topic is also of deep interest: The Captain of the Lord's Host. Of this we read in verses 13 to 15:

**And it came to pass, when Joshua was by Jericho, that he lifted up his eyes and looked, and behold, there stood a man over against him with his sword drawn in his hand: and Joshua went unto him, and said unto him, Art thou for us, or for our adversaries? And he said, Nay; but as captain of the host of the Lord am I now come. And Joshua fell on his face to the earth, and did worship, and said unto him, What saith my Lord unto His servant? And the captain of the Lord's host said unto Joshua, Loose thy shoe from off thy foot; for the place whereon thou standest is holy. And Joshua did so.**

Joshua had evidently gone out to reconnoiter. He was looking upon Jericho, doubtless considering what might be the best method of attacking it in order to insure the capture of that walled city; but he was to learn that it was not for him to direct the armies of Israel except as the Lord Himself gave instruction. Suddenly he saw standing before him a man with a drawn sword in his hand. Joshua, apparently without fear, immediately went over to him and asked the question: "Art thou for us or for our adversaries?" The answer was most instructive. This stranger warrior replied, "Nay but as captain of the host of Jehovah am I now come." It was the angel of the covenant appearing in human form to take command of the armies of Israel. Joshua was to be subject to his control.

Recognizing immediately the supernatural character of this visitor, Joshua fell, we are told, on his face to the earth and worshiped, inquiring, "What saith my Lord unto His servant?" The answer was simple, but designed to impress Israel's great chieftain with the sanctity of the Being who addressed him, "Loose thy shoe from off thy foot, for the place whereon thou standest is holy." Instantly obeying, Joshua remained prostrate before this supernatural Captain. We are not told of anything further that passed between them, but it is evident that Joshua recognized in this theophany the blessed fact that Jehovah Himself had come to lead His people to victory. The Captain of the Lord's host is, of course, none other than that Great Captain of our salvation: the Lord Jesus Christ Himself. The angel of the covenant of the Old Testament is the Jesus of the New Testament, God manifest in flesh. May it be ours ever to yield glad subjection to His guidance and so as we follow Him and obey His Word, we shall be assured of victory over all our foes.

## BACK TO GILGAL

*Back to Gilgal, back to Gilgal,*
  *Let me, O my spirit, go!*
*Where the stones of death lie buried*
  *'Neath the mighty Jordan's flow;*
*When the manna ceased from falling*
  *On the resurrection day—*
*Back to where the shame of Egypt*
  *From the host was rolled away.*

*Back to where the stones of witness*
  *Silent by the river stand;*
*Where was ate the feast unleaven'd,*
  *And the old corn of the land;*
*Where Jehovah's ransomed army*
  *For the Canaan conquest start;*
*Back to where death and resurrection*
  *Meet the eye and fill the heart.*

*When, by strength of God, victorious*
  *Thou dost bear the spoil away,*
*Back unto the camp of Gilgal*
  *Hasten in that joyful day!*
*If, defeated in the conflict,*
  *Thou dost flee before the foe,*
*Back to Gilgal, O my spirit—*
  *In thy shame and sorrow go!*

*Till the land shall* all *be conquer'd,*
  *And the palm thy hand shall bear—*
*Till the tent is pitched at* Shiloh,
  *And Jehovah worshipped THERE.*

*Camp at Gilgal, start from Gilgal,*
  *Back to Gilgal ever come!*
*Anchor by the ford of Jordan*
  *Till all Canaan is thy home.*
                    —WILLIAM BLANE

# The Fall of Jericho

**Now Jericho was straitly shut up because of the children of Israel; none went out and none came in (verse 1).**

THE walled city of Jericho was the first obstacle that met the people of Israel as they looked forward from the camp at Gilgal to taking possession of the inheritance, which was theirs already by title, that is, by Jehovah's gift, but which they had to make their own experimentally by driving out or destroying the inhabitants of the land, who had become so vile in the sight of the Lord that He could no longer tolerate them. Because of their unspeakably corrupt lives the land was about to vomit them out (Lev. 18:25). In Abraham's day we are told that the iniquity of the Amorites was not yet full (Gen. 15:16). God therefore had waited in long-suffering mercy, but now all the nations of Canaan had sunk into such depths of depravity and the land had become so utterly defiled that it could only be cleansed by judgment.

Canaan speaks, as we have seen, not primarily of heaven itself—the eternal inheritance of the believer in Christ, for there will be no foes to contest our possession there. But it speaks of our present inheritance : that rest of heart and mind which is the abiding portion of all who take God at His Word and go forward in confidence to overcome their spiritual foes. "We wrestle not against flesh and blood"—our conflict is not with men—but with wicked spirits in the heavenlies, the world-rulers of this darkness—that is, with Satan and his hosts, who control the minds of those who know not God and who would seek to hinder Christians from entering into and enjoying their privileges in Christ.

There is a life of blessing and victory which is the birthright portion of each child of God, but which many of us fail to appropriate by faith and enjoy practically because of indolence and selfishness.

Jericho stood as the barrier to Israel's advance and had to be destroyed before the host of the Lord could move forward.

But how were they to subjugate this walled city when they had no battering-rams or other engines of war whereby to make a breach in its defenses ? The answer is given in the eleventh chapter of Hebrews. By faith the walls of Jericho fell down after they were compassed about seven days (verse 30). Surely there never was another siege of so strange a character !

The Captain of the Lord's host outlined the plan of procedure, as we find it in verses 2 to 5 :

**And the Lord said unto Joshua, See, I have given into thine hand Jericho, and the king thereof, and the mighty men of valour. And ye shall compass the city, all ye men of war, and go round about the city once. Thus shalt thou do six days. And seven priests shall bear before the ark seven trumpets of rams' horns: and the seventh day ye shall compass the city seven times, and the priests shall blow with the trumpets. And it shall come to pass, that when they make a long blast with the ram's horn, and when ye hear the sound of the trumpet, all the people shall shout with a great shout; and the wall of the city shall fall down flat, and the people shall ascend up every man straight before him.**

The instructions were implicit. There was no room for human schemes or approved military tactics. All was ordered of the Lord and Joshua and Israel had but to obey.

What is the Jericho that has kept many of us from fullness of blessing? With some it is a selfish ambition: the desire for fame or for success in some chosen pursuit. With others it is covetousness: the yearning to accumulate wealth and to live in opulence. With others again it is the love of worldly pleasure: the effort to find enjoyment in the vain things that the Christless crave. Only by faith can such obstacles be overcome. The frowning walls of Jericho must fall before there can be spiritual progress and enjoyment of the riches of grace in Christ Jesus.

In obedience to the Word of the Lord, Israel marched once about the city the first day, as recorded in verses 8 to 11:

And it came to pass, when Joshua had spoken unto the people, that the seven priests bearing the seven trumpets of rams' horns passed on before the Lord, and blew with the trumpets: and the ark of the covenant of the Lord followed them. And the armed men went before the priests that blew with the trumpets, and the rereward came after the ark, the priests going on, and blowing with the trumpets. And Joshua had commanded the people, saying, Ye shall not shout, nor make any noise with your voice, neither shall any word proceed out of your mouth, until the day I bid you shout; then shall ye shout. So the ark of the Lord compassed the city, going about it once: and they came into the camp, and lodged in the camp.

Doubtless the people of Jericho wondered at the strange sight as the army of the Lord, led by the priests with their trumpets, and the ark of the covenant, speaking of Christ Himself, marched around the city. Little did they realize that the sounding of those trumpets was both a summons to surrender and a warning of coming judgment if they refused. Such is the message God's anointed priests are sounding out to the world today.

For six days these strange proceedings went on.

And Joshua rose early in the morning, and the priests took up the ark of the Lord. And seven priests bearing seven trumpets of rams' horns before the ark of the Lord went on continually, and blew with the trumpets: and the armed men went before them; but the rereward came after the ark of the Lord, the priests going on, and blowing with the trumpets.

Still nothing happened. The walls stood broad and high just as before and no doubt the people of Jericho congratulated themselves upon the strength of their defenses and ridiculed the folly and absurdity of Joshua and his army.

But on the seventh day the change came.

**And it came to pass on the seventh day, that they rose early about the dawning of the day, and compassed the city after the same manner seven times: only on that day they compassed the city seven times. And it came to pass at the seventh time, when the priests blew with the trumpets, Joshua said unto the people, Shout; for the Lord hath given you the city.**

As Israel obeyed the command of Joshua the Lord acted for them. The walls of Jericho fell and the host of the Lord entered in triumph, driving all their foes before them and setting the city on fire.

Implicit instruction was given to the Israelites to keep themselves from the accursed thing when the fall of the city ensued. All that was worth preserving was to be dedicated to the Lord, even as today whatever God-given talents or wealth men have are to be consecrated to Him who gave them. No Israelite was to appropriate anything for himself. What was worthless was to be burned with fire.

**And the city shall be accursed, even it, and all that are therein, to the Lord: only Rahab the harlot shall live, she and all that are with her in the house, because she hid the messengers that we sent.**

**And ye, in any wise, keep yourselves from the accursed thing, lest ye make yourselves accursed, when ye take of the accursed thing, and make the camp of Israel a curse, and trouble it. But all the silver and gold and vessels of brass and iron, are consecrated unto the Lord: they shall come into the treasury of the Lord.**

At last the long silence (save for the sounding of the trumpets) was broken.

**The people shouted when the priests blew with the trumpets: and it came to pass, when the people heard the sound of the trumpet, and the people shouted with a great shout, that the wall fell down flat, so that the people went up into the city, every man straight before him, and they took the city. And they utterly destroyed all that was in the city, both man and woman, young and old, and ox, and sheep, and ass, with the edge of the sword.**

So the first great obstacle to taking possession of the land had been overcome. "This is the victory that overcometh the world, even our faith."

But what of the promise made to Rahab, she who hid the spies because of her faith and who asked for a true token? God had not forgotten her. Neither had Joshua. Provision was made for the protection of her and all who found shelter in her house, where the scarlet cord hung in the window.

Once more our minds turn to the eleventh chapter of Hebrews, where in verse 31 we read: "By faith the harlot Rahab perished not with them that believed not, when she had received the spies with peace."

Her house was upon the wall and therefore exposed to grave danger, but because of her confidence in God that part of the wall fell not when the rest was destroyed. We read in verses 22 to 25:

But Joshua had said unto the two men that had spied out the country, Go into the harlot's house, and bring out thence the woman, and all that she hath, as ye sware unto her. And the young men that were spies went in, and brought out Rahab, and her father, and her mother, and her brethren, and all that she had; and they brought out all her kindred, and left them without the camp of Israel. And they burnt the city with fire, and all that was therein: only the silver, and the gold, and the vessels of brass and of iron, they put into the treasury of the house of the Lord. And Joshua saved Rahab the harlot alive, and her father's household, and all that she had; and she dwelleth in Israel even unto this day; because she hid the messengers, which Joshua sent to spy out Jericho.

Thus the promise of the spies to Rahab was fulfilled and she and her father's household were preserved alive. She became an honored mother in Israel, for we learn in Matthew 1:5 that she was united in marriage to Salmon, a leader in Israel, and she became the mother of Boaz, who in turn became the husband of Ruth, the grandmother of King David. Thus Rahab, of unsavory character before she was reached by divine grace, became an ancestress, after the flesh, of our blessed Lord Jesus Christ. How wondrous are the ways of God; how great His loving-kindness!

We notice in the following verses of our chapter that Joshua put Jericho under a curse, so that in after days it would be thought of from that standpoint— "The city of the curse." This is what the world is and ever will be until the Lord Jesus Christ is recognized as King of kings and Lord of lords.

**And Joshua adjured them at that time, saying, Cursed be the man before the Lord, that riseth up and buildeth this city of Jericho: he shall lay the foundation thereof in his firstborn, and in his youngest son shall he set up the gates of it.**

This prophecy was fulfilled long years afterwards in the days of the ungodly King Ahab, as we are told in 1 Kings 16:34. The destruction of Jericho was the beginning of the fulfillment of God's Word given to Moses so long before and repeated to Joshua. It was evident that no enemy would be able to stand before His people—that is, Jehovah's people—so long as they put their trust in Him and kept themselves from the accursed thing. So we are told in the last part of the chapter that "the Lord was with Joshua; and his fame was noised through all the country."

As we read and ponder over this record today we should remember that the things that were written aforetime were written for our learning that we might be encouraged to take the path of obedience to the Word of the Lord, and to trust in the living God in order that we may overcome every spiritual foe and so go up in faith to possess that which has been given us in Christ. No power can stand against us if we are careful to give God His rightful place in our lives and so press with confidence to take possession of our rich inheritance.

# Sin in the Camp

But the children of Israel committed a trespass
in the accursed thing: for Achan, the son of Carmi,
the son of Zabdi, the son of Zerah, of the tribe of
Judah, took of the accursed thing: and the anger
of the Lord was kindled against the children of
Israel. And Joshua sent men from Jericho to Ai,
which is beside Bethaven, on the east side of
Bethel, and spake unto them, saying, Go up and
view the country. And the men went up and viewed
Ai. And they returned to Joshua, and said unto
him, Let not all the people go up; but let about two
or three thousand men go up and smite Ai; and
make not all the people to labour thither; for they
are but few. So there went up thither of the people
about three thousand men: and they fled before the
men of Ai. And the men of Ai smote of them about
thirty and six men: for they chased them from before the gate even unto Shebarim, and smote them
in the going down: wherefore the hearts of the
people melted and became as water. And Joshua
rent his clothes, and fell to the earth upon his face
before the ark of the Lord until the eventide, he
and the elders of Israel, and put dust upon their
heads.

THE fall of Jericho in such a miraculous way, without any real effort on Israel's part, evidently led to overconfidence and forgetfulness of the fact that it was God alone who had destroyed this first barrier to their possession of the land. The next city to be subdued was small compared to Jericho and a detachment sent out to reconnoiter reported that it would be easily captured and that it would be quite unnecessary for the entire host to move against it. So about three thousand men undertook to destroy it, but were defeated ignominiously. We are told they fled before the men of Ai and thirty-six of them were slain. It was a great shock naturally to Joshua and to the people as a whole, but we are told at once of the reason for the defeat.

God had commanded Israel to take nothing for themselves of the spoil of Jericho. The silver and the gold and metallic vessels were to be devoted to the service of the Lord, but all else was under a curse and was to be destroyed. One man and his family failed to obey the Word of the Lord and committed a trespass in the accursed thing. Thus Israel had no power to stand against their foes.

There are two important lessons that we may take to our own hearts from this incident. First, note how God looked upon the twelve tribes of Israel as a unit. They formed one nation, and what affected one part of the nation affected all. Though strife and division came in afterwards, God still speaks of the twelve tribes of Israel. To them the Epistle of James is addressed and the Apostle Paul speaks of the Resur-

rection as that to which "our twelve tribes, instantly
serving God day and night, hoped to come." In the
Christian dispensation one of the great outstanding
truths set forth in the Word is that of the entity of the
body of Christ. So intimately are the members of
Christ linked to one another by the Spirit that it is
written : "If one member suffer, all the members suffer with it ; if one member be honored all the members
rejoice with it." This is very precious, but it is also
exceedingly solemn. As individual members of Christ
we need to realize that our attitude and behavior has
an effect for good or ill upon the body as a whole. We
know how true this is in the human body : often some
affected hidden gland is the cause of great discom-
fort and misery to the entire body. When this condition is rectified the whole body is freed of its distress.

And so the secret of Israel's defeat at Ai was the
fact that one man and his family had disobeyed
the Word of the Lord and committed a trespass in the
accursed thing. When the defeated soldiers of Israel
came fleeing for their lives back to their brethren in
the camp, the hearts of the people melted. All their
hopes of a speedy defeat of their enemies seemed to be
at an end and they were utterly bewildered and discouraged. Their great leader himself was shocked
and perplexed at what had taken place, and we are
told that "Joshua rent his clothes and fell to the
earth upon his face before the ark of the Lord until
the eventide, he and the elders of Israel, and put dust
upon their heads." This was the expression of utter
self-abnegation and grief.

We have Joshua's prayer recorded in verses 7 to 9:

**And Joshua said, Alas, O Lord God, wherefore hast Thou at all brought this people over Jordan, to deliver us into the hand of the Amorites, to destroy us? would to God we had been content, and dwelt on the other side Jordan! O Lord, what shall I say, when Israel turneth their backs before their enemies! For the Canaanites and all the inhabitants of the land shall hear of it, and shall environ us round, and cut off our name from the earth: and what wilt Thou do unto Thy great name?**

Note the two things that troubled him: "O Lord," he exclaimed, "what shall I say when Israel turneth their backs upon their enemies?" The story of their defeat at Ai would spread rapidly throughout the land and the other nations of Canaan would be encouraged to defend their cities with renewed valor, whereas before the fear of the Lord had fallen upon them. Then Joshua also asked: "What wilt Thou do unto Thy great name?" But Jehovah can be depended upon to defend His own name. He will not condone sin in His own people to do this. Sin must be dealt with before God will manifest Himself openly on their behalf.

We are told that the Lord said unto Joshua:

**Get thee up; wherefore liest thou thus upon thy face? Israel hath sinned, and they have also transgressed My covenant which I commanded them: for they have even taken of the accursed thing, and have also stolen, and dissembled also, and they**

**have put it even among their own stuff (verses 10, 11).**

This was the cause of their defeat. Prayer is always good in its place, but this was not the time for prayer. It was the time to deal in unsparing judgment with the family who had committed the sin that had weakened Israel before their foes. It was because of this sin that they had no strength to stand before their enemies, and God declared that He would not be with them any more until they destroyed the cursed thing from among them.

How often similar conditions have prevailed even in the churches of God in this dispensation of grace! Hidden sin, unconfessed, unjudged, has made the people of the Lord as weak as water when they came in conflict with their satanic foes.

In accordance with the Word of the Lord all Israel was called to stand before God, and Joshua cast lots to determine the particular tribe in which the guilty party was to be found. The casting of lots was an Old Testament way of determining the mind of the Lord. We read in the book of Proverbs: "The lot is cast into the lap; but the whole disposing thereof is of the Lord" (16:33). Again and again we find this method used in determining the will of God. The last time which God seems to have recognized is that recorded in the book of Acts, when the apostles cast lots to determine whether Joseph or Matthias should be appointed as successor to Judas. After the coming of the Holy Spirit on the day of Pentecost, no such method is ever indicated in the New Testament. The believer today is able to determine the will of God as he searches the Scriptures in dependence on the Holy Spirit.

The story is told of a young curate in the Church of England who was greatly helped in his understanding of the Scriptures by frequent conversations with an uneducated cobbler, who was, nevertheless, well acquainted with the Word of God. On one occasion when a friend of his, a young theologian, was visiting him, he mentioned the remarkable knowledge of the Bible which this cobbler possessed. The young theologue, in a spirit of pride, expressed a desire to meet him, saying he felt sure he could propose some questions to him on the Scriptures which he would be quite unable to answer. Upon being introduced to him in his little shop the question was put: "Can you tell me what the Urim and Thummim were?" The cobbler replied: "I don't know exactly; I understand that the words apply to something that was on the breastplate of the high priest. I know the words mean 'Lights and Perfection' and that through the Urim and Thummim the high priest was able to discern the mind of the Lord. But I find that I can get the mind of the Lord by just changing one letter. I take this blessed Book and Usim and Thummim, and I get the mind of the Lord that way."

When the lots were cast in this particular instance, the tribe of Judah was taken; then the various families of Judah stood before the Lord; lots were cast for them and the family of the Zarhites was taken. The

households of this family were then brought before
God and lots were cast and the household of Zabdi
was taken. His household was brought man by man
before the Lord and the lot fell on Achan, the guilty
person whose disobedience to the word of the Lord
was responsible for Israel's defeat at Ai. Adjured by
Joshua to make confession of his sin and tell what he
had done, Achan answered:

**Indeed I have sinned against the Lord God of Is-
rael, and thus and thus have I done: When I saw
among the spoils a goodly Babylonish garment, and
two hundred shekels of silver, and a wedge of gold
of fifty shekels weight, then I coveted them, and
took them; and, behold, they are hid in the earth
in the midst of my tent, and the silver under it.**

Unhappily, this confession came too late. Had
Achan come to God of his own accord and acknowledged his sin and brought a proper offering, doubtless
there would have been forgiveness for him. But the
confession wrung from him only after the lot had indicated who the wicked one was, could not avail to
shield him from judgment.

We need to remember that this event occurred in
the dispensation of the law. Law knows no mercy;
law is absolutely just. Therefore Achan and his family had to be destroyed because of their sin. It is very
evident that the family were implicated in the evil
deeds of the head of the house, because the law
strictly forbade putting the children to death for the
sins of the parents, but inasmuch as all were devoted

to judgment, it is evident that all participated in the evil. They were brought down into the Valley of Achor; that is, the valley of trouble. As they stood there before the Lord and His people,

**Joshua said, Why hast thou troubled us? the Lord shall trouble thee this day. And all Israel stoned him with stones, and burned them with fire, after they had stoned them with stones. And they raised over him a great heap of stones unto this day. So the Lord turned from the fierceness of His anger. Wherefore the name of that place was called, The valley of Achor, unto this day.**

It is a sad story, but it has a serious lesson for God's people everywhere. Sin in the camp will weaken the host of the Lord and hinder blessing and victory. Sin judged and dealt with leaves God free to work in the way in which He delights.

In the book of Hosea there is a word of comfort even in connection with this sad story. The Lord tells Israel that in the latter days He is going to recover them from their wandering and restore them to Himself and He will give them the valley of Achor for a door of hope (Hos. 2:15). The valley of Achor speaks of the trouble that we bring upon ourselves by our own sins: retributive justice because of our departure from the Lord. But if we judge ourselves before God and turn to Him in sincerity of heart, He will give deliverance, and even the valley of Achor will become an entrance into blessing.

We need to remember that grace does not set aside

government. It is still true that "whatsoever a man soweth that shall he also reap," and "he that doeth wrong shall receive for the wrong that he hath done and there is no respect of persons with God." We cannot sin with impunity because we are saved by grace. But on the other hand, if we judge ourselves we shall not be judged of the Lord.

# The Fall of Ai and the Proclamation of the Law

## Joshua 8

T HE present chapter readily divides into two sections. In verses 1 to 29 we have the account of the destruction of Ai. In verses 30 to 35 we read of the proclamation of the law, with the blessings for the obedient and the curses that would fall upon the disobedient.

When God's people fail to act in accordance with His will the first time they have to face some barrier to progress, they find it far harder to overcome upon making a second effort. Had it not been for hidden sin in the camp, Israel would have overcome Ai very easily, even as they overcame Jericho when they acted in accordance with the Word of the Lord. But when, after dealing with Achan and his covetous household, they prepared to make a second onslaught on the little city by whose inhabitants they had been defeated before, they found it a difficult task indeed which they had to undertake.

We read in verses 1 to 8:

And the Lord said unto Joshua, Fear not, neither be thou dismayed: take all the people of war with thee, and arise, go up to Ai: see, I have given into thy hand the king of Ai, and his people, and his city, and his land: And thou shalt do to Ai and her king as thou didst unto Jericho and her king: only the spoil thereof, and the cattle thereof, shall ye take for a prey unto yourselves; lay thee an ambush for the city behind it. So Joshua arose, and all the people of war, to go up against Ai: and Joshua chose out thirty thousand mighty men of valour, and sent them away by night. And he commanded them, saying, Behold, ye shall lie in wait against the city, even behind the city: go not very far from the city, but be ye all ready: And I, and all the people that are with me, will approach unto the city: and it shall come to pass, when they come out against us, as at the first, that we will flee before them, (For they will come out after us) till we have drawn them from the city; for they will say, They flee before us, as at the first: therefore we will flee before them. Then ye shall rise up from the ambush, and seize upon the city: for the Lord your God will deliver it into your hand. And it shall be, when ye have taken the city, that ye shall set the city on fire: according to the commandment of the Lord shall ye do. See, I have commanded you.

Thus did God outline the plan they were to carry out; a plan intended to impress upon them the folly of underrating the power of the enemy as they had done before, and also the lesson of their own helplessness and insufficiency apart from the divine enabling.

Acting on the instruction given, we are told that

Joshua rose up early in the morning, and numbered the people, and went up, he and the elders of Israel, before the people to Ai. And all the people, even the people of war that were with him, went up, and drew nigh, and came before the city, and pitched on the north side of Ai: now there was a valley between them and Ai. And he took about five thousand men, and set them to lie in ambush between Bethel and Ai, on the west side of the city. And when they had set the people, even all the host that was on the north of the city, and their liers in wait on the west of the city, Joshua went that night into the midst of the valley.

Thus all was in readiness for the test of the morrow, when the men of Ai were to learn that, after all, they were no match for Israel so long as they acted in accordance with the Word of God.

Ai was a little city, and it is the little things that become great obstacles in the onward march of the host of the Lord, unless they are dealt with in the light of His Word. In this instance, Israel was to learn how strong a little city may be and what wisdom and dependence on God is needed in order to overcome it.

As anticipated and foreseen by Joshua, acting under divine direction, the men of Ai came rushing forth early in the morning expecting an easy victory, and at first it seemed as though they were right. We read:

And it came to pass, when the king of Ai saw it, that they hasted and rose up early, and the men of

the city went out against Israel to battle, he and all
his people, at a time appointed, before the plain;
but he wist not that there were liers in ambush
against him behind the city. And Joshua and all
Israel made as if they were beaten before them, and
fled by the way of the wilderness. And all the
people that were in Ai were called together to pursue after them: and they pursued after Joshua, and
were drawn away from the city. And there was not
a man left in Ai or Bethel, that went not out after
Israel: and they left the city open, and pursued
after Israel.

Recklessly the self-confident men of Ai left their
city utterly unprotected as they pursued after the re-
treating Israelites. At Joshua's signal the 3000 men in
ambush then rose up and carried out the orders given
on the night before (verses 18, 19):

And the Lord said unto Joshua, Stretch out the
spear that is in thy hand toward Ai; for I will give
it into thine hand. And Joshua stretched out the
spear that he had in his hand toward the city. And
the ambush arose quickly out of their place, and
they ran as soon as he had stretched out his hand:
and they entered into the city, and took it, and
hasted and set the city on fire.

This ruse resulted in the capture of Ai and the
destruction of its inhabitants, as we read in verses
20-23:

And when the men of Ai looked behind them,
they saw, and, behold, the smoke of the city ascended up to heaven, and they had no power to

flee this way or that way: and the people that fled
to the wilderness turned back upon the pursuers.
And when Joshua and all Israel saw that the ambush had taken the city, and that the smoke of the
city ascended, then they turned again, and slew
the men of Ai. And the other issued out of the city
against them; so they were in the midst of Israel,
some on this side, and some on that side: and they
smote them, so that they let none of them remain
or escape. And the king of Ai they took alive, and
brought him to Joshua.

It was a signal victory for Israel, though achieved
in a manner designed to impress upon them the folly
of acting in accordance with their own thoughts and
failing to discern the mind of the Lord. They were
strong only as they acted in obedience to His commands.

Details of the close of the battle are given in verses
24 to 29:

And it came to pass, when Israel had made an
end of slaying all the inhabitants of Ai in the field,
in the wilderness wherein they chased them, and
when they were all fallen on the edge of the sword,
until they were consumed, that all the Israelites returned unto Ai, and smote it with the edge of the
sword. And so it was, that all that fell that day,
both of men and women, were twelve thousand,
even all the men of Ai. For Joshua drew not his
hand back, wherewith he stretched out the spear,
until he had utterly destroyed all the inhabitants of
Ai. Only the cattle and the spoil of that city Israel
took for a prey unto themselves, according unto
the word of the Lord which He commanded Joshua.

And Joshua burnt Ai, and made it an heap for
ever, even a desolation unto this day. And the king
of Ai he hanged on a tree until eventide: and as
soon as the sun was down, Joshua commanded that
they should take his carcase down from the tree,
and cast it at the entering of the gate of the city,
and raise thereon a great heap of stones, that remaineth unto this day.

Observe that in this instance God permitted Israel
to take the cattle and the wealth of the city as a prey
for themselves. He did not put a ban on the spoil of
Ai as on that of Jericho. There are certain things of
an earthly character which God's children are permitted to use for sustenance and enjoyment, even
though they are called upon to judge the world as an
ordered system opposed to the Cross of Christ.

We turn now to the second section. Moses had
commanded the children of Israel that when they entered into the land they were to proceed to the Mounts
Gerizim and Ebal and there set up an altar and a pillar and proclaim the law, with its statutes and judgments, as given first at Sinai and amplified in the
plains of Moab. Of this we read in Deuteronomy 27
and 28.

In accordance with this command, we are told that

Joshua built an altar unto the Lord God of Israel
in mount Ebal, As Moses the servant of the Lord
commanded the children of Israel, as it is written
in the book of the law of Moses, an altar of whole
stones, over which no man had lift up any iron:
and they offered thereon burnt-offerings unto the
Lord, and sacrificed peace-offerings.

This altar, observe, was built of whole stones, upon which no tool had been lifted, as Moses had told them in Exodus 20:25. The altar speaks of Christ, as does the offering placed upon it. He had to be who He was in order to do what He did. Therefore, there was to be no effort by man to shape the stones. They were to be put together just as they were provided by God. Upon this altar burnt offerings and peace offerings were placed. These speak of Christ offering Himself without spot unto God on our behalf and thus making peace by the blood of His Cross.

It was most blessed that such a foreshadowing was seen at the base of Mount Ebal—for from that mount the curses were declared by one half of the Levites. All are under the curse to whom the law comes, for "Cursed is every one that continueth not in all things that are written in the book of the law to do them." That smoking altar told of Him who, sinless Himself, was to make propitiation for the sins of the world.

The blessings were proclaimed by the other half of the Levites from Mount Gerizim (Deut. 27:12) but as these blessings depended entirely upon the obedience of the people, it was soon manifest that no man could claim them as being rightfully his. All blessing must be on the ground of pure grace.

After the sacrifices were offered, the altar was, as it were, turned into a monument. It was covered with plaster, on which, when hardened, the blessings and the curses were written as a memorial "according to all that is written in the book of the law." This was to be an abiding testimonial that it might not be forgotten in days to come (verse 35) :

**There was not a word of all that Moses commanded, which Joshua read not before all the congregation of Israel, with the women, and the little ones, and the strangers that were conversant among them.**

Thus had Joshua begun to take possession of the land which by this monument was dedicated to Jehovah. But because of Israel's disobedience, the time came when God could no longer own them as His covenant people and so He gave them over to the power of their enemies. It is not possible for fallen man to keep God's perfect law. That law which in itself is "holy, just, and good," can only curse and condemn those who are under it. In the fullness of time Christ came to redeem from that curse all who believe in Him. Now His redeemed people stand before God on the ground of pure grace, and their obedience, far from being of a legal character, is the glad service of love to Him who has made them His own.

# The Wiles of the Devil

JOSHUA 9

I T HAS been well said that "Satan plays with
loaded dice." He knows all the weaknesses of
human nature and is an expert in the black art
of deception. So in the New Testament believers are
exhorted to "put on the whole armour of God, that
[they] may be able to stand against the wiles of the
devil" (Eph. 6:11).

We have a very striking illustration of the devil's
deceptive practices in this ninth chapter of Joshua.
As the word went out to the other Canaanite peoples
that Jericho and Ai had fallen before the victorious
Israelites, the dwellers in a certain Hivite city, named
Gibeon, decided that if they would avert the destruction of themselves and their city, they must act at
once and that in a manner calculated to mislead
Joshua and his forces regarding their identity and the
location of their homeland.

So we are told in verses 3 to 6:

**And when the inhabitants of Gibeon heard what
Joshua had done unto Jericho and to Ai, They did
work wilily, and went and made as if they had been**

92

ambassadors, and took old sacks upon their asses,
and wine bottles, old, and rent, and bound up; And
old shoes and clouted upon their feet, and old garments upon them; and all the bread of their provision was dry and mouldy. And they went to
Joshua unto the camp at Gilgal and said unto him,
and to the men of Israel, We be come from a far
country: now therefore make ye a league with us.

This was on the part of these Hivites a very clever
ruse and it accomplished its purpose, for when the
strange-looking "ambassadors" arrived at the camp
of Israel in Gilgal, Joshua and his officers were deceived by their appearance and the story that they
concocted. The ragged garments, the worn-out san-
dals, the rotting wine-skins, and the mouldy bread
all seemed to authenticate the plea that these Gibeonites made.

And the men of Israel said unto the Hivites,
Peradventure ye dwell among us; and how shall we
make a league with you? And they said unto
Joshua, We are thy servants. And Joshua said
unto them, Who are ye? and from whence come ye?
And they said unto him, From a very far country
thy servants are come because of the name of the
Lord thy God: for we have heard the fame of Him,
and all that He did in Egypt, And all that He did
to the two kings of the Amorites, that were beyond
Jordan, to Sihon king of Heshbon, and to Og king
of Bashan, which was at Ashtaroth. Wherefore our
elders and all the inhabitants of our country spake
to us, saying, Take victuals with you for the journey, and go to meet them, and say unto them, We
are your servants: therefore now make ye a league

with us. This our bread we took hot for our provision out of our houses on the day we came forth
to go unto you; but now, behold, it is dry, and it is
mouldy: And these bottles of wine, which we filled,
were new; and, behold, they be rent: and these our
garments and our shoes are become old by reason
of the very long journey.

There was something so apparently genuine about
this recital, with its hypocritical pretense of having
come to fear Jehovah, the God of Israel, that those
who listened to it were quite carried away by it. We
are told, "the men took of their victuals, and asked
not counsel of the Lord" (verse 14). This was a fatal
mistake. It is always wrong to act on our own judgment instead of seeking to know the mind of God as
revealed in His Word.

Had Joshua and the rest remembered the instruction given them to destroy utterly the corrupt nations
of Canaan, they would have been careful to make
further inquiry before accepting the story of the men
of Gibeon at face value. But, as we so often are inclined to do, they trusted their own judgment and
so were misled completely. Verse 15 tells us:

And Joshua made peace with them, and made a
league with them, to let them live: and the princes
of the congregation sware unto them.

How the wily Gibeonites must have laughed in
their sleeves as they noted the success of their scheme!
Joshua had failed to discern their hypocrisy. When he

and the princes of the congregation had made a league with these deceivers, the latter departed in high glee, to inform their fellow citizens that they were now allies of Israel and so the danger of their extirpation had passed!

May we not see in this how Satan works today? Knowing he cannot by any means affect the eternal destiny of the people of God, he uses all kinds of schemes to mislead them here on earth and to turn them aside from full obedience to the will of God. He never comes to a Christian presenting himself in his true character. He appears as an angel of light with suggestions which appeal to the natural mind, just as he came to Eve of old, who was deceived by his wiles and thus the old creation went down with a crash.

Whatever plan he suggests will be seen in its true light if tested by what God has revealed in His Word: "To the law and to the testimony: if they speak not according to this Word, it is because there is no light in them" (Isa. 8:20). Yet those who should know better are often led astray by specious suggestions and flattering words and so enter into associations and are led to pursue plans which work havoc to their own spirituality and make them useless to others who need their help.

Perhaps there is nothing whereby Satan has lured more young Christians into paths of disobedience and lifetime wretchedness than by the snare of mixed marriages. God has plainly forbidden the unequal yoke (2 Cor. 6:14); yet when Satan manages to get

the affections engaged and the hearts of two are
drawn together—the one a Christian and the other
an unbeliever—it is easy to allow one's personal desires to overrule God's plain testimony. In the hope
that after all He will be better than His Word, the
child of God enters into a union entailing lifelong
misery. The same is true as to many other relation-
ships: business partnerships with the ungodly, joining lodges and other societies that link saved and
unsaved together, and, most insidious of all, the union
of children of God and children of the devil in church
fellowship!

Israel soon discovered the mistake they had made,
but it was then too late to extricate themselves from
the mess into which they had fallen (verses 16-18) :

**And it came to pass at the end of three days after
they had made a league with them, that they heard
that they were their neighbours, and that they
dwelt among them. And the children of Israel journeyed, and came unto their cities on the third day.
Now their cities were Gibeon, and Chephirah, and
Beeroth, and Kirjath-jearim. And the children of
Israel smote them not, because the princes of the
congregation had sworn unto them by the Lord
God of Israel. And all the congregation murmured
against the princes.**

In an effort to alleviate the condition to some extent, it was determined that the spared Gibeonites
should become servants to the Israelites, as we read
in verses 19-21 :

But all the princes said unto all the congregation, We have sworn unto them by the Lord God of Israel: now therefore we may not touch them. This will we do unto them; we will even let them live, lest wrath be upon us, because of the oath which we sware unto them. And the princes said unto them, Let them live; but let them be hewers of wood and drawers of water unto all the congregation; as the princes had promised them.

This was the best they could do under the circumstances which they had brought upon themselves, and many a believer since has sought in a similar way to bend the results of his folly to his own service, only to find that it has entailed conditions which have been perplexing and bewildering through all the years ahead.

Joshua was the spokesman for the princes. He said to the Gibeonites:

Wherefore have ye beguiled us, saying, We are very far from you; when ye dwell among us? Now therefore ye are cursed, and there shall none of you be freed from being bondmen, and hewers of wood and drawers of water for the house of my God.

Glad to have saved their lives at any cost, the Hivites accepted the situation as gracefully as they could.

And they answered Joshua, and said, Because it was certainly told thy servants, how that the Lord thy God commanded His servant Moses to give you all the land, and to destroy all the inhabitants of

the land from before you, therefore we were sore
afraid of our lives because of you, and have done
this thing. And now, behold, we are in thine hand:
as it seemeth good and right unto thee to do unto
us, do.

In this way, the matter was closed for the time, as
we read in verses 26 and 27:

And so did he unto them, and delivered them out
of the hand of the children of Israel, that they
slew them not. And Joshua made them that day
hewers of wood and drawers of water for the congregation, and for the altar of the Lord, even unto
this day, in the place which he should choose.

How much better it would have been, both for
Israel and for Gibeon, if these Canaanites had come
to Joshua in all honesty and made peace with Israel
by accepting the amnesty which was offered freely
to all who acknowledged the claims of Jehovah, the
one true and living God, even as we are told in
Deuteronomy 20:10-12: "When thou comest nigh
unto a city to fight against it, then proclaim peace
unto it. And it shall be, if it make thee answer of
peace, and open unto thee, then it shall be, that all the
people that is found therein shall be tributaries unto
thee, and they shall serve thee. And if it will make no
peace with thee, but will make war against thee, then
thou shalt besiege it."

According to this Word of the Lord, had the men
of Gibeon and the adjoining cities come to Joshua
and frankly acknowledged the power and authority

of Jehovah, seeking to make peace with Israel by complete surrender, their cities would have been spared, their lives saved, and an honorable league would have been entered into. But they chose instead to take the path of deception which led to bondage and servitude.

Today God has commissioned His servants to go to all men everywhere, "preaching peace by Jesus Christ." All who receive the message in faith, who bow in repentance at the feet of the risen Saviour are justified by faith and have peace with God. For Christ has made peace by the blood of His Cross. Those thus saved are united to the Church of the living God and become in turn His messengers to carry the gospel to others.

There is no occasion for deception or hypocrisy, which can only result in greater disaster, for "the hypocrite's hope shall perish." But when there is frank confession of sin, God stands ready in faithfulness and justice to forgive all sin and to cleanse from all unrighteousness. None can be too vile for Christ. None need fear to come to Him for salvation, for He has said, "Him that cometh to Me I will in no wise cast out." Blessed are they who take Him at His Word and trust His grace!

# When the Sun Stood Still

THE evil effects of the unhappy alliance with the men of Gibeon soon began to be manifested. When the nations of the contiguous territories learned what had taken place, they formed a confederation, headed by Adonizedek, king of Jerusalem, and set out to attack Gibeon, as a warning to the people of other districts, not to make peace with Israel. This at once led the Gibeonites to call for help from their new allies, and in order to redeem their pledges it became necessary for Joshua to lead the host of the Lord up from Gilgal to attack the confederated armies. Had it not been for the blunder into which they had been betrayed by failing to consult the Lord, they would not have had to meet so vast an army at one time, but the conquest of Canaan would have proceeded in a more orderly way as city after city should have fallen before them, even as Jericho and Ai had done.

We have seen that the seven nations of Canaan, who were determined to contest Israel's right to take possession of the land, picture for us the spiritual foes who ever seek to hinder our entering into the enjoyment of the inheritance which is ours by title from the moment we are saved. We wrestle not with flesh and blood but with wicked spirits in the heavenlies, the world-rulers of this darkness, or, the rulers of this dark world. Of these Satan is the chief, even as Adonizedek headed up the coalition against Israel.

We know that a former king of Jerusalem, Melchizedek, was priest of the Most High God and was a type of our resurrected Lord, made a high priest forever after the order of Melchizedek, a name that means "King of Righteousness." Adonizedek means "lord of righteousness." He was not a priest of the Most High, but was the avowed enemy of the people of God. In this he pictures Satan, the accuser of the brethren, who accuses them before our God day and night. Pretending to be concerned about the maintaining of righteousness on the part of those who profess faith in Christ, he both seeks to lead them into sin and then accuses them of unrighteousness when or if they yield to the temptations he sets before them. Thus he seems to be the lord of righteousness, and his ministers, we are told, pass for ministers of righteousness (2 Cor. 11:13-15). In meeting such, we need to remember that "the weapons of our warfare are not carnal, but mighty through God to the pulling down of strong holds; casting down imaginations, and every high thing that exalteth itself against the knowledge of God, and bringing into captivity every thought to the obedience of Christ."

It is of this conflict in the heavenlies that the opening verses of our chapter speak if we look at them in their typical aspect.

Now it came to pass, when Adonizedek king of
Jerusalem had heard how Joshua had taken Ai, and
had utterly destroyed it; as he had done to Jericho
and her king, so he had done to Ai and her king;
and how the inhabitants of Gibeon had made peace
with Israel, and were among them; That they
feared greatly, because Gibeon was a great city, as
one of the royal cities, and because it was greater
than Ai, and all the men thereof were mighty.
Wherefore Adonizedek king of Jerusalem sent
unto Hoham king of Hebron, and unto Piram king
of Jarmuth, and unto Japhia king of Lachish, and
unto Debir king of Eglon, saying, Come up unto
me, and help me, that we may smite Gibeon: for
it hath made peace with Joshua and with the children of Israel. Therefore the five kings of the
Amorites, the king of Jerusalem, the king of Hebron, the king of Jarmuth, the king of Lachish,
the king of Eglon, gathered themselves together,
and went up, they and all their hosts, and encamped before Gibeon, and made war against it.

In their terror and alarm, the Gibeonites appealed to
Joshua for help.

And the men of Gibeon sent unto Joshua to the
camp of Gilgal, saying, Slack not thy hand from
thy servants; come up to us quickly, and save us,
and help us: for all the kings of the Amorites that
dwell in the mountains are gathered together
against us. So Joshua ascended from Gilgal, he,
and all the people of war with him, and all the
mighty men of valour.

Although this conflict was precipitated by their
own failure, yet God in His grace gave assurance to

His servants that He would destroy their foes as they
went up against them in dependence on His might:

**And the Lord said unto Joshua, Fear them not:
for I have delivered them into thine hand; there
shall not a man of them stand before thee.**

Acting in accordance with the Word of the Lord,
Joshua came upon the allied Canaanite armies suddenly, going up from Gilgal all night. He attacked the
detachments besieging Gibeon first, and defeated
them utterly. As they fled with Israel pursuing, panic
overtook the other Canaanites and they did not even
attempt a united stand against the host of the Lord.

The battle raged all day long, and as twilight was
falling the event occurred at which skeptics have
sneered for all the centuries since.

**Then spake Joshua to the Lord in the day when
the Lord delivered up the Amorites before the children of Israel, and he said in the sight of Israel,
Sun, stand thou still upon Gibeon; and thou, Moon,
in the valley of Ajalon. And the sun stood still, and
the moon stayed, until the people had avenged
themselves upon their enemies. Is not this written
in the book of Jasher? So the sun stood still in the
midst of heaven, and hasted not to go down about
a whole day. And there was no day like that before
it or after it, that the Lord hearkened unto the
voice of a man: for the Lord fought for Israel.**

Just what did take place we may not know;
whether an actual day was lost in astronomical reck-

oning, as some reputable scientists have insisted, or whether by the phrase, "the sun stood still," we are to understand a miracle of refraction, we cannot say, but we do know from the inspired record that the light continued for nearly another whole day, until all the battered hosts of the allies were destroyed and their kings taken captive. Scripture uses the language to which men are accustomed. We speak of the sun rising and setting, even though we understand that this is not literally true. So with the expression "the sun stood still." To human sight this was a fact. How it came to pass we can leave with God.

Following this great victory, Joshua returned to Gilgal, the place of self-judgment. There the five confederate kings were brought out from the caves in which they had been imprisoned while the battle went on and we are told that:

**When they brought out those kings unto Joshua, that Joshua called for all the men of Israel, and said unto the captains of the men of war which went with him, Come near, put your feet upon the necks of these kings. And they came near, and put their feet upon the necks of them.**

How this reminds us of Romans 16:20: "The God of peace shall bruise Satan under your feet shortly."

This great victory was followed by attacks upon city after city and the discomfiture and utter destruction of their defenders. After each new victory the triumphant Israelites returned to Gilgal, there to give thanks to God, who had thus given deliverance, as He had promised.

The series of victories is summed up for us in verses 40-43:

**So Joshua smote all the country of the hills, and of the south, and of the vale, and of the springs, and all their kings: he left none remaining, but utterly destroyed all that breathed, as the Lord God of Israel commanded. And Joshua smote them from Kadesh-barnea even unto Gaza, and all the country of Goshen, even unto Gibeon. And all these kings and their land did Joshua take at one time, because the Lord God of Israel fought for Israel. And Joshua returned, and all Israel with him, unto the camp to Gilgal.**

Thus had God fulfilled His Word, for "He is faithful that promised." The judgment of the Canaanites long deferred until the patience of God came to an end was the manifestation of His holy detestation of the abominable idolatrous rites and the vile immoral habits that characterized these nations. The description of the heathen world given in Romans 1 will give the reader some idea of the filthy behavior of these people. They had defiled the land by their lasciviousness and God commanded their destruction accordingly.

Thus the way was opened for Israel to take full possession of the inheritance which God had given them although there were yet other enemies to be destroyed.

# God's Word Tested
# and Proven

JOSHUA 11 AND 12

ADMITTEDLY these chapters and most of those
to follow do not lend themselves readily
to expository preaching. Yet we would not
forget that "All Scripture is God-breathed and profitable"; so we may be sure that these portions were
written for our admonition and have in them precious
lessons we cannot afford to pass over lightly.

In the opening verses of chapter 11 we read of the
second, and, as it turned out, the last great coalition
of Canaanite nations that Joshua and the Lord's host
had to face before they could take possession of their
promised inheritance. This time it was a confederation headed by Jabin, king of Hazor, and with him
were associated Jobab, king of Madon, and the kings
or sheiks who held authority over the tribes on the
north of the mountains of Palestine and in the great
plains south of Chinneroth, that is, the sea of Galilee.
The Canaanites who dwelt in the east and on the
west, and the remnants of the Amorites, Hittites,
Perizzites, Jebusites, and Hivites also sent their

quotas. It was a formidable host indeed, but Joshua
went out to meet them strong in the Lord and in the
power of His might; and the result is given us in
verses 6 to 9:

**And the Lord said unto Joshua, Be not afraid
because of them: for tomorrow about this time will
I deliver them up all slain before Israel: thou
shalt hough their horses, and burn their chariots
with fire. So Joshua came, and all the people of
war with him, against them by the waters of Merom
suddenly; and they fell upon them. And the Lord
delivered them into the hand of Israel, who smote
them, and chased them unto great Zidon, and unto
Misrephoth-maim, and unto the valley of Mizpeh
eastward; and they smote them, until they left
them none remaining. And Joshua did unto them
as the Lord bade him: he houghed their horses, and
burnt their chariots with fire.**

Hazor was the metropolis of that entire section, it
would seem, and having defeated its king and his allies, we read that:

**Joshua at that time turned back, and took Hazor,
and smote the king thereof with the sword: for
Hazor beforetime was the head of all those kingdoms. And they smote all the souls that were
therein with the edge of the sword, utterly destroying them: there was not any left to breathe:
and he burnt Hazor with fire.**

As intimated before, it is only as we realize something of the unspeakably vile character of these
wretched people that we can understand why God

ordered their utter extermination. He had borne with them until the cup of their iniquity was full to overflowing; then, in His righteousness as the Moral Governor of the universe, He decreed their destruction. Joshua was His instrument in carrying out this judgment and he did his work faithfully, as we are told in verses 15 to 20. God's love had given the Canaanites many years in which to repent, had there been on their part any desire to be delivered from their manifold iniquities. Instead of that they had sunk deeper and deeper into the pit of corruption and vileness until there was no remedy. The very mercy of God had but hardened them in their sins; so judgment had to be meted out according to their works.

Some of the ancient inhabitants of the land, the Anakim, a race of men of giant stature who had been driven back into the mountains by those who came in later, were also destroyed, except for a small remnant who dwelt in the Philistine cities, some of whom were slain by David and his associates in after years.

We read in verse 23:

**So Joshua took the whole land, according to all that the Lord said unto Moses; and Joshua gave it for an inheritance unto Israel according to their divisions by their tribes. And the land rested from war.**

Thus God's Word had been tested and proven. He had kept every promise He made when He first commissioned Joshua to go over the Jordan and take possession of the land; He had assured him that He would destroy the enemies before Israel and that if they kept His law and acted in accordance with His commands they would never know defeat! And so it had come to pass.

The twelfth chapter gives us a list of the many kings who had fallen before Israel's triumphant march, from the day that they met the Amorites and the king of Bashan on the eastern side of the Jordan and of the lake of Chinneroth until the last of the cities of Canaan had submitted to them. The lands of Sihon and of Og had been allotted already to the tribes of Reuben and Gad and the half tribe of Manasseh. The territories of the kings on the west of the Jordan were now to be divided among the other nine and a half tribes. Of this the following chapters treat in detail.

Joshua's victories illustrate the Christian's triumph over the unseen hosts of evil who, acting under the leadership of Satan, the god and prince of this world, would seek to hinder believers from possessing practically that which God has given them in Christ Jesus.

Many of us are defeated, when we ought to be victors, because of unjudged sin in our lives, or because of sloth and lethargy which hinder our laying hold of that for which God has laid hold of us. Blessed it is, if, like the Apostle Paul, we recognize the importance of pressing on toward the mark for the prize of the calling of God on high in Christ Jesus (Phil. 3:14, literal rendering). When God has promised to lead us on from victory to victory if we but cleave to Him with purpose of heart, it is the greatest folly to hold back and to fear lest we may not be able to overcome in the day of adversity. We may well take to heart the admonition of Philippians 3:15 and 16: "Let us therefore, as many as be perfect, be thus minded: and if in any thing ye be otherwise minded, God shall reveal even this unto you. Nevertheless, whereto we have already attained, let us walk by the same rule, let us mind the same thing." Let us hold fast what God has revealed to us already and go forward in dependence upon His Holy Spirit to appropriate the precious things into which we have not yet entered.

We often sing contentedly:

*There are depths of love that I cannot know,*
*Till I cross the narrow sea;*
*There are heights of joy that I may not reach*
*Till I rest in peace with Thee.*

While this is true, and there will ever be more to enter into and enjoy than we can possibly know on earth, yet we should not settle down contented to make no further progress because God has led us on into the enjoyment of some measure of His truth.

A dear brother used often to suggest that this verse be changed so that we should sing:

*There are depths of love that I yet may know*
*Ere I cross the narrow sea;*
*There are heights of joy that I yet may reach*
*Ere I rest in peace with Thee.*

This is surely true. We should ever be moving on from one victory to another, proving anew from day to day the faithfulness of our gracious God and the trustworthiness of His promises!

# Caleb, the Wholehearted, or the Energy of Faith

JOSHUA 13 AND 14

THE wars of Canaan were largely at an end. Israel had to a great extent found at least temporary rest in the land that God had promised them. We know from the history that follows that this condition, however, did not continue. In the Epistle to the Hebrews we are told, "If Jesus had given them rest, He would not have spoken of another rest." Many, perhaps, have not realized that *Jesus* and *Joshua* are the same: that is, Joshua is the Hebrew form of the name that our blessed Lord bore here on earth. *Jesus* is an anglicization of the Greek form. So the passage in Hebrews is referring to the rest into which Joshua led the people, which did not prove to be lasting because of the faithlessness of Israel, and yet in the beginning of their history there was certainly much to give them confidence as they saw how marvelously God undertook for them.

As the thirteenth chapter opens we hear the Lord addressing Joshua, now an aged man. God said to him:

111

**Thou art old and stricken in years, and there re-
maineth yet very much land to be possessed.**

Then in the rest of the chapter we have pointed out
vast tracks of the land not yet settled by Israel, even
though they had to a very large extent overcome their
enemies and taken possession of many of their cities
and villages.

We learn too of the judgment meted out to Balaam, who sought to destroy Israel by giving evil ad-
vice to Balak. Verse 22 tells us also,

**Balaam did the children of Israel slay with the
sword among them that were slain by them.**

Several of the tribes had already obtained their inheritance, but the others had not yet taken possession
of the land that was to be allotted to them; and so the
challenge was given: "There remaineth yet very
much land to be possessed."

Surely these words may speak loudly to our hearts.
Many of us have known the Lord for years. To what
extent have we really entered into the enjoyment of
the precious things of Christ which are ours by title?
Have we not been content to know that our souls are
saved and that we shall spend eternity in heaven, while
failing to enter into the reality and blessedness of a
"life hid with Christ in God" as we pass through this
scene? Then, too, think of the great treasure committed to us in the Word of God. Those of us who
have given the most time to careful study and meditation over God's blessed Book must realize that still

there remaineth very much land to be possessed. Large portions of Scripture are still to most of us a kind of a literary *terre incognita*. We are familiar, perhaps, with the great outstanding truths of Scripture, and certain precious chapters have ever been our joy and delight, but there is so much more in the Scriptures that we need to make our own by careful study in dependence on the Holy Spirit of God. In the energy of faith we are called upon to take possession of that which is already ours through the gift of God.

In the story of Caleb we see this energy of faith blessedly illustrated. We read in chapter 14, beginning with verse 6:

Then the children of Judah came unto Joshua in Gilgal: and Caleb the son of Jephunneh the Kenezite said unto him, Thou knowest the thing that the Lord said unto Moses the man of God concerning me and thee in Kadesh-barnea. Forty years old was I when Moses the servant of the Lord sent me from Kadesh-barnea to espy out the land; and I brought him word again as it was in mine heart. Nevertheless my brethren that went up with me made the heart of the people melt: but I wholly followed the Lord my God. And Moses sware on that day, saying, Surely the land whereon thy feet have trodden shall be thine inheritance, and thy children's for ever, because thou hast wholly followed the Lord my God. And now, behold, the Lord hath kept me alive, as he said, these forty and five years, even since the Lord spake this word unto Moses, while the children of Israel wandered in the wilderness: and now, lo, I am this day fourscore and five years old. As yet I am as strong this day as I was in the day that Moses sent me: as my strength was then, even so is my strength now, for war, both to go out, and to come in. Now therefore give me this mountain, whereof the Lord spake in that day; for thou heardest in that day how the Anakims were there, and that the cities were great and fenced: if so be the Lord will be with me, then I shall be able to drive them out, as the Lord said. And Joshua blessed him, and gave unto Caleb the son of Jephunneh Hebron for an inheritance. Hebron therefore became the inheritance of Caleb the son of Jephunneh the Kenezite unto this day, because that he wholly followed the Lord God of Israel. And the name of Hebron before was Kirjath-arba; which Arba was a great man among the Anakims. And the land had rest from war.

There is something very stirring in this record. Caleb, as we know, was one of the two spies who brought back a minority report when the ten spies discouraged the people of Israel. The ten admitted that the land was all God said it would be, and the grapes of Eschol bore witness to its fruitfulness, but they were terrified as they beheld the walled cities and the sons of Anak, mighty giants, in whose sight they were but as grasshoppers, and so they declared it would be impossible to overcome these people of Canaan. But Caleb and Joshua brought back a good report, exclaiming, "Let us go up and take the land, for we are well able to overcome it."

But the people refused to listen and so, as we know, were turned back into the wilderness, there to wander until all that generation, except Caleb and Joshua, had passed away. Now their children had entered into and taken possession of the land. Caleb, though eighty-five years of age, came to Joshua to remind him of the promise that Moses had made, that because he had wholly followed the Lord he should have whatever inheritance his heart desired. He did not look about for some secluded valley where he would be safe from the prying eyes of enemies, nor did he ask for some town or village from which the Canaanites had been driven out already, but he requested Joshua to give him the mountain on which Kirjath-arba was located. Arba was a great man among the Anakims. Kirjath-arba meant the City of Arba. The Anakims still dwelt there, but strong in faith Caleb declared: "If so be the Lord will be with me, then I shall be able to drive them out, as the Lord said." Acting upon Caleb's request, Joshua blessed him and gave him the hill for which he asked as his inheritance. Caleb took possession of it, drove the Anakims out of the city and changed its name to Hebron, a word that means *fellowship* or *communion*. The name Caleb means *wholehearted* and aptly describes this doughty warrior and faithful servant of God. He did not immediately get possession of Hebron, but he fought stubbornly and determinedly until he had driven out the ancient inhabitants and so took possession of it. Later it became a Levitical city and a city of refuge, but the suburbs belonged to Caleb and his descendants.

As we contemplate this ancient record it should surely stir our hearts and lead us to act as Caleb did—

in the energy of faith taking possession of that which God has declared He has given to us in Christ. No foe can withstand the man of God who presses forward in power of the Spirit and in obedience to the Word.

An old hymn says,

> *"Faith, mighty faith the promise sees*
> *And looks to that alone;*
> *Laughs at impossibilities*
> *And cries, "It shall be done."*

Such a faith was Caleb's and in this he is an example for us all. We are too apt to take the line of least resistance, to be content with that which seems the easiest thing instead of valiantly going on in faith to lay hold of the best that God has for us, no matter what difficulties may seem to make it impossible for us to overcome the foe and to enter into and enjoy our allotted portion.

# The Inheritance of the Tribes and the Story of Othniel and Achsah

JOSHUA 15-19

WE COME now to a portion of the book of Joshua which, while it would richly repay careful and minute examination, we must pass over cursorily because of the nature of these messages. In chapters 15 to 19 we have the account of the division of the land west of the Jordan among the nine and one-half tribes that had not chosen to remain in the country of Bashan and the land of Gilead on the east side of the river, as had the two and one-half tribes, who found there such fine accommodation for pasturing their great herds of cattle. They preferred to settle down in the countries taken from Og, king of Bashan, and Sihon, king of the Amorites, and Moses gave them that permission, as we have seen, providing their warriors went into the land to help their brethren against the Canaanites.

The tribe of Judah had the first portion. Their inheritance was in the high country, adjacent to, and south and west of Jerusalem. Judah was the royal tribe and was honored of God in a very special way, but the other tribes also had their portion in different parts of the land, each one having its own particular values, but divided by the casting of lots. In the book of Proverbs we read, "The lot is cast into the lap; the whole disposing thereof is of the Lord." He directed Joshua to use this method, doubtless in order to avoid what might have seemed like partiality in giving the tribes their inheritances. That there are great spiritual lessons to be learned from these records there can be no question. Others have gone into this in a way we do not attempt here, notably, God's honored servant, F. W. Grant, who in his enlightening notes on these passages in the *Numerical Bible* has shown that the Hebrew names of the cities, towns, and districts all have remarkable significance, and when translated help us to understand more fully something of the richness and preciousness of our inheritance in the heavenly places in Christ. We need to remember that "all these things were written for our learning" and are types of what God has given us to enjoy in this present age of grace.

It is pathetic, however, to note that tribe after tribe failed to make a full end of their enemies and so were obliged to permit these Canaanites to dwell among the Israelites. All this was but a compromise and compromise with evil never pays. In days to come, these foes who had been spared when they should have been exterminated, either became a snare to the people of God by leading them off into idolatry, or else wrought great havoc by their warlike behavior, attacking and often destroying cities and farms of the Israelites who had permitted them to remain unmolested among them. God had warned Israel of this beforehand, telling them that those who were not destroyed would be thorns in their sides and would cause them untold trouble.

Concerning Judah we read in chapter 15 : 63:

**As for the Jebusites the inhabitants of Jerusalem, the children of Judah could not drive them out: but the Jebusites dwell with the children of Judah at Jerusalem unto this day.**

Then in chapter 16 : 10, we learn that the children of Joseph

**drave not out the Canaanites that dwelt in Gezer: but the Canaanites dwell among the Ephraimites unto this day, and serve under tribute.**

Of Manasseh, the children of the elder son of Joseph, we are told that they

**could not drive out the inhabitants of those cities; but the Canaanites would dwell in that land. Yet it came to pass, when the children of Israel were waxen strong, that they put the Canaanites to tribute; but did not utterly drive them out.**

In spite of their failure, we find these children of Joseph grumbling because they had only one lot and one portion to inherit; whereas they declared they were "a great people"! Joshua's answer was fitting indeed:

**If thou be a great people, then get thee up to the wood country, and cut down for thyself there in the land of the Perizzites and of the giants, if mount Ephraim be too narrow for thee.**

Still these children of Joseph were not satisfied, but they replied:

**The hill is not enough for us: and all the Canaanites that dwell in the land of the valley have chariots of iron, both they who are of Bethshean and her towns, and they who are of the valley of Jezreel.**

To this Joshua answered somewhat ironically perhaps:

**Thou art a great people, and hast great power: thou shalt not have one lot only: But the mountain shall be thine; for it is a wood, and thou shalt cut it down: and the outgoings of it shall be thine: for thou shalt drive out the Canaanites, though they have iron chariots, and though they be strong.**

We may well learn from the failures of Israel to beware lest we ourselves fail to judge every evil thing that Satan would use to hinder our enjoyment of the things of Christ. We are called to deal unsparingly with every unholy thought and every sinful tendency, cleansing ourselves from "all filthiness of the flesh and spirit, perfecting holiness in the fear of God." It is only thus that we can appreciate truly and enjoy, in the way God would have us, the great privileges and manifold blessings He has bestowed upon us. Sin unjudged results in weakness and loss of communion, which can only be restored as we face the sin in the presence of God, confessing and forsaking it, and thus obtaining mercy and the assurance that all is forgiven.

But now let us turn back and consider briefly an incident that shines out brightly in the midst of all these long lists of Hebrew names, which to many of us seem unintelligible. We have already considered the energy of faith as seen in Caleb, the wholehearted. He comes before us again in the thirteenth verse of chapter 15, where we read:

**And unto Caleb the son of Jephunneh he gave a part among the children of Judah, according to the commandment of the Lord to Joshua, even the city of Arba the father of Anak, which city is Hebron. And Caleb drove thence the three sons of Anak, Sheshai, and Ahiman, and Talmai, the children of Anak. And he went up thence to the inhabitants of Debir: and the name of Debir before was Kirjath-sepher.**

Kirjath-sepher means *the city of the book.* It was probably so named because an ancient library was located there. Its name was changed later to Debir, which means the *oracle* or *the word,* and suggests that Word of God through which He speaks directly to His people. Caleb's energy set a splendid example to younger men and this comes out clearly in what follows. We are told in verse 16:

**And Caleb said, He that smiteth Kirjath-sepher, and taketh it, to him will I give Achsah my daughter to wife.**

Achsah means *anklet,* and, as others have suggested, speaks of the decorated foot, reminding us of the word in the prophecy of Isaiah, "How beautiful upon the mountains are the feet of him that bringeth good tidings, that publisheth peace." In Ephesians 6 the soldier of Christ is commanded to have his feet shod with the preparation of the gospel of peace. Surely, no lovelier decoration could be found for any foot than this.

In response to Caleb's challenge, we are told that Othniel, his nephew, took Kirjath-sepher, and thus the city of the book, or the word, became his inheritance. In accordance with his promise, Caleb gave him Achsah to be his wife. Thus the cousins were united. Achsah suggested to her husband that he ask of her father a field, a petition which Caleb readily granted, but the young woman realized that a field without water was practically worthless; so she herself approached her father in an attitude of supplication. In response to his inquiry, "What wouldest thou?" she replied,

**Give me a blessing; for thou hast given me a south land; give me also springs of water.**

We are told that Caleb gave her the upper springs and the nether springs. This is all very suggestive. A believer may have rich treasure indeed in the fact that the oracles of God are committed to him, but he can only enjoy to the full this blessed gift of God when the Holy Spirit is given in power to open up the truth to him. In this dispensation of grace the Spirit dwells in every believer. He is likened by our Lord Jesus to a fountain of living water springing up in the heart. It is as we appreciate and value the work of the Holy Spirit that we enjoy the refreshing influences which flow from His acknowledged presence. May the faith of Othniel and of Achsah be duplicated in us, who through grace have been blessed with all spiritual blessings in heavenly places in Christ. May we be so yielded to the indwelling Holy Spirit that He will make very real to us the precious things of Christ, and thus give us to enjoy our inheritance to the full.

The Spirit and the Word are linked together, both in connection with the new birth and in later Christian experience. The Spirit-filled believer is one in whom the Word of Christ dwells richly. May this be true of all who read these lines!

# The Cities of Refuge

JOSHUA 20

I T IS very evident that God has hidden some
special lessons for us in the types of the City of
Refuge, of which we now read in chapter 20, as
otherwise we would find ourselves wondering why
they are mentioned so frequently. In four previous
passages the Spirit of God drew the attention of Israel
to the importance of these cities and the expression
of His grace toward the unwitting or unintentional
manslayer in Israel. First, we have the brief intimation in Exodus 21 : 13, telling Israel that when they
reached the land, God would provide such a refuge:
"And if a man lie not in wait, but God deliver him
into his hand; then I will appoint thee a place whither
he shall flee." Then we have much fuller information
in Numbers 35 : verses 6 and 9-28:

"And among the cities which ye shall give unto
the Levites there shall be six cities for refuge, which
ye shall appoint for the manslayer, that he may flee
thither : and to them ye shall add forty and two cities.

And the Lord spake unto Moses, saying, Speak
unto the children of Israel, and say unto them, When
ye be come over Jordan into the land of Canaan; then

124

ye shall appoint you cities to be cities of refuge for you; that the slayer may flee thither, which killeth any person at unawares. And they shall be unto you cities of refuge from the avenger : that the manslayer die not, until he stand before the congregation in judgment. And of these cities which ye shall give six cities shall ye have for refuge. Ye shall give three cities on this side Jordan, and three cities shall ye give in the land of Canaan, which shall be cities of refuge. These six cities shall be a refuge, both for the children of Israel, and for the stranger, and for the sojourner among them: that every one that killeth any person unawares may flee thither. And if he smite him with an instrument of iron, so that he die, he is a murderer : the murderer shall surely be put to death. And if he smite him with throwing a stone, wherewith he may die, and he die, he is a murderer : the murderer shall surely be put to death. Or if he smite him with an hand weapon of wood, wherewith he may die, and he die, he is a murderer : the murderer shall surely be put to death. The revenger of blood himself shall slay the murderer : when he meeteth him, he shall slay him. But if he thrust him of hatred, or hurl at him by laying of wait, that he die; Or in enmity smite him with his hand, that he die : he that smote him shall surely be put to death; for he is a murderer : the revenger of blood shall slay the murderer, when he meeteth him. But if he thrust him suddenly without enmity, or have cast upon him any thing without laying of wait, Or with any stone, wherewith a man may die, seeing him not, and cast it upon him, that he die, and was not his enemy, neither sought his harm: Then the congregation shall judge between the slayer and the revenger of blood according to these judgments: And the congregation shall deliver the slayer out of the hand of the revenger of blood, and the congregation shall restore him to the city of his refuge, whither he was fled: and he shall abide in it unto the death of the high priest, which was anointed with the holy oil. But if the slayer shall at any time come without the border of the city of his refuge, whither he was fled; And the revenger of blood find him without the borders of the city of his refuge, and the revenger of blood kill the slayer; he shall not be guilty of blood: Because he should have remained in the city of his refuge until the death of the high priest: but after the death of the high priest the slayer shall return into the land of his possession."

It is perhaps hardly necessary for our purpose to quote the remaining passages, both of which are found in the book of Deuteronomy, namely, 4:41-43 and 19:1-10. With these Scriptures our present chapter is in perfect harmony. It gives us the complete fulfillment of God's command concerning these cities of refuge, of which there were six in all: three on the east of Jordan and three on the west. Clear, open roads were to be kept leading from all parts of the land to one or other of these cities, with definite signs indicating the nearest one, so that the man who had slain another in Israel without hating him in his heart or intending to kill him, might flee at once to the city of refuge and so be protected from the avenger of blood.

It is important to observe that there was no refuge offered to the one who was guilty of deliberate and wilful murder. God had declared, "Ye shall take no satisfaction for the life of a murderer": but for the manslayer there was ever the open gate in order that he might be secure from the vengeance of the relatives of the one he had killed. When we come over to the New Testament we read in Hebrews 6:19 of those "who have fled for refuge to lay hold of the hope set before them." The reference is to those who, though conscious of their own sinfulness have availed themselves of the salvation procured for them by our Lord Jesus Christ upon the Cross. All who find a refuge in Him are safe forever from the judgment of a Holy God. But if He be rejected after the gospel has been clearly proclaimed, and men deliberately crucify to themselves the Son of God afresh, putting Him to an open shame, there is for them no hope of deliverance. Christ rejected means eternal judgment.

The whole world, Jew and Gentile, stands guilty before God as having participated in that which brought about the death of His son, but inasmuch as Christ came to give Himself a ransom for all, His sacrifice on the Cross has opened up, as it were, a city of refuge for all who put their trust in Him.

Of old, the manslayer was to remain in the city of refuge until the death of the high priest. Christ is not only the Man slain and the city of refuge Himself, but He too is the High Priest, and as such He will never die again. His is an everlasting priesthood; so those who find refuge in Him are eternally saved.

> *Once in Christ, in Christ forever,*
> *Thus the eternal Covenant stands.*

He settled the sin question on the Cross and He put all mankind on the ground of manslaughter instead of murder when He prayed for those who had been so active in rejecting Him, and even in nailing Him to the Cross, "Father, forgive them, for they know not what they do." In other words, the Father might consider them guilty of the sin of ignorance or unintentional manslaughter rather than the wilful murder of the Son of God.

The Apostle Peter in addressing the Jews shortly after Pentecost, said: "And now, brethren, I wot that through ignorance ye did it, as did also your rulers. But those things which God before had showed by the mouth of all His prophets, that Christ should suffer, He hath so fulfilled." And in view of this Peter called upon them to repent, saying: "Repent ye therefore, and be converted, that your sins may be blotted out, when the times of refreshing shall come from the presence of the Lord; And He shall send Jesus Christ, which before was preached unto you: Whom the heaven must receive until the times of restitution of all things, which God hath spoken by the mouth of all His holy prophets since the world began."

The Apostle Paul emphasizes the same thing when in 1 Corinthians 2 : 6-8, he says: "Howbeit we speak wisdom among them that are perfect: yet not the wisdom of this world, nor of the princes of this world, that come to nought: But we speak the wisdom of God in a mystery, even the hidden wisdom, which God ordained before the world unto our glory: Which none of the princes of this world knew: for had they known it, they would not have crucified the Lord of glory."

According to these passages God looks upon the whole world as guilty of the sin of manslaughter in connection with the death of Christ, but has opened up a new and living way into the place of refuge for all who go to Him, confessing their sins and thus availing themselves of His grace. What folly, then, for men to turn a deaf ear to the call of God and to persist in the rejection of the salvation He offers them!

We have an outstanding example in the Old Testament of a man who was slain just outside the wall of a city of refuge, who would have been safe inside. I refer to Abner, of whom David lamented, crying, "Died Abner as a fool dieth?" With no malice aforethought on his part, Abner had slain Asahel, the brother of Joab. Abiding in the city of refuge, he would have been secure from the avenger of blood, but Joab found him outside the city and put him to death in retaliation for the killing of Asahel.

What fools men are who now deliberately refuse the security that God offers in Christ Himself, and so by spurning Him become guilty before God of the murder of His Son.

It would seem as though the names of the six cities

of refuge have suggestive meaning: at least, they may well bring to our minds some of the privileges that are ours in Christ. The three cities on the western side of the Jordan were: Kedesh in Galilee, Shechem in Mt. Ephraim, and Hebron in the mountains of Judah. On the other side of Jordan the three selected were: Bezer in the tribe of Reuben, Ramoth in Gilead, and Golan in Bashan.

Kedesh is *the sanctuary* and it is in Christ Himself that the troubled soul finds sanctuary in the midst of a world of strife and sin. Shechem means *a shoulder,* when our blessed Lord is said to carry the government of the world on His shoulder (Isaiah 9) and the Good Shepherd places the sheep that was lost upon His shoulders. And so all believers are sustained by Him, who is our strength and who undertakes to carry us safely through all the trials of life. Hebron means *communion* and suggests that precious fellowship with Christ into which believers are brought through Christ.

The names of the cities on the east of Jordan would seem to be definitely significant, although the meaning of some of them is a little uncertain. Bezer is said to come from a root meaning *munitions* or *fortress,* and may speak to us of Christ Himself, who is for all who believe a strong tower and fort of security. Ramoth is generally understood as meaning *the heights,* and may be an intimation of the precious truth that God has raised us up together and seated us together in the heavenlies in Christ. Golan is perhaps the most uncertain of all, but one meaning given to it is *their rejoicing,* which may remind us that "the joy of the Lord is our strength."

In obedience to the Word of God, given so long before, Joshua set aside these cities of refuge, each one of them a Levitical city and each one with an open door to receive the poor, distressed soul who is fleeing from the avenger of blood. Looked at individually or corporately, they all tell us of Him who is our refuge and strength, our Saviour from judgment.

> *In the refuge God provided,*
>  *Though the world's destruction lowers,*
> *We are safe to Christ confided;*
>  *Everlasting life is ours.*

# The Last Days of Joshua's Leadership

W E MAY consider these closing chapters of the book of Joshua as a group, as the matters with which they deal are all so intimately linked together. In chapter 21 we read of the separation of forty-eight cities from among the various tribes of Israel, which were allotted to the Levites. In chapter 22 we get the return of the warriors of the two and a half tribes to the homes which had already been given to them by Moses on the east of the Jordan. In chapters 23 and 24 we listen to Joshua as he seeks solemnly to impress upon the nation, which he had led into the possession of the land, the importance of cleaving closely to the Word of the Lord and not being turned aside through following any of the customs of the surrounding nations.

The Levites, as we know, were not to be numbered among the people of Israel; therefore they did not inherit any special portion of the land of Palestine. They had been chosen by God instead of the firstborn, who were dedicated to Him because of the de-

liverance wrought on the Passover night in Egypt
and were set apart for special service in connection
with the sanctuary and also ministering and teaching
the Word of God among the people. The Lord Himself was their portion and their inheritance. So long
as the people were obedient to Him, the Levites would
be well cared for. In after years, when the nation
drifted away from God, the Levites suffered greatly
and in many instances were obliged to forsake the
special service committed to them in order to care
for their fields and vineyards, that they might properly provide for their families and themselves. Of
old, God's people were divided into three classes:
priests, Levites, and warriors. The priests were the
worshipers and had to do with the way of approach
to God. The Levites were the ministers of the Lord,
serving, as we have seen, in various capacities. The
warriors fought to take possession of the land and
to hold it against their enemies in days to come. In
the present dispensation of grace, the three groups
are combined in each believer. All have been set apart
of God as priests, holy and royal, to offer unto God
spiritual sacrifices and to make known the riches of
His grace to a lost world. All are Levites, whose joy
it should be to serve with gladness the One who has
redeemed them. All, too, are warriors, responsible
to contend earnestly for the faith once for all committed to the saints.

Cities, with their suburbs, were set apart for the
possession of the Levites throughout the entire land,
taken from the inheritances of the various tribes.

Thus it was the privilege of all to share with the servants of the Lord that which He had given them and which they had appropriated in faith. This provision for the Levites was made after the Lord had given Israel all the land which He sware to give unto their fathers, and they possessed it and dwelt therein. God had fulfilled his Word to the letter. It was now the responsibility of His people to hold by obedience that which they had inherited.

In chapter 22 (verses 1-6) we learn that these warriors had done their part faithfully. Although they speak of those who prefer to settle down on the borders of the world rather than to enter in and possess in fullness all that God has for them, nevertheless, according to the light which they seemed to have, they were true and faithful to the promise they had given to Moses and so they were now entitled to return to Bashan and Gilead and adjoining districts east of the Jordan to settle down with their families and care for their flocks and herds.

On their way to their homes an incident occurred which is very suggestive and might well be kept in mind by us today—we who are so apt to misunderstand one another's motives and to judge each other wrongly because we do not know what is going on in the heart. It is against this that our Lord warns us when He says, "Judge not, that ye be not judged; for with what judgment ye judge, ye shall be judged; and with what measure ye mete, it shall be measured unto you."

In Joshua 22, verse 10 we read:

**And when they came unto the borders of Jordan, that are in the land of Canaan, the children of Reuben and the children of Gad and the half tribe of Manasseh built there an altar by Jordan, a great altar to see to.**

When word got abroad regarding the building of this altar, those who had their inheritances west of the Jordan immediately jumped at the conclusion that their brethren were setting up some separate kind of worship and so were making a breach in Israel. Without sending messengers to make proper inquiry, word was sent to all the nine and one-half tribes that a rebellion against the Word of the Lord had begun and they were summoned together to quell it. Led by that devoted man Phineas, the son of Eleazar the priest, they charged their brethren with trespass against the Lord, and reminding them how judgment had fallen upon them because of previous iniquities, they warned them of what they might expect if they continued to rebel against God by setting up some other center of worship than that which He had already established at Shiloh. But when thus charged by their excited brethren, the two and one-half tribes, through their leader, made it clear that they had no such thought whatever.

On the other hand, the altar they had built was in order to remind their children and the children of the nine and one-half tribes that they were one nation and that together they worshiped the one true and living God. When the facts of the case came out clearly, Phineas and the host following him were satisfied, and they thanked God that division was averted. The altar that the children of Reuben and of Gad had built was simply a replica of that which was set up at the tabernacle and was designed to keep in mind the unity of the nation rather than to foment division. Thus what might have been a very serious breach between brethren was avoided. How often through the centuries have Christians attacked one another and separated one from another on even less provocation, simply because they acted in haste and did not take time to acquaint themselves with one another's motives!

As we turn to chapter 23 we read:

**And it came to pass a long time after that the Lord had given rest unto Israel from all their enemies round about, that Joshua waxed old and stricken in age. And Joshua called for all Israel, and for their elders, and for their heads, and for their judges, and for their officers, and said unto them, I am old and stricken in age: And ye have seen all that the Lord your God hath done unto all these nations because of you; for the Lord your God is He that hath fought for you.**

Joshua then went on to remind them how he had divided the land by lot among them and how the Lord their God had expelled their enemies in the past. If they continued to walk in obedience He could be depended on to drive out those that remained, in order that Israel might possess the land in peace and quietness, even as God had promised them. It was for them to be courageous and obedient and to seek to walk in all the commandments of the Lord, as set forth in the law of Moses. Then they could depend upon God to keep His Word and act on their behalf. If, on the other hand, they failed in this and did not cleave to the Lord their God, but turned from His law to walk in the ways of the nations surrounding Palestine or of the remnant of those remaining in the land, then their own God would turn against them and they would learn in bitterness of soul the folly of disobedience to His truth.

**And, behold, this day I am going the way of all the earth: and ye know in all your hearts and in all your souls, that not one thing hath failed of all the good things which the Lord your God spake concerning you; all are come to pass unto you, and not one thing hath failed thereof. Therefore it shall come to pass, that as all good things are come upon you, which the Lord your God promised you; so shall the Lord bring upon you all evil things, until He have destroyed you from off this good land which the Lord your God hath given you. When ye have transgressed the covenant of the Lord your God, which He commanded you, and have gone and served other gods, and bowed yourselves to them; then shall the anger of the Lord be kindled against you, and ye shall perish quickly from off the good land which He hath given unto you.**

Following this, Joshua now an aged man, gathered all the tribes of Israel to Shechem to give them his last charge. He reminded them how God had called Abraham from Mesopotamia and set him apart, that through him all nations of the world might be blessed.

It is evident from chapter 24, verse 2 that Abraham himself had been brought up in idolatry and belonged to an idolatrous family at the time that God revealed Himself to him. Joshua said,

**Your fathers dwelt on the other side of the flood [that is, of the river Euphrates], even Terah, the father of Abraham, and the father of Nachor: and they served other gods.**

Abraham was not called out from the nations because he was inherently different from other people, but God in His sovereignty chose him from an idolatrous family and revealed Himself to him. They were His children. They knew how wonderfully the Lord had fulfilled His word to their fathers, and now they were responsible to yield implicit obedience to His word. Joshua recited briefly an account of God's dealings with them under Moses in Egypt and in the wilderness, and then reminded them of recent events after they entered into the land. Everything Jehovah had promised was fulfilled. He had given them the land for which they had not labored and cities which they did not build. In these they dwelt securely with the vineyards and the olive yards which they had not planted but of which they ate. They were responsible, therefore, to fear the Lord and serve Him in sincerity and in truth and put away the gods which their fathers had served on the other side of the flood and in Egypt and to serve the Lord alone (verse 14).

This is very illuminating and shows us that even in Egypt idolatry had a hold on some in Israel, even as

we know was true in the wilderness, and now that
they were settled in the land there were still idols to
be brought out into the light and destroyed. So long
as anything is given the place in our hearts that
belongs to God Himself, there can never be the fullness of blessing that He would have us enjoy.

Joshua's own steadfast purpose is emphasized in
verse 15. After calling upon Israel to choose at once
whom they would serve, whether Baal or Jehovah,
he declares,

**As for me and my house, we will serve the Lord.**

For the doughty old warrior who had seen so much
of the mighty acts of the one true and living God
there could be no thought of any other god. Nor
would he allow for one moment that those subject to
his headship in the family relation should take any
other course. Jehovah was his God and the God of his
household. His was an unflinching and unquestioning
loyalty to the Holy One of Israel whom he had served
for so long.

Responding to Joshua's words, we are told in
verses 16 to 18:

**And the people answered and said, God forbid
that we should forsake the Lord, to serve other
gods; For the Lord our God, He it is that brought us
up and our fathers out of the land of Egypt, from
the house of bondage, and which did those great
signs in our sight, and preserved us in all the way
wherein we went, and among all the people through**

whom we passed: And the Lord drave out from
before us all the people, even the Amorites which
dwelt in the land: therefore will we also serve the
Lord; for He is our God.

All this sounded very good and no doubt at the
moment those who made such protestations of loyalty
to Joshua meant every word they uttered. But time
was to prove how untrustworthy the human heart is.
Joshua realized it and warned the people accordingly,
as we read in verses 19 and 20:

And Joshua said unto the people, Ye cannot serve
the Lord: for He is an holy God; He is a jealous
God; He will not forgive your transgressions nor
your sins. If ye forsake the Lord, and serve strange
gods, then He will turn and do you hurt, and consume you, after that He hath done you good.

However, the people replied, "Nay, but we will serve
the Lord." And God called Joshua to witness against
them that they had thus confirmed their devotion to
Him. Again the command came (verse 23):

Now therefore put away, said he, the strange
gods which are among you, and incline your heart
unto the Lord God of Israel.

The people protested their full intention to be obedient. So we are told,

Joshua made a covenant with the people that day,
and set them a statute and an ordinance in Shechem. And Joshua wrote these words in the book

of the law of God, and took a great stone, and set
it up there under an oak, that was by the sanctuary
of the Lord. And Joshua said unto all the people,
Behold, this stone shall be a witness unto us; for
it hath heard all the words of the Lord which He
spake unto us: it shall be therefore a witness unto
you, lest ye deny your God.

After such solemn adjuration the people departed
to their homes.

The death of Joshua followed shortly after and he
was buried in the borders of his inheritance in Tim-
nath-serah.

In verse 31 we learn that Israel served the Lord all
the days of Joshua and all the days of the elders which
overlived Joshua and which had known all the works
of the Lord that He had done for Israel. The history
that follows in later books tells us how terribly the
people failed to carry out their part of the covenant
which the fathers had made.

One thing remains to be noticed ere we close our
present study of this book. We read in verse 32:

And the bones of Joseph, which the children of
Israel brought up out of Egypt, buried they in
Shechem, in a parcel of ground which Jacob bought
of the sons of Hamor the father of Shechem for
an hundred pieces of silver: and it became the inheritance of the children of Joseph.

Before Joseph died, by faith he gave commandment
concerning his bones, exhorting his brethren not to
allow his embalmed body to remain in the land of

Egypt, but to carry it with them to Canaan and bury it there. So when Moses led the people out of Egypt, we are told he took the bones of Joseph with him. All through the forty years in the wilderness when they were bearing about in the body the dying of Joseph, the memorial of death, the death of the one who had been used of God for their deliverance, who might be described as their saviour, was with them. Now that all had been fulfilled and they were settled in the land, they buried the bones of Joseph in the parcel of ground which he himself had indicated.

May we not learn from this the importance of always bearing about in the body the dying of the Lord Jesus, that the life also of Jesus might be manifested in us until that day when, the wilderness journey ended, we shall enter into our final rest in the Paradise of God above.

# Ezra

## INTRODUCTION

THAT the book of Ezra contains much-needed
truth for the present time is my firm belief.
A re-affirmation of early principles is necessary
on account of the attempt on the part of many
to set aside "that which is written" as to the
gathering and fellowship of children of God in
separation from evil; and this, because of break-
downs on the part of some who sought, through
grace, to take a scriptural position years ago.
Corporate failure has been supposed (in some
way incomprehensible to one who would be
guided alone by the word of God) to sanction
individual turning from the path of the truth,
and thus excuse and palliate what the late W.
Kelly very appropriately called "nothingarianism
in Church relations."

No amount of failure alters divine truth. We
to-day are as responsible as our fathers were to
go back to "that which is written" and act in
faith upon it.

It is true difficulties and perplexities abound
as might be expected, because of the near close
of the dispensation. But "God and the word
of His grace" are still all-sufficient for every
peril or disaster. A careful study of the books

of Ezra and Nehemiah would, I feel certain, preserve from a gloomy pessimism as to the carrying out of the truth of gathering to the Name of the Lord and furnish many needed warnings against the abounding snares of the last times.

This little book has been written far away from the opportunities of consulting the writings of others, while laboring in the gospel among the Pueblo Indians. Here in the wilderness the same blessed work is going on among our red-skinned fellow-believers, of making Christ the one only Centre. The principles put before them, and blessed to the souls of many, are, in this brief exposition, presented for the consideration afresh of those older in the truth.

I should add that while, as noted above, unable *now* to consult the works of others, I have in times past read several expositions of Ezra with profit, and, no doubt, much suggested in their writings now appears in this work. "We can do nothing against the truth, but for the truth." That what is of God may prevail, is my earnest desire; and to forward this, is my only object in sending out these unpretentious pages, which are now committed to the care of "the Spirit of truth" in the worthy name of the Lord Jesus Christ.

H. A. IRONSIDE.

*Casa Blanca, New Mexico.*

# NOTES

# THE BOOK OF EZRA

## CHAPTER I

### Separated Vessels

THERE are seven Old Testament books
most intimately linked together;—three
historical, three prophetic and one both historical and prophetic. I refer to Ezra, Nehemiah
and Esther in the first group, Haggai, Zechariah
and Malachi in the second; and Daniel standing
alone as the third.* All have to do largely with
a special work of God, subsequent to the close
of the seventy years' captivity predicted by
Jeremiah in which the land of Palestine was to
make up her lost sabbatic years (Jer. 25:11–14;
2 Chron. 36:21; Dan. 9:2). During this period
of desolation her people were in bondage to the

---

* I have previously sent forth a little book called "Notes on
the Book of Esther," and have published a volume of "Lec-
tures on the Book of Daniel." The three post-captivity
prophets are in measure expounded in my "Notes on the
Minor Prophets." If God will, a volume on "Nehemiah" will
follow the present work.

king of Babylon first, and after his overthrow, to the king of Persia. Babylon was the fountain-head of idolatry, and in its false worship, demon-inspired, was found in germ every evil teaching that Satanic ingenuity has ever devised for the turning away of unbelieving men from the revelation given by God in His holy Word.

It was to cure the people of Judah of their deeply-rooted love for idolatry that Jehovah gave them up to serve the Chaldeans, "that bitter and hasty nation." Dwelling in the midst of the heathen, surrounded on all sides by the detestable creations of the human mind energized by wicked spirits, they learned to the full the folly and wretchedness of forsaking "the Guide of their youth" for the "gods many and lords many" of the nations. Their experiences in this stronghold of paganistic corruption cured them effectually of the worship of images, and resulted in a gracious revival under God's good hand which gave to His word a place of importance in their souls that it had not previously held. Unhappily, this blessed work of God's Spirit soon lost its power and degenerated into a mere cold intellectual bibliolatry, in which the letter of the Word was clung to tenaciously while the spirit was quite ignored. So devoted were the Pharisaic successors of "the men of the great synagogue" (as Ezra and his companions were afterwards called) to the study of the sacred

writings, that they even counted the words and
letters of the law, while a great body of expository literature was produced, most of it pedantic
and imaginative in the extreme, but all testifying to the veneration in which the Scriptures
were held.   Yet when He who is Himself the
Spirit of the entire Old Testament, and of whom
Moses and all the prophets wrote, appeared in
their midst, He was not discerned by faith and
was rejected and crucified by the descendants of
the very remnant whose zeal for God is com.
mended in the book of Ezra.   Though He came
in fulfilment of the very writings they read every
Sabbath in public, and often in private, as the
Babe of Bethlehem Ephrata, the Light of Galilee
of the nations, and the lowly Prince of Peace riding upon an ass, they fulfilled other prophecies
in rejecting Him and spurning His claims.

As a result of this stupendous blunder, in a day
yet to come and now undoubtedly drawn very
near, the mass of the Jews are to sink to a lower
form of idolatry than ever, when they receive
and own the Antichrist of the future as Messiah
of Israel and minister of "a god whom their fathers knew not," the Roman Beast who will be
worshiped by the apostate Jews and Christendom
alike as "the god of forces" (Dan. 11: 36 to end;
Rev. 13).

This perversion of the word of God and insen-
sibility to the Spirit's work is exceedingly solemn.

and may well have a voice for saints of God in this last end of the present dispensation of His grace, who have been largely delivered from Romish abominations and Protestant misconceptions of Scripture, and brought again to own in simplicity the headship of Christ, the presidency of the Holy Spirit in the Church, and the authority of the written Word over the consciences of all who call upon the name of the Lord.  Here also there is grave danger of holding fast the letter, while losing sight of the tremendous importance of walking in the Spirit in living, realized fellowship with the Lord Jesus Christ, to whose peerless name God would gather all His own.  Already a declension of no slight character has come in, and against those who seek to hold fast the Word and not deny the one only Name, the world, the flesh and the devil have combined to render powerless the testimony to the failure of the Church at large, and the abiding unity of the body of Christ.

It cannot therefore be other than salutary to prayerfully trace again some of God's dealings with a remnant of old, that we may learn afresh His mind for His people to-day.  In this spirit we would turn to the record of Ezra the scribe, a portion of Holy Scripture of intensely practical character, and abounding with suggestive teaching for believers in all ages.

The first two and a half verses of chapter one
are quoted from the ending of 2 Chron., thus sug-
gesting that Ezra was, perhaps, the chosen instrument to complete the earlier record, and
which God would not have concluded without a
pledge of restoration.

But these first verses of Ezra are not really
the beginning of the work of God of which he
treats.   The true starting point will be found in
the 9th of Daniel.   There we find a man of God
on his knees over the word of God—a lovely sight
and one that ever foretells coming blessing.
There are three 9th chapters in this series of
books that are in large measure of the same
character, namely, the 9th of Ezra, of Nehemiah
and of Daniel.   In all three alike we have men,
each one whose heart is under the power of the
truth for his times, in the place of confession before God.   Such an attitude of soul well becomes
all who recognize in any degree the advancing
apostasy and the growth of the spirit of insub-
jection to the Holy Scriptures now so prevalent.

In Daniel's case, " he understood by books " that
the seventy years of affliction were very nearly
run.   He was a student of prophecy, and as he
pored over Jeremiah's serious messages, he recognized that the time for their fulfilment of the
Word as to the restoration had drawn near. What
is the result ?   It drives him to his knees.   He
was no mere intellectual Bible student like so

many to-day. The Scriptures had power over his soul and brought him to prayer and confession. He made the approaching deliverance a matter of earnest supplication coupled with a self-judgment that was the outcome of being in the realized presence of God. He confessed his own sin and the sin of his people. There was no harsh criticism of others while congratulating himself on his own faithfulness. He had been faithful, no doubt, but he does not claim anything on that ground. He confesses the failure of the nation to which he belongs and acknowledges their sin as his own. "*We* have sinned" is his cry, not "*they* have sinned."

And what is the happy outcome of all this? We get it in the beginning of Ezra. "Now in the first year of Cyrus, king of Persia, that the word of the Lord by the mouth of Jeremiah might be fulfilled, the Lord stirred up the spirit of Cyrus, king of Persia" (ver. 1). Thus had God begun to hear and answer His servant's prayer, in fulfilment of His own word given through Jeremiah.

People are often stumbled as to the relations of prayer and the purpose of God. If God has counseled, shall He not bring it to pass, whether we pray or not? The answer is that prayer is a part of God's purpose. He has willed to act when His people pray; and one of the first evidences that He is about to perform a certain thing is that the spirit of prayer and supplication is poured out upon His people in regard to that particular work.    Here He moves the heart of a king in his palace to accomplish His word, after Daniel has made it a matter of prayer.

Cyrus issues a decree saying, "The Lord God of heaven hath given me all the kingdoms of the earth; and He hath charged me to build Him a house at Jerusalem, which is in Judah.    Who is there among you of all His people?    His God be with him, and let him go up to Jerusalem, which is in Judah, and build the house of the Lord God of Israel (He is the God), which is in Jerusalem.    And whosoever remaineth in any place where he sojourneth, let the men of his place help him with silver, and with gold, and with goods, and with beasts, beside the freewill offering for the house of God which is in Jerusalem" (vers. 2–4).

In the beginning of this proclamation we see how evidently Cyrus was inspired of the Lord in the very title given to Jehovah.    He is the "God of heaven."    This is the name by which He is largely known in the series of books indicated above.    It was a title He took when His throne was removed from the earth, and He gave His people into the hands of the Gentiles.    He went and "returned to His place," as Hosea puts it.    He forsook the temple at Jerusalem, dissolved the theocracy and became "the God of heaven."

Such He is still to His ancient people, and so He will remain till He returns to Jerusalem to establish His throne again as "the Lord of the whole earth."

It is likewise of note that Cyrus issues no *command* for any one to return to Jerusalem. There is to be nothing legal in this movement. It must be the result of grace working in the soul. So the king gives permission, and all who have heart for it are free to go up to the place where of old the Lord had set His name.

For nature there was little indeed to attract any one to Jerusalem. It lay a burned, ruined heap in the midst of a land of desolation. But for faith there was an attraction which nature could not understand. It was the city of God, the place of the Name,—the only place on earth to which a grateful people could scripturally bring their offerings and where the guilty could bring a sacrifice for sin.

For believers now there is no such hallowed spot in this scene; "Neither in Jerusalem, nor at this mountain" is our place of worship. But our Lord has said: "Where two or three are gathered together unto My name, there am I in the midst." Where He is acknowledged as sole Head and Lord and His redeemed are gathered to Himself, is what answers to the place where He set His name of old. As so gathered He leads His saints into the heavenly sanctuary, and there draws out their

hearts to offer the sacrifice of praise and thanksgiving. To get back to this simplicity, as it was
at the beginning, may well be the desire of our
hearts. Ever since the rising light of the Reformation there have been such stirrings of heart
and conscience among the children of God;—
yearnings after more of the simplicity of early
days, with a larger appreciation of Christ, a separation from the unholy and profane.

It would be a grave blunder to make the scenes
of Ezra typical of any one movement in Christendom. It rather has suggestive lessons by
which saints may profit when any special work
of gathering back to Christ in the Spirit's power
is going on. And this is one of the first and most
important lessons. Such a movement must be of
the working of grace. It cannot be a legal thing
or all its freshness and power are lost. Hence the
unwisdom of trying to force people into a position
where grace has not been drawing them.

It is customary in some quarters to rail against
human systems and to put the leaving them on
people's consciences as a matter of duty. By
this means many take an outward place of separation who are not really drawn to *Christ*. It
follows that such are very likely to be hard and
legal in their ways and words, and will know
little of that stirring of heart and attraction to
the Lord Himself that we have pictured here in
Ezra. The 5th verse tells us that certain of the

chief of the fathers of Judah and Benjamin, together with priests and Levites, and "all them whose spirit God had awakened," arose "to go up to build the house of the Lord which is in Jerusalem." This was most precious to God. The voluntariness was a lovely evidence of grace working in their souls.

Some there were, perhaps the majority, who did not go up, and it is not for us to judge them as to this; for we cannot tell what natural hindrances there may have been. But the book of Esther is witness that God did not take the same pleasure in those who remained as in the company who "for the Name's sake" ascended to Jerusalem. He watched over them still, but He did not link His name openly with them as He did with the rest.

There was no enmity or spirit of judgment between the two classes. Those who remained helped their brethren who went up "with vessels of silver, with gold, with goods, and with beasts, and with precious things beside all that was willingly offered" (ver. 6).

The action of Cyrus to which our attention is next directed, in separating the vessels that had of old belonged to Jehovah's temple, from the treasure of the kings devoted to the heathen deities, is most suggestive, reminding us of the word of the Lord in 2 Tim. as to separating between vessels to honor and vessels to dishonor.

What was of and for God must be purged out
from the mixture.   And this remains true for
to-day.

The separated vessels are all numbered and
committed to Sheshbazzar, called generally
Zerubbabel (a stranger in Babel) the prince of
Judah.   It is noteworthy that this prince of David's line claims no honors by virtue of his illus-
trious descent.   It was a day of weakness and of
small things.   Zerubbabel therefore takes his
place as one whose faith others can follow, but
he claims nothing as David's son and heir.

This may speak to the hearts of those who to-
day are exercised as to the lack of sign-gifts and
who desire something great that the eye may see.
The time for great things is over, the dispensation is closing in failure on man's part as to all
committed to him.   It becomes those who really
"have understanding of the times" to be through
with pretension, and in simplicity to go along
with the lowly.   " The meek will He guide in
judgment; the meek will He teach His way."

## CHAPTER II.

## Back to the Place of the Name

IT is to a sample-page from the books of eternity that we are next introduced. A leaf out of God's memorial record is spread before us for our inspection. Similar specimen lists are given us in other parts of the book of God. Gen. 49 is one. The two accounts of David's mighty men, as set forth in 2 Sam. and in 1 Chron., are of the same character. In Neh. 3 (and also in 7, where this 2nd of Ezra is duplicated), God shows how carefully He was taking note of each individual, each family, and the work they accomplished for Him. Rom. 16 is much on the same line, though at first sight only a chapter of apostolic greetings, and in Heb. 11 we have an honor-roll that shall yet be consulted at the judgment-seat of Christ.

There is something peculiarly solemn about records such as these. Many, yea, most of the names in them are for us only names, but God has not forgotten one of the persons once called by these names on earth, and "in that day" He will reward according to the work of each. Some too must "suffer loss" for opportunities neglected, or half-hearted service. Nothing of good or ill shall be overlooked by Him who seeth not as man seeth, who looks not on the outward appearance but on the heart. How little did any of these devoted Jews of Ezra's day think that God would preserve a registry of their names and families for future generations to read, and thus to learn how highly He values all that is done from devotion of heart to Himself and for the glory of His name!

" Now these are the children of the province that went up out of the captivity, of those which had been carried away, whom Nebuchadnezzar the king of Babylon had carried away unto Babylon, and came again unto Jerusalem and Judah, every one unto his city " (ver. 1). And then follows the long list of forty-two thousand three hundred and sixty, besides their servants and two hundred choristers (vers. 64, 65). Even the number of their beasts of burden is recorded, for God takes note of all that may be connected with His people, if only in a temporal way (vers. 66, 67).

As one's eye runs down the list of Hebrew names, there are many that stand out in a special way, and some have most suggestive comments attached.

In verse 2 we read both of a Nehemiah and a Mordecai: but the first must not be confounded with the writer of the next book, who came up later, after the re-building of the temple, and in accordance with the " commandment to restore and build Jerusalem," mentioned as the starting point of the seventy heptads of Dan. 9: 24. Nor should the record be identified with the aged

consin of Queen Esther, who remained in the
city of Shushan, and so far as we know, never
went up to Jerusalem after being carried away
as a child (Esther 2: 5, 6).

"The men of Anathoth," of verse 23, recalls
Jeremiah's purchase of the field of Anathoth, so
long before, and the sealed title-deeds awaiting
their lawful claimant. It looked like the height
of folly to purchase a field in a doomed district;
but faith looked on to the restoration, and now
the long-expected day had come when the sealed
scroll would prove of real value (Jer. 32).

It is noticeable that so few Levites went up
at this time (ver. 40). Only seventy-four! A
small company indeed, and what wonder if we
look only at the human side of it. They were to
have no inheritance save in the Lord. He alone
must be their portion. But it took genuine faith
to enable these dear servants of God to count
upon His abundant resources at a time when
neither wealth nor prestige were found among
His remnant people. That a time of testing had
soon to be faced we may see by consulting Neh.
13: 10. If God's people are going on with Him
His servants will not be neglected, however little
there may seem to be for sight to look upon.
And on the other hand, if the people of the Lord
do prove forgetful, it is for the servant to realize
the more his dependence on God Himself—not
on saints, however amiable and benevolent.

There were more of the children of Asaph, the temple singers, than of the Levites in Zerubbabel's company (ver. 41). Of them one hundred and twenty-eight went up. The spirit of praise supports the soul and easily passes over rough ways.

Some there were who could not show their genealogy. "These were they that went up from Tel-melah, Tel-harsa, Cherub, Addan and Immer: but they could not show their father's house and their seed, whether they were of Israel: the children of Delaiah, the children of Tobiah, the children of Nekoda, six hundred fifty and two " (vers. 59, 60). They formed a large company, but there was an uncertainty about their origin which was perplexing indeed. And, alas, of how many in Christendom to-day is this the case! Characterized by zeal and earnestness often, they are yet quite unable to give a clear, scriptural answer for the hope that is in them. We need to beware of passing hasty judgment on such people; but, on the other hand, a degree of care and caution is needed, that is often resented, but which godly concern for what is dear to Christ demands.

Even of the priests, of whom more than a thousand went up (vers. 36–39), were there found some who could not fully establish their title to serve in Jehovah's temple. "Of the children of the priests: the children of Habaiah, the children of Koz, the children of Barzillai, who took a wife of the daughters of Barzillai the Gileadite, and was called after their name: these sought their register among those that were recorded by genealogy, but they were not found: therefore were they, as polluted, put from the priesthood, and the Tirshatha (Governor) said unto them, that they should not eat of the most holy things, till there stood up a priest with Urim and with Thummim " (vers. 61–63). These were not declared positively to be laying false claim to the priestly title; they were simply set to one side because they could not prove it, until an inspired priest should rise up who could speak with authority.

So we may well treat some now, who cannot trace their genealogy, but nevertheless insist on the Christian place as rightfully theirs. We dare not say they are not born of God—and those who do so essay to speak are guilty of gross presumption; but we cannot own them as such till they can give clear evidence of being indeed of the priestly company and partakers of the divine nature.    We can in such case but fall back upon the word, "The Lord knoweth them that are His," and wait until our Great Priest shall Himself pronounce authoritatively as regards them. Till then, we dare not give them the full Christian place; and if they resent the seeming discourtesy, it but indicates a state of soul that calls for self-judgment and repentance.

The 68th and 69th verses show that God was taking note of what was given with a willing heart "for the house of God to set it up in its place." And when the journey was ended, and the returned company stood upon the site of the ruined city where the Lord had set His name, the desolation did not lead to despair, but stirred afresh the hearts of "some of the chief of the fathers," who "gave after their ability" of both silver and gold and garments for the priests. And all this ere even the altar had been set upon its base. It was a gracious work, surely, and evidenced the healthful spiritual state of these aged men, who longed to see the temple rise from its ashes ere being called hence.

It is to be feared that very few Christians are faithful in giving after their ability. The rule laid down in 1 Cor. 16: 2, "Upon the first day of the week, let each one of you lay by him in store *as God hath prospered him*," is one that seldom claims a second thought with many. At the weekly gathering a coin is dropped in the box, often with no previous forethought, and certainly not as a result of a prayerful laying by at home according as God has prospered the giver during the past week. Were this genèrally acted upon, there would be no dearth of means to carry on the work of the Lord in the home and foreign fields, nor any lack of provision for the poor among the saints. God will never forget that these fathers of old gave according to their ability. Will He forget that many have done nothing of the kind?

Verse 70 closes the chapter with the statement that the priests and Levites, the singers and porters, and the Nethinims* dwelt in their cities, "and all Israel in their cities." Who would have expected to read of "all Israel" at such a time as this! Yet God sees in this weak and feeble remnant a company occupying the ground of all Israel, and He refuses to consider the nation other than in its unity.

So to-day, it is not possible to re-gather the whole Church of God in one outward visible unity.    But it *is* possible for a feeble few to meet on the ground of the Church of God, refusing all sectarian names and ways, "endeavoring to keep the unity of the Spirit in the bond of peace." The last phrase must never be forgotten. When strife and discord come in, the unity of the Spirit is at once violated.   It can never be forced.   It is a practical thing, maintained alone as believers walk in the Spirit and recognize in each other all that is of God, while each one individually seeks to "follow peace with all men, and holiness, without which no man shall see the Lord."

---

* A word of uncertain meaning; they are supposed by many to be the descendants of the wily Gibeonites.

In no other way can the unity of the Spirit be truly kept. The unity of the body of Christ is in no sense in our keeping. "There *is* one body"—only one; and no failure on man's part can alter that. But we are responsible to act on the *ground* of that one body, in accordance with the Word, "The loaf which we break is it not the communion of the body of Christ?" (1 Cor. 10: 16.) Thus in the very act of breaking bread at the table of the Lord, we set forth our unity as members of the one body. Why should we then recognize any other body—any narrower circle?

In principle, christian fellowship, to be scriptural, must embrace all believers; but just as of old there were those whose register could not be found, so now there are many whom one dare not say are not believers, with whom those who would maintain the truth of God cannot have fellowship, because of their doctrine or manner of life. And under this latter heading must be included the being partakers of other men's sins, by associating with what is unholy and defiling. It is here that faith is tested; for only godly discernment can enable saints to act consistently without human rules and regulations, owning all fellow-members of Christ's body, but walking only with those who, following "righteousness, faith, love, peace, call on the Lord out of a pure heart" (2 Tim 2: 19–22).

## CHAPTER III

## The Altar and the House

THERE is an evident hiatus to be understood between chapter 2 and 3; but of how
long a time we have no record. Doubtless there
were weeks, or possibly months, of earnest labor,
in which the returned remnant builded homes
for themselves, and made preparations for the
re-building of the desolated temple by clearing
away the rubbish and debris that marked the impiety of the Babylonian conqueror.

At last the seventh month, the month in which
the Feast of Tabernacles was celebrated of old,
had been reached, and it was decided to set up
the altar of Jehovah at once, and with the word
of God as their only guide to seek to carry out
the instructions as to its observance. There
could be nothing so grand nor so stable as of old,
but it would be of the same order; and the
Word was as truly sufficient for direction and
"instruction in righteousness " as in the palmiest
days of the fathers.

There was no thought of substituting human
expediency for what God had spoken through
Moses in the distant past. No one was called on
for ideas or suggestions as to the most suitable
way to act in these their adverse circumstances,
and under such different conditions to those of

old. They simply searched the Scriptures, and when "they found it written," that was an end of controversy. The Bible was their authority; expediency was barred out.

This is a principle of all importance to any who to-day value the divine approbation above the approval of carnal men. The Scriptures are all-sufficient still. They contain all the instruction needed for the guidance of those who would be faithful to God in any particular period of the Church's history. The moment expediency usurps the place of subjection to the revealed will of the Lord, the whole principle of faith is given up, and a walk by sight takes its place. For we cannot walk by faith except as we yield unhesitating obedience to the word of God, which leaves no place for human will or human arrangements.

In the first verse of this lovely chapter we have a beautiful picture of that unity which should ever characterize the children of God. "And when the seventh month was come, and the children of Israel were in their cities, the people gathered themselves together *as one man* to Jerusalem." This is indeed blessed. "Behold how good and how pleasant a thing it is for brethren to dwell together in unity! . . . There the Lord commanded the blessing, even life for evermore " (Ps. 133). It is of this we have an example, delightful to contemplate, in the case

before us. The people were gathered together
as one man to the place of the Name; and in full
accordance with the psalm just quoted from,
"The Lord commanded the blessing." Of this the
balance of the chapter affords ample proof.    It
was fulfilled again in wondrous measure at the
beginning of the Church's history: "When the
day of Pentecost was fully come, they were all
with one accord in one place" (Acts 2: 1).    And
what was the happy result? Nothing less than
the outpouring of the Holy Spirit, the baptism
whereby the one body was formed, the conversion of three thousand persons, and the edification of the whole company, while the name of
the crucified Jesus was with great power magnified and lauded.

When we look back to the Church's natal day,
and contrast the sweet and holy unity then manifested, with the heart-breaking divisions and
cruel separations now seen among Christians, we
may well weep and cry, "O Lord, how long?"

Heal all these schisms we cannot; but we can
judge the whole thing as of the flesh, and, turning from all we learn to be contrary to the mind
of God, cease to own any narrower body than the
body of Christ; refuse allegiance to any other
head than Him who sits at God's right hand; and,
while gathering back to the one only Name—
turning away from all that bears the Babylonian
trade mark—open our hearts, "to all who call

upon the name of our Lord Jesus Christ, both theirs and ours," and thus, in obedience to the word of God, we may yet "endeavor to keep the unity of the Spirit in the bond of peace."

So stirring a theme tempts us to wander from our subject, but space and time alike forbid; so we turn back to consider what is further presented for our learning and admonition in the verses that follow.

The altar of the God of Israel (not of the few re-gathered ones, be it noted—but of the whole nation which, though scattered and peeled, is seen by faith in its integrity), was rebuilt by Jeshua the son of Jozadak and his brethren the priests, together with Zerubbabel and his brethren of the Davidic line. The testimony is both priestly and royal, even as Christians, whatever their weakness, are called of God a holy and royal priesthood, to worship in reverence and to show forth the praises of Him who has called us by His glories and virtue.

The rebuilding of the altar answers to the establishment of believers in the fundamental truths connected with the person and work of the Son of God. "We have an altar whereof they have no right to eat who serve the tabernacle" (Heb. 13: 10). Christ Himself is our altar, for as of old it was the altar that sanctified the gift, so was it the perfection of Christ personally that gave all the value to His work. Therefore, in any true recovery of the Spirit's inditing, it will always be found that Christ Jesus and His atonement are magnified. True revival there cannot be if He is not the soul's object.

The altar established upon its basis—answering to the truth as to Christ and His work, set forth in accordance with the Word of God—the morning and evening sacrifices or burnt offerings were, without any delay, re-instituted. Now the burnt offering speaks of Christ offering Himself without spot unto God, an offering and sacrifice of a sweet-smelling savor, as contrasted with the sin and trespass offering, wherein Christ made sins is set forth. As the highest offering, it speaks of the believer's heart-felt appreciation of what Christ and His work were and are to God, leading to worship in spirit and in truth. Surely all is here in perfect and lovely accord. If the Lord Jesus be Himself before the soul, and His work be rested in, there can but be unceasing worship and adoration ascending in His name to the Father.

For the Christian, the Lord's table should ever be linked with thoughts such as these. It is in a most distinctive way the eucharistic feast—a festival of thanksgiving in grateful acknowledgment of what our Lord in infinite grace has accomplished, and of the Spirit's delight in contemplating the excellencies of His glorious person. Where this is indeed the case, participation

in the Lord's supper can never be a matter of
legal, ritual, or lifeless form. It will be with a
holy, chastened joy that the redeemed of the
Lord will be found gathered by the Spirit to the
precious name of Jesus, now made Lord and
Christ, to remember Him.

The alacrity with which the remnant of Judah
set about re-establishing the daily offerings and
the set feasts is most refreshing to contemplate.
There was a holy eagerness, a godly enthusiasm,
to walk in the old paths which is delightful to
dwell upon.

The feast of tabernacles was kept "as it is
written," and all the appointed burnt offerings
made "according to the custom, as the duty of
every day required" (ver. 4). There were apparently none to object that it was folly at so late
a day to attempt to pattern all "according to the
custom" of the early days of their glorious history. Had there been such an one, he would
have been met by the firm, decided answer and
rebuke, "It is written." And for each believer
this should ever be enough, outweighing all
carnal suggestions, modern notions and unscriptural innovations.

The continual burnt offering, the special sacrifices of the new moons, and all the set feasts
were properly provided for ; and when willing
hearts suggested at any time special thank offerings to the Lord, priestly hands were ever ready

to attend to the temple requirements as Moses in the book of the law had given commandment.

And all this before the house itself was built, even as there must first be true appreciation of Christ Himself and delight in His work ere there can be any proper entering into the truth of the house of God. The offerings began on the first day of the seventh month, but the work had not yet progressed far enough for the laying of the foundation of the house of the Lord. Indeed some nine months must have elapsed ere this house was properly begun (see ver. 8). But conjointly, we judge, with the setting up of the altar on its bases, money was given to the masons and carpenters, and full provision made to care for the temporal needs of those who were to bring cedar trees and rebuild the house, "according to the grant that they had of Cyrus, king of Persia" (ver. 7).

In the 8th verse, the date of the laying the foundation is given. It is said to be "in the second year *of their coming to the house of God at Jerusalem*, in the second month," that the work of setting forward the house of the Lord began. They had come "to the house of God," though to sense and sight there was only a blackened ruin before them! What a withering rebuke is this to man's unbelief. All that is of God abides, however we may fail in maintaining it.

We often speak, and rightly, of the truth as to

the Church being lost for over a thousand years after Romish usurpation and Judaistic legality had made the special ministry of Paul to be all but forgotten. But though the truth might be lost, so far as man's apprehension of it was concerned, the fact of the Church—both as the body of Christ and the house of God—remained, though only to be recovered to the knowledge and heart of God's people when faithful men turned from human traditionalism to Christ Himself, and from human authorization to the Word alone. Then how soon did the Spirit begin to work in revealing the long-lost truth as to God's habitation, "The house of God, which is the Church of the living God, the pillar and ground of the truth."

The truth as to all this can never be known in power in one's soul so long as practices and systems contrary to God's revealed will are tolerated or endorsed. Hence is it true that the best view of all ecclesiastical systems is to be had outside of them, when the believer can take his stand in simplicity with God's Word open in his hand and discern what is according to His mind, and what is but the product of the human will and fleshly energy. Then also can the outlines of the foundations of the house of God be discerned, and grace found to act in accordance with the truth now learned.

For we are not called to rebuild the Church.

Such has been the vain dream of more than one great mind, only to result in a rude awakening as the ruin became worse than ever. We are simply called to get back to what is written, and act on the truth as though the ruin had never come in, while yet recognizing our feebleness and dependence.

Where there is fellowship in this, it is most blessed; and this leads us to notice a word for our times, found in this and the next chapter. I refer to the fellowship-word " together," which we have already noticed in verse 1. In verse 9 we read: " Then stood Jeshua with his sons and his brethren, Kadmiel and his sons, the sons of Judah, *together*, to set forward the workmen in the house of God." Here are " laborers together." Then in verses 10 and 11, after telling of the priests, Levites, and the sons of Asaph standing in rank in their apparel, "when the builders laid the foundation of the temple of the Lord," we learn that " they sang *together* by course in praising and giving thanks unto the Lord; because He is good, for His mercy endureth forever toward Israel." Here they are praising together, each heart as one with every other, employed in exalting the loving-kindness of the Lord.

In the next chapter, verse 3, Zerubbabel and the rest, in answer to the Samaritans' offer of assistance, say : " We ourselves *together* will

build unto the Lord." Thus they are builders
together, raising the walls of the temple in holy,
happy fellowship, and in separation from the
unclean.   And so would God ever have His people going on together, remembering that they
have been "called unto the fellowship of His
Son, Jesus Christ our Lord" (1 Cor. 1: 9).

Turning again to verse 11, we note how the
people were stirred when at last the foundation
of the house of the Lord was laid.  In their godly
exaltation at this slight measure of recovery,
they "shouted with a great shout."

But all were not so exuberant, for "many of
the priests and Levites and chief of the fathers,
who were ancient men, that had seen the first
house, when the foundation of *this* house was
laid before their eyes, wept with a loud voice;
and many shouted aloud for joy: so that the
people could not discern the noise of the shout
of joy from the noise of the weeping of the people: for the people shouted with a loud shout,
and the noise was heard afar off" (vers. 12, 13).

Youth is the period of enthusiasm and exuber-
ance of spirit, while age is the time of sobriety
and serious contemplation.   Young men are apt
to be over-sanguine looking on to the future;
aged men, on the other hand, are likely to be
reminiscent and unduly occupied with the past.
It is often difficult for youth to comprehend the
fears of the old and experienced regarding any

new work in which they are involved. It is equally hard, frequently, for the elder men to recognize any special work of God entrusted chiefly to the young and in which they cannot share for long. They are too apt to forget their own youth; and as they think of ruined hopes would put the brake on any who do not now occupy their standpoint. Hence much patience is ever needed in a movement such as we have been tracing. The young need grace to profit by the godly, sober counsels of the fathers, who, in their turn, need grace to rejoice in what God is doing through those as yet immature.

Critical, fault-finding old men, even though devoted saints, may be a great hindrance to young brethren, ardent in faith and love till chilled by continual carping or objecting on the part of their elders. On the other hand, cheery, fatherly brethren, who are ever ready to see God's leading in any fresh work of His Spirit, who have grown old gracefully, and are "mellowing for heaven," as one has put it, can be both helpers and counsellors of great value to their younger brethren.

There is room both for the weeping and the shouting. As we think of the failure of man to carry out, and hold fast, the truth committed to him, we may well shed tears. As we note the matchless grace of God, rising above all failure, and ever raising up a fresh testimony to His truth in times of declension, we may well shout aloud for joy. The two are not discordant, but blend in one majestic strain, of which the treble is carried by the joyous, youthful shouters, and the bass by the weeping patriarchs—all alike to the praise and glory of the God of all grace, who is also the God of infinite holiness and intrinsic righteousness.

## CHAPTER IV

## The Adversaries

THE first discordant note in connection with this gracious symphony is struck in the chapter we are now to be occupied with, not however, at first from within, but from without; then affecting those within, so that the song of joy is silenced and a brief season of apathy supervenes.

There were those who, all along, had watched with a jealous eye the work of restoration going on at Jerusalem. They were the Samaritans, the descendants of the mixed races settled in the land by heathen kings after the capture of the ten tribes, who had long ago been carried away to Assyria, and have since been lost so far as positive identification by man is concerned.

We learn something of these conscienceless people by turning back a few pages in our Bibles, to 2 Kings, chap. 17; from ver. 24 to the end we have the record of these men who were brought from the various parts of the Assyrian dominions and settled in the land. At first they made no pretence at being anything but idolaters; but upon becoming alarmed by wild beasts increasing among them, they concluded they needed to know "the manner of the God of the land." Entreating the king of Assyria for help, he sent unto them

some of the captive priests of Jeroboam's order,
who "taught them how they should fear the Lord."
But the unreality of it all is seen in verses 32 and
33: "So they feared the Lord, and made unto
themselves of the lowest of them, priests of
the high places, who sacrificed for them in the
houses of the high places. They feared the Lord,
and served their own gods after the manner of
the nations whence they had been carried away."
And their subsequent degraded state is depicted
in the closing verse, in contrast to what God
required of His people Israel.

These Samaritans were largely of the same
character as thousands in this day of grace who
make a profession of Christianity but have never
even pretended to own Christ as Lord, and who
know nothing of the saving value of His blood.
They, too, fear the Lord, but serve their own
gods; and it is a sad mistake for the believer to
be linked up with such in Church fellowship.
Such "Christians" as these will ever prove a
snare and a hindrance, like "the mixed multitude" who came up with the children of Israel
out of Egypt.

In the case before us, we learn that "when
the adversaries of Judah and Benjamin heard
that the children of the captivity builded the
temple unto the Lord God of Israel, then they
came to Zerubbabel, and to the chief of the
fathers, and said unto them, Let us build with

you: for we seek your God, as ye do; and we do sacrifice unto Him since the days of Esar-haddon, king of Assur, who brought us up hither" (vers. 1, 2). Their words sounded friendly, but their true character is given in the opening clause— they were *adversaries*. They sought the ruin of the little company to whom they made such fair protestations. These were indeed "the wiles of the devil." Had they once gotten a foothold in the city of God they would have destroyed everything that bore the sign of His approval. To have received and encouraged them would have made the remnant company numerically stronger, but actually much weaker. It would have been admitting the enemy within the fortress. The safety of the people of God was in separation. They were set apart to Him whose name they bore. To mingle with the nations could but insure ruin and disaster.

Note the profession of these Samaritans. They declared that they too served the God of Israel, —but they could not go back far enough. They knew nothing of redemption by blood, nothing of Jehovah's covenant-sign; they had not known God's mighty works. What they knew was mere hearsay, and based on that was an empty acknowledgment of His power, while ignorant of His grace, and no subjection of heart to His will. How like the empty professions one so frequently hears. Men talk glibly of serving the Lord and

having made a start for the kingdom, who know
nothing of repentance toward God and faith in
our Lord Jesus Christ.  Till such are brought to
self-judgment before God, and heart-confidence
in Christ as Saviour, they are only a hindrance
to any Christian company, and will be adversaries to everything that is really of the Holy Spirit.

Yet the flesh hates to be accounted unfit to
take part in what is of God.  Natural men, however little place they have for the truth in their
souls, resent being given the place the truth
puts them in.  So here, when Zerubbabel and
Jeshua and the ancient men of Judah refused the
help of these unholy Samaritans, great indignation was aroused.  The leaders in Israel said:
"Ye have nothing to do with us to build a house
unto our God; but we ourselves together will
build unto the Lord God of Israel, as king
Cyrus, the king of Persia, hath commanded us"
(ver. 3)).  The last words show how plainly they
recognized their servitude, and felt the difference of present conditions from those of old.
But withal there is a splendid boldness, an un-
equivocal declaration of adherence to the principle of separation, the neglect of which in the
past had been responsible for all their troubles.
It is the spirit of the 50th psalm—taking sides
with God, who says to the wicked, "What hast
thou to do to declare My statutes, or that thou
shouldst take My covenant in thy mouth?"

This is divine independence; and only as believers learn to take this attitude toward the Christless profession around them, will they be maintained in integrity and uprightness before God.  As a testimony for Him in the world, amalgamation with the ungodly cannot help *them*, and will only hinder saints.  " Wherefore come out from among them, and be ye separate, saith the Lord; touch not the unclean, and I will receive you, and will be a Father unto you, and ye shall be My sons and daughters, saith the Lord Almighty " (2 Cor. 6: 17, 18).

But this always provokes the ire of the wicked, who will ever be ready to make unsubstantiated charges of pride and pharisaism against those who would be faithful to God at whatever cost.  So we read: " The people of the land weakened the hands of the people of Judah, and troubled them in building, and hired counsellors against them, to frustrate their purpose "—and this not for a brief season, but persistently, " all the days of Cyrus . . . even until the reign of Darius," including the years of Ahasuerus (probably Xerxes).

Thus their real nature is made manifest.  If they cannot have a hand in the work, they will do their best (or, their worst) to ruin it.  They cannot brook the refusal of their offer of fellowship; so, by spreading evil reports and misrepresenting the motives and actions of the separated company, they will hinder all they can.  A letter is even drawn up and dispatched to the king, who is here called Artaxerxes, in which there is just enough truth to make it likely to accomplish its purpose, while the question at issue is not touched upon at all.

From chap. 4: 6 to chap. 6: 18 the language used is Chaldean, or Aramaic; so we have here undoubtedly transcripts of the actual letters that passed between the kings and their subjects.

It is significant that the first letter proceeds not exactly from the "nations" but from the *societies* settled in Canaan. (See vers. 9, 10.) The various names used are rather the names of clans, or guilds, than national designations. The little Jewish company's exclusiveness drew out their hatred.

In their epistle they profess great concern for the king's interests, and grave fears lest his revenues or honor be touched. They charge the Jews with rebuilding Jerusalem, with having set up its walls and joined the foundation (ver. 12). Now all this was flagrantly false, as Nehemiah's record proves. No permission had yet been granted "to restore and build Jerusalem;" and this was not the work in which the remnant were engaged. They were rebuilding the house, or temple—not the city—of God; and their work is wilfully misrepresented.

The past history of Jerusalem is briefly reviewed, at least such part of it as would serve their purpose, and the charge is confidently made that the restoration of "the rebellious city" will mean the destruction of Persian power "on this side the river" (ver. 16).

The cunningly worded document accomplished its purpose, and a messenger soon returned with an imperial mandate declaring that search had been made, and all the evil accusations against Jerusalem as a centre of rebellion and sedition established. Then an order is given to "cause these men to cease, and that this city be not builded until another commandment shall be given from me" (vers. 17–21).

With this official communication in their hands, Rehum and Shimshai and their companions made a hasty visit to Jerusalem and caused the work to cease by force and power. Yet, clearly they acted with no real authority whatever, inasmuch as the matter of carrying out the decree of Cyrus as to the building of the *temple* had not been touched at all. That edict remained unrepealed, and had there been the energy of faith the work of restoring the house of God would have gone on despite the wrath of Rehum and his allies.

But already, first love had begun to wane, and we are told, "Then ceased the work of the house of God which is at Jerusalem. So it ceased unto the second year of the reign of Darius king of Persia" (ver. 24).

During the interval a period of apathy came in, so that the first energy for what was of God declined, and each one began to think rather of his own comfort and the comforts of his family. They turned to building their own ceiled houses, to storing up goods, and to attending carefully to their own interests. Of this the prophet Haggai accuses them. For, it should be noted, the ministry of both Haggai and Zechariah comes in here. The reader might with profit turn from the present account and read thoughtfully the two books bearing their names, ere going on with Ezra's record.

There is no hint of any suffering inflicted by the adversaries of the Jews while they were attending to their own interests. It was *what was of God* these wicked workers hated. To behold those gathered to His name devoting their time and strength to building for themselves excited no enmity, and the enemies' purpose to stop the building of the house of God succeeded.

So it ever is, the world and the world-church are quite content to see Christians prospering in temporal ways. The line of demarkation soon goes down when riches increase and self-interest prevails. It is the *spiritual* prosperity, the energy of *faith*, that offends the world; for when the light shines brightly, it exposes the selfishness, the pride, the hypocrisy of those who have a name to live but are dead.

## CHAPTER V

## Prophetic Ministry

IT has often been said, and truly, that it is one thing to occupy a right *position*, and quite another to be in a right *condition*. The remnant of Judah were in the right position when gathered back to the place of the Name. But we have just seen that they had dropped from the happy state in which they were when they first returned to Jerusalem, and had lapsed into a condition that made them easily disheartened.

What then was the remedy? Give up all and go back to the place they had left? Not at all; for they had God's word for remaining where they were, and He could be depended on to send them suited ministry to arouse and revive that they might thus reach a healthier state.

Yet how often do we see the opposite of this. People learn certain lines of truth from the Word of God, and seek grace to walk in them. To do so involves a special position as gathering alone to the name of the Lord Jesus in separaration from what is unholy. But by and by the freshness of early days passes away, and a period of lethargy and apathy succeeds. The love of many waxes cold, and the dew of their youth is gone. What should those do who would be right with God? Forsake the position and go

back to what they once left for Christ's sake?
Surely not; but in the position cry to God for the
Spirit's ministry that there may be revival and
blessing. Maintain the right position at all costs
and cease not looking up to the Head for what
each member needs.

But God's eye was on His discouraged people,
and in gracious concern for their state, He
raised up among them Haggai and Zechariah,
both "the Lord's messengers in the Lord's message" (Hag. 1: 13). In the name of the God of
Israel these two devoted servants exhorted the
remnant to consider their ways, and be strong,
or courageous, for they were directly under Jehovah's care as brands plucked from the fire.
Haggai dealt more especially with the consciences of the people. His are stirring, cutting
words. Zechariah was commissioned to speak
more to their hearts, enthusing them to holy
boldness in view of the coming glory. Both
lines of ministry were needed; for God's people
are possessed of conscience and heart, and each
must be appealed to.

The immediate result was the stirring of spirit
among the leaders. "Then rose up Zerubbabel the
son of Shealtiel, and Jeshua the son of Jozadak, and
began to build the house of God which is at Jerusalem: and with them were the prophets of
God helping them" (ver. 2). Such was the happy effect of this Spirit-given ministry.

And, as might have been expected, their insolent adversaries are once more immediately active. Hardly have trowel and hammer begun to be used in the work of rebuilding or completing the house, when Tatnai, the Samaritan governor, and Shethar-boznai (new names to us), and their companions appear, and indignantly enquire, "Who hath commanded you to build this house?" (ver. 3.) To explain to men like these would have been useless, and would have been but casting pearls before swine. "The secret of the Lord is with them that fear Him," and with no one else. Natural men could not understand a divine call and divine authorization. Therefore Zerubbabel and his helpers made no reference to the prophetic messages which had so stirred their own souls, but simply answered those fools according to their folly. "What are the names of the men that make this building?" they asked in their reply. This was but another way of saying that the business they were concerned in was one in which their questioners had no part or responsibility.

And though persuasion and threats were evidently used, "the eye of their God was upon the elders of the Jews, that they could not cause them to cease, till the matter came to Darius;" and then God so directed the king's heart that he gave an answer of peace and encouragement.

The Darius here mentioned should not be con-

founded with the king of the same name in
Daniel 6. This was evidently the successor to
Xerxes the Great, while the other was but a
vice-king under Cyrus. The splendid reign of
Artaxerxes, as he is called in this record, had
come to an end, and Darius ascended the throne.
To him therefore the enemies of the Jews addressed themselves in a lengthy epistle which, at
first sight, is of a much more straightforward
character than the one drawn up by Rehum and
Shimshai. No false evidence as to rebuilding
the *city* is manufactured, but the simple facts
stated that "the house of the great God" was in
process of construction, and "the work goeth
fast on and prospereth." One point is probably
a falsification, in that they say, "We went into
the province of Judea," and beheld these things,
as though their going there was only casual,
without malice aforethought ; whereas, as we
know, it was deliberate hostility to the Jews
that led them to thus trespass in a district where
they had no authority ; they were but evil-minded
busy-bodies. This they skilfully endeavor to
cover, and write as though a mere accident had
given them to see what made them fear for the
the king's honor.

It is a question whether in the light of verse 4,
already noted, they are not drawing on a previous knowledge in putting the lengthy answer
into the mouths of the elders which is given in

verses 11 to 16. All this was actually done, but it hardly seems likely that it was made known to Tatnai and his friends at this particular time. It was, rather, what they had heard when the work first began—the very thing that had rankled in their minds for so long.

They tell how they had questioned these elders as to who had commanded them to build these walls; and then, for very shame, in place of the abrupt and contemptuous reply of the Jews, they tell that (which Zerubbabel apparently did not say) which would have a great effect upon Darius, in throwing him back upon the unalterable decrees of the Persian king.

They declare that an answer was given to this effect: That these builders were the servants of the God of heaven and earth* and were restoring the house which a great king of Israel (whose name is evidently unknown to these plotters) had set up. But after their fathers had provoked the God of heaven unto wrath, He had permitted the Babylonian captivity, under Nebuchadnezzar, by whom the house was destroyed and the people carried away. But declaration had been made of what, to their minds, was evidently a most unheard of and preposterous thing: namely, that in the first year of Cyrus a decree

---

* Their addition of the words "and earth" shows their ignorance of God's relation with Israel at that time.

had been given to rebuild this house of God; and
that the vessels of that old and destroyed temple
had been restored to these Jews with a command
given to Sheshbazzar (the Persian name of
Zerubbabel), who was reported to have been
made governor, to take these vessels and carry
them to the temple that is in Jerusalem, and
"let the house of God be builded in his place."
Accordingly the said Sheshbazzar had come to
Jerusalem and laid the foundation, and (here
followed clear prevarication) "since that time
even until now hath it been in building" (as
though in contravention of the decree of Artaxerxes, which they supposed fully covered the
case), "and yet it is not finished."

These busy-bodies evidently felt sure that this
entire report was without authentic foundation,
so they urged that search be made to see if such
a decree had ever been issued by king Cyrus,
and loyally concluded, "Let the king send his
pleasure to us concerning this matter" (ver. 17).

And so their letter was drawn up and de-
spatched; and doubtless they felt assured that
the king's reply would put an effectual *quietus*
upon the work of these obnoxious Jews, and forever stop the erection of a building which was as
a sermon directed against their evil and idolatrous ways.

Meantime the work went right on, "for the
people had a mind to build," as we elsewhere

read and the prophets of the Lord encouraged them in carrying out His revealed will, in holy independence of their active and crafty adversaries.

The result could not be in doubt, for God never fails faith. He always makes bare His arm on behalf of those who acknowledge the authority of His Word. He has said, " Them that honor Me I will honor, and they that despise Me shall be lightly esteemed."

All that is needed is the faith that fears not the face of man, because the fear of the Lord, which is the beginning of wisdom is upon the soul.

## CHAPTER VI

# The House Completed

THAT God never fails an obedient and trusting people is preciously exemplified in this stirring chapter of His ways with the separated remnant of the Jews.

As when, in the book of Esther, the search of the royal records but vindicated Mordecai and led to the confusion of Haman, so here, when "search was made in the house of the rolls, where the treasures were laid up in Babylon, there was found at Achmetha, in the palace that is in the province of the Medes, a roll," in which was found the record of king Cyrus, containing the very decree cynically referred to in the epistle of Tatnai and Shethar-boznai. There the command that the house be builded was plainly declared, together with the specifications and plans, and the order for returning the vessels of the house of God from among the pollutions of heathen idolatry to their proper home in Jerusalem, the city where Jehovah had put His name (vers. 1–5).

King Darius accordingly wrote at once warning Tatnai and his confederates to "let the work of this house of God alone; let the governor of the Jews and the elders of the Jews build this house of God in his place" (vers. 6, 7).

This stinging rebuke was all that these enemies of the Jews and professed loyalists to the
king got for their pains. Nay, there was even
greater humiliation than this for them. The decree went on to command what they should do to
further this work: "That of the king's goods,
even of the tribute beyond the river, forthwith
expenses be given unto these men, that they be
not hindered; and that which they have need of,
both young bullocks and rams and lambs for the
burnt offerings of the God of heaven, wheat, salt,
wine, and oil, according to the appointment of
the priests that are at Jerusalem, let it be given
them day by day without fail: that they may
offer sacrifices of sweet savors unto the God of
heaven, and pray for the life of the king, and of
his sons" (vers. 8–10). Moreover, it was directed,
that if any one dared in any way to contravene
this decree, his house was to be made a dunghill,
and he himself hanged upon a scaffold made of
its timbers (ver. 11).

We must remember that all this was the decree of a king, who, whatever the measure of his
enlightenment (as a Persian disdaining the idols
of the Babylonians), nevertheless gives no evidence of that direct inspiration of God which is
declared to have been the case in regard to
Cyrus and his commandment; he was definitely
raised up of God, and designated before his birth
by name (Isa. 44: 28), and as "the righteous man

from the east " who was to fulfil Jehovah's will as
to the restoration of His people (Isa. 41:2). With
Darius it was otherwise. He writes as one who
had great respect for the decrees of his prede-
cessors, and he will therefore invoke fearful penalties on any who venture to act contrary to
them.

The last part of his letter is such as we might
expect from a king of his character, under the
circumstances that had arisen: "And the God
that hath caused His name to dwell there destroy
all kings and people, that shall put to their
hand to alter and to destroy this house of God
which is at Jerusalem " (ver. 12). It is a solemn
fact that this curse was literally fulfilled in every
instance. Antiochus defiled this house and died
unnaturally under the anger of God. Herod
presumed to alter and enlarge it for his own
aggrandizement, and died under divine displeasure. The Romans utterly destroyed it
when the days of grace for Israel had expired;
but in doing so, sealed their own doom, and their
mighty empire is to-day but a memory.

The celerity with which the humbled and
astonished Tatnai and his friends undertook to
carry out the provisions of the decree must have
been a great relief to the hitherto despised
Jews. It reminds one of the Lord's words to
another feeble remnant, the church of Philadelphia, who had a little strength and kept

Christ's word, not denying His name. To them them He says: "Behold, I will make them of the synagogue of Satan, which say they are Jews and are not, but do lie; behold, I will make them to come and worship before thy feet, and to know that I have loved thee" (Rev. 3: 9).

What is really of God may be despised for the moment by the unsubject and hypocritical, but the day of manifestation ever shows where the Lord has found His pleasure. Not always does this manifestation take place on earth, but in the day of Christ all that God has owned will be made plain. Yet, even here, often He shows where He has set the seal of His approval, to the discomfiture of haughty pretenders to an authority and spirituality they do not possess.

Happily, we see no evidence of carnal exultation or of haughtiness of spirit on the part of Zerubbabel and his fellow-laborers over the exposure and humbling of their opponents. Rather do we see a sincere cleaving to the Lord and rejoicing in Him who has made their mountain to stand strong. It was His work they were concerned in, not their own vindication. So, in holy serenity, "the elders of the Jews builded, and they prospered through the prophesying of Haggai the prophet and Zechariah the son of Iddo" (ver. 14).

I would call the reader's attention to the designations given these servants of God, now for

the second time. Haggai is called "the prophet"
as though pre-eminently that, while his compan-
ion-servant is simply declared to be "the son of
Iddo." Yet, as men generally speak, the latter
it is who possesses the fullest claim to the prophetic office; for he unfolds in a wonderful manner the future in store for Israel and Judah.
And this opening up of the unseen future is
what is generally called prophecy. But it is
otherwise in the word of God. The true prophet
is the one whose words come from heaven to
men on earth, searching the heart, reaching the
conscience and exposing the evil that may have
come in. "He that prophesieth speaketh unto
men to edification, and exhortation (or stirring up)
and comfort (or encouragement)" (1 Cor. 14: 3).
Now this was exactly what Haggai did. His
pungent, conscience-arousing messages were distinctly of this character, and so he is pre-eminently "the prophet." Zechariah's needed ministry of future things was equally of God, but it
was subservient to the rousing words of his
brother prophet, whose ministry was in view of
the state of soul in God's people.

A ministry like Zechariah's will more probably
be enjoyed than one of the character of Haggai's.
Carnal believers often find great pleasure in lis-
tening to dispensational and eschatological discourses, in attending what are often mis-called
"prophetic" conferences; but what such really

need is the trumpet-like call to consider their ways, rather than eloquent and beautiful discourses about things to come. The Haggais may not be so popular with the mass as the Zechariahs, but their ministry is ever a much needed one. He who goes on with God will welcome truth, and will thus hold the truth in its right proportions.

At last the house was finished, in the sixth year of Darius the king—a long time indeed since the work had been begun. But persistent effort had eventually prevailed, and the temple, whose foundations had been laid with praise and weeping, and whose walls had been erected with faith and prophecy, was now ready to be dedicated to the service and worship of the Lord God of Israel.

If one goes back and compares, or contrasts, the account of the dedication of the temple of Solomon with that of this house of the captivity, he cannot but feel how meagre was the service of the latter; but, on the other hand, one cannot but recognize it as of the same character. It was, in very deed, a going back to that which was from the beginning. The hundred bullocks, two hundred rams, and four hundred lambs for a peace offering, were few indeed as compared with the twenty-two thousand oxen, and the one hundred and twenty thousand sheep offered by Solomon; but all spoke of the same Christ who, "having made peace by the blood of His cross" is now the ground of the soul's communion with God.

In solemn contrast with the sweet savor offerings, alone mentioned in connection with Solomon's dedication, we here read of twelve he-goats as a sin-offering *for all Israel*, according to the number of the tribes of Israel (ver. 17). This was eminently fitting, for all Israel had sinned; and on behalf of all Israel, the remnant confessed and judged the sin in which all had participated. Only an active conscience, truly in the light, could have led to this blessed result. The dedication was kept, we are told, with joy, and "they set the priests in their divisions, and the Levites in their courses, for the service of God which is at Jerusalem; as it is written in the book of Moses" (ver. 18).

And so, once again, we are reminded of the only way to learn the mind of God, even to consult His holy Word, in dependence on the Spirit who inspired it. "As it is written" would settle many a needless controversy among Christians if there were only grace to "search the Scriptures" and to obey what is found therein. With "It is written," Jesus met every assault of Satan; and when he, for his own ends, misquoted, or partially quoted, from the same Word, concealing an important phrase, he was met with "It is written again," to silence his impious suggestions. This is the path of safety for each saint,

only let none suppose that a mere slavish adherence to "book, chapter and verse," is what is
here indicated.   This there cannot always be;
but the tenor of Scripture, the broad principles enunciated and exemplified therein, are
what one needs to be familiar with.  There was
no specific scripture that instructed Zerubbabel
to offer on this particular occasion twelve goats
as a sin offering for all Israel.  But it was fully
in accord with the word of God so to do; it was
in the *spirit* of the law He had given through
Moses, and therefore well-pleasing to Him.

And, in the next place, in obedience to the
same Word, "The children of the captivity kept
the passover upon the fourteenth day of the first
month " (ver. 19).  Great was the care exercised
that all should be as God had directed.   "The
priests and the Levites were purified together; all
of them were pure, and killed the passover for all
the children of the captivity, and for their brethren the priests, and for themselves.  And the
children of Israel who were come again out of
captivity, and all such as had separated themselves unto them from the filthiness of the nations of the land, to seek the Lord God of Israel,
did eat " (vers. 20, 21).

All this is most instructive and enlightening,
furnishing a helpful principle for those to act
upon in any age, who would please the Lord in
their public feasts of love, and their fellowship

one with another. The passover was the great central feast of Israel. It was to them what the Lord's supper is to Christians. In fact, our Lord links the two most intimately, in that it was during the celebration of the one that He instituted the other. The loaf in His hand was the unleavened Passover bread, while the cup was the Passover cup, for which Scripture gives no direct authority, but which was a natural accompaniment of a Jewish meal. Both spoke of the same blessed event—the death of Christ. The one set forth that death in prospect, the other declares that death as already having taken place. "For as oft as ye eat this bread and drink this cup, ye do show (or *announce*—it might even be rendered, *preach*) the Lord's death till He come" (1 Cor. 11: 26).

In the beginning all confessing Christ's name had their place at that holy table. Then divine instruction was given not to eat with any one, called a brother, whose life was wicked. Teachers of false doctrine were likewise debarred from all Christian fellowship, which could not but include participation in the communion supper. With this, God has also warned lest any be partakers of other men's sins, by going on with those unfitted for fellowship, thereby unfitting themselves. And so, with these broad principles to guide, it may be confidently asserted that God has not left believers to decide for themselves

the grave question of who is to be received and
who refused at the table of the Lord. The unholy have no place there. Being the *Lord's* table,
it implies subjection to Him as such. Hence,
we see the priests all purified together. To-day
all believers are priests. This then is the scriptural ideal of a Christian gathering—"all of
them were pure."

To this company were received "all such as had
separated themselves from the filthiness of the
nations of the land to seek the Lord." What an
enlightening word is this! There are those who
object to an expression long current among certain believers: "Separation from evil is God's
principle of unity." But is not that exactly what
we have here ? Were not these dear Israelites
one as a separated company from the abominations of the people of the land ? Only as so
separated could they cleave together. And in
any dispensation, I apprehend, the same principle abides for faith. There can be no true
practical unity save as evil is refused, and Christ
becomes the object of each soul. And separation from evil involves turning to the Lord alone,
for He is the one only centre, apart from all the
evil. Given His rightful place, the incongruity
of endeavoring to cling to what is unholy while
seeking to please God, is at once made manifest.

But argument avails little here. This truth,
like all others, has to be learned through

the conscience. Men may reason and contend about what to faith is most simple, if there be activity of conscience, enlightened by the word of God. The feeble few of Zerubbabel's day were far beyond some now, who, despite greatly increased light, are quite unable to discern the mind of God because persons are before them instead of the glory of Christ. Much grace is needed if any truth be apprehended that it may be held in the Spirit's power; and this is especially true as to what Scripture reveals in regard to gathering to the name of the Lord Jesus.

## CHAPTER VII

## A Second Awakening

WE reach a new beginning, as it were, in the present chapter, when Ezra for the first time, is definitely identified with the movement for returning to the place where God had set His name.

Another Artaxerxes is now on the throne, and in his reign God revives the spirits of many who had hitherto remained in Babylon, and fills their hearts with a desire to go up to Jerusalem. Of these Ezra himself is the leader. He was a direct lineal descendant of Phinehas, the man whose javelin had turned aside the wrath of the Lord in the days of Baal-peor, when Balaam taught Balak how to seduce Israel by unholy alliances with the daughters of Moab (Num. 25). To him had been granted an everlasting priesthood, and of this pledge Ezra is witness.

He was, we are told, "a ready scribe in the law of Moses," and one who had the confidence of the king; so when he preferred a request to be permitted to lead another company up from Babylon to the city of God, his petition was heard, and full permission given, "according to the good hand of the Lord his God upon him." This expression is characteristic. In all his ways Ezra recognized "the good hand of the Lord," and to that alone he attributes every forward step.

With Ezra went up a considerable company of the children of Israel, including priests, Levites, singers, porters and Nethinim, who left Babylon in the seventh year of Artaxerxes, and in about four months arrived in Jerusalem to join the former company, and there to set forward the work of the Lord.

Of Ezra we read that he "had prepared his heart to seek the law of the Lord, and to do it, and to teach in Israel statutes and judgments" (ver. 10). His was just the ministry now needed among the returned company, and "the good hand of the Lord" supplied it. A competent, sober man of sound judgment, a man mighty in the Scriptures, and an able instructor of his brethren; how invaluable he would be at this time.

Not a mere intellectual student of the word of God, nor one teaching others what had not gripped his own heart and controlled his ways, was Ezra. He had begun by earnestly preparing his own heart to seek the law of the Lord. "The preparation of the *heart* in man is of the Lord." This Ezra recognized. So it is not said that he prepared his head—but his heart. His inmost being was brought under the sway of the truth of God. His affections were controlled by the Scriptures. He might have said, with Jeremiah; " Thy words were found, and I did eat them; and Thy word was unto me the joy and rejoicing of my heart." He was personally right with God, and so was prepared to help set others right. Then there was more than inward preparation. Having learned the mind and will of God, he undertook to *do* it. He did not preach truth that he was not living. When under the good hand of God the king granted him all his requests, to leave Babylon and go to Jerusalem for the sake of the Name, he considered not circumstances (which might well have held him where he was, in place of going up to a desolated land and a ruined city), but he at once prepared to go forth trusting " the good hand of the Lord upon him."

One reason there is so little power with much of the preaching and teaching of the day is a lack of consistently *doing* the truth ere proclaiming it. Men preach the Lord's near coming, who give no evidence that the "blessed hope" has moulded their ways. Men teach the truth of the mystery of the one body, who yet, for filthy lucre's sake, or because of other circumstances, abide in what practically denies it. Men proclaim the heavenly calling who have never learned to walk on earth as strangers and pilgrims. Is it any wonder their words are without

power and their ministry but as clouds without
water? The path of blessing is *doing*—then
teaching. It was thus with the true Servant.
Luke writes "of all that Jesus began both to do
and to teach" (Acts 1: 1). Woe be to any man,
however able and gifted, who ventures to neglect
the first while carrying on the second. Ezra
was a pattern man in this respect. He undertook to do what he found written ; then "to
teach in Israel statutes and judgments." Let
every servant of God lay this 10th verse to heart,
and ask himself: Am I thus serving my Master?
No doubt such a question will at once bring before every conscientious soul much that calls for
self-judgment; and Ezra himself, doubtless, would
have felt the same. But the aim, the bent of
the life, is what I refer to—the endeavor to carry
out the order here indicated.

A copy of the letter of Artaxerxes is given in
verses 12 to 26, and, as in the case of the previous decrees, this passage is reproduced in Aramaic or Chaldean, directly transcribed from the
Persian records. There is something very beautiful in the salutation of this letter: "Artaxerxes,
king of kings, unto Ezra the priest, a scribe of
the law of the God of heaven, perfect peace,"
and so forth (ver. 12). How marked the contrast
between the two. How different their titles.
And, in God's sight, how much higher was
Ezra's rank than that of him who vain-gloriously

designated himself by a title that properly belongs alone to the Lord Jesus Christ: "Who, in His own times shall show, who is that blessed and only Potentate, King of kings and Lord of lords!"

Who that lived in those olden days would have supposed that in the course of the centuries the name and achievements of Artaxerxes would be almost unknown by millions to whom Ezra's name and work would be as familiar as if he had lived but yesterday! There are many such contrasts in the word of God. Ahasuerus is not even certainly identified to-day, but Mordecai is known wherever the word of God has been carried. The Pharaoh of the Exodus has been supposed to be one of half a dozen different monarchs, but no one makes a mistake as to Moses. Gamaliel is only remembered as the teacher of the devoted apostle Paul, and because of his moderation in treating the despised Nazarenes. And so with many more. Better far is it to be a child of God and to walk with Him than to wear earth's proudest diadem or have the widest reputation among carnal men.

Nor, in writing thus, would I reflect adversely upon Artaxerxes. His letter gives good evidence of sincere regard for the glory of the God of heaven. But he takes the place of a patron, Ezra of a servant. And between the two there is a vast difference.

The decree is largely after the order of that of Cyrus. As in the former, so here, stress is laid upon the voluntariness of the project. Permission is given to any or all of the people of Israel "that are minded of their own free will to go up to Jerusalem," to go with Ezra. God would have no coercion, but He removes every legal barrier for those who have the heart to take the arduous journey and to retrace their fathers' steps back to the place where His house is established.

Silver and gold, a free-will offering from the king and his counsellors, as well as from the people, for the habitation of God, Ezra is bidden to carry up to Jerusalem for sacrificial offerings, to be offered on Jehovah's altar in Jerusalem; while full liberty was granted to use any superfluity in any way that seemed best "after the will of their God" (vers. 16–18). Goodly vessels were also supplied for the service of the house of God out of the king's own treasure; and assurance was given that if more were needed, they would be forthcoming (vers. 19, 20).

Commandment was likewise laid upon the king's treasurers beyond the river to help forward the work by giving " whatsoever Ezra the priest, the scribe of the God of heaven," might require, "unto a hundred talents of silver, and to a hundred measures of wheat, and to a hundred baths of wine, and to a hundred baths of oil, and salt without prescribing how much " (vers. 21, 22).

All that they needed for the service of "the God of heaven " was to be done; and His priests and servants were to be freed from all toll or tribute. Besides all this, Ezra was commissioned to establish order throughout the province, by appointing magistrates and judges, and teaching the law of God to all ignorant of it (vers. 24, 25). And the decree closed as did that of Darius by denouncing severe penalties upon any who were hardy enough to act contrary to its provisions (ver. 26).

Ezra's heart was filled with rejoicing as he received and perused the letter. He recognized it was a greater King who had thus moved Artaxerxes so to favor His people. In holy exultation of spirit he cries, " Blessed be the Lord God of our fathers, who hath put such a thing as this in the king's heart, to beautify the house of the Lord which is at Jerusalem: and hath extended mercy unto me before the king and his counsellors, and before all the king's mighty princes." Thus had the king's gracious act produced thanksgiving to God, and joy of heart in the breast of His servant.

Again Ezra speaks of "the hand of God." He was a man who seemed never to look at mere human instrumentality, but, back of the hand of man, he saw the guiding, or controlling, hand of the Lord. "I was strengthened," he says, "as the hand of the Lord my God was upon me, and I gathered together out of Israel chief men to go up with me" (ver. 28).

Of the going up we have already had a brief epitome in verses 6 to 9, but we are to have a fuller description, to learn something of the difficulties to be overcome, the perils to be faced, and the testings of faith, as also its glorious triumph in the next chapter.

Every work that is really of God will have to be tried; but to the man of faith, instructed in the mind of the Lord, difficulties are never insurmountable; but he will be able in holy confidence to say with Paul, "None of these things move me." Of such a spirit was Ezra the scribe, and of such must be all who would count for God in a day of ruin.

## CHAPTER VIII

# The March of Faith

WHAT I would especially press upon the conscience of my reader at this juncture is this: Albeit the movement in which Ezra and his company were participants was distinct from that of Zerubbabel, Jeshua and their brethren, there were no new principles involved than those the former company had already learned from the word of God. No new centre was ever thought of. No new place to gather was suggested. Jerusalem was the one only place and Jehovah the one only Name. He had set His name at Jerusalem : consequently thitherward were the faces of all Ezra's company turned. They were soon to learn that those who had preceded them had " made a mess and a failure" * of the whole thing; but that did not set them inquiring if it would not be wise to gather elsewhere, to give up the principle of separation, to step aside from the movement and contentedly go back to Babylon. Not at all. God's word remained. God's centre remained. God's Spirit

---

* I quote by memory from J. N. D. [Failure in what is of God calls for suited ministry—for exhortation and correction unto righteousness. But false principles and false position leave no divine basis for recovery. The false principles or position of necessity must be abandoned.]—*Ed.*

remained. And for this fresh company there was nothing to do, as guided by that Spirit, but to return to and continue to own the one centre in accordance with the unchanging Word.

Surely in this we may learn a lesson which some are fast letting slip—a lesson which really learned would save from much discouragement as well as from many a blunder here and from much loss at the judgment-seat of Christ.

We turn now to our chapter, and here again we have a table of the chief of the fathers—a table that God delighted to put on record, and which, like the former one, stands on the books of eternity. All will be forever remembered by Him who never overlooks anything done in faith and subjection to His Word. Had one of these turned back to Babylon He would have noted it too ; and had any stopped half way between the land of Shinar and the city of God, His eye would have discerned it and His hand recorded it. Solemn considerations are these for any who might be disposed to trifle with divine truth.

Not one of the names here listed may be otherwise known to us; but all stand in God's sight for distinct living personalities, all of whose acts and words are as clear in His mind as though they still tabernacled in flesh and blood, and walked the earth as strangers and sojourners, servants of the God of heaven, cleaving to His name in the midst of ruin.   It is for us to occupy this very position to-day, as though in their place; and, if faithful in it, rest assured, He who forgets not one of them will pass by nothing in our history that He can reward in that day.

When the whole company were assembled together by Ezra's orders, by "the river that runneth to Ahava," they abode in tents—the sign of pilgrimage—for three days, the period of full display or testimony; and then all were reviewed before their priestly leader, who soon observed that the sons of Levi were sadly conspicuous by their absence.   Not one was found among the pilgrim band.   What did it mean? Evidently it was harder for these men whose whole portion must be in God, to rise to the blessedness of such a place, than for those who expected to have an inheritance in their ancient home.   The Levites were settled in a large measure of comfort in the land of the stranger. To forsake it all and go forth in simplicity to the place of the Name, meant more to them than to some others.*   But, on the other hand, how

---

* Similar tests occur now-a-days.   I know a clergyman who, years ago, was convinced of the unscripturalne-s of his position ; but, opposed by his family when contemplating "going forth, for His name's sake, outside the camp," said : " For my children's sake I will remain where I am, but will preach the truth as far as I can."   He lived to see his son a convicted felon outlawed by the State; his daughter, an actress

much greater the blessing, when one thus puts
God to the test and finds Him ever the all-
sufficient One anticipating every need, and leading the soul out in a way that others seldom know.

Ezra at once sent a deputation of faithful men
to lay before the Levites and the Nethinims,
who were of old appointed by David to the service of the Levites, to lay before them the importance of going forth with them, "That they
should bring unto us ministers for the house of
our God" (vers. 15–17). And thus it was that a
number of both classes were, as Ezra so beautifully puts it, " by the good hand of our God upon
us," led to join their company. Among these
one is especially mentioned as "a man of understanding." Valuable indeed in any movement
of God's Spirit are such men; like those of old,
who " had understanding of the times, to know
what Israel ought to do."

The company was now, one might have supposed, ready to go up to the house of God at Jerusalem. But Ezra has other thoughts. He knows
the way is long and lonely. Dangers abound.
There are perils of robbers and perils of wild
beasts. A safe convoy is surely needed, and

---

on the world's unholy stage; and he himself made practical
shipwreck of the faith.

Not in vain has God said, "Them that honor Me I will
honor, and they that despise Me shall be lightly esteemed ;"
and again, " The Lord is with you while ye be with Him."

where shall such be found but in the living God ?
"The angel of the Lord encampeth round about
them that fear Him and delivereth them." So a
fast is proclaimed by the river-side, and all the
people are urged to humble themselves before
God, to entreat of Him "a prosperous way for
us, and for our little ones, and for all our substance" (ver. 21). What a lovely sight in the
eyes of the Lord was that self-judged, fasting
company, in the dust before Him, crying to Him
to be their Guide and Deliverer. No ark, borne
on the shoulders of anointed priests, was there
to lead them now. No pillar of cloud by day and
of fire by night was there to guide. But they
knew that He who of old had led them through
the wilderness changeth not; and they sent up
their petition to Him to be indeed their Shepherd, preserving them from every danger and
meeting every need, all along their march of faith.

It would have been easy to have applied to
their royal patron, Artaxerxes, for a convoy, but
this would have given the lie to the profession
Ezra had made in his presence. It stirs the
heart to read his reasons, so artlessly given in
verse 22, for turning alone to God. "For I was
ashamed," he says, "to require of the king a
band of soldiers and horsemen to keep us against
the enemy in the way; because we had spoken
unto the king, saying, The hand of our God is
upon all them for good that seek Him; but His

wrath is against all them that forsake Him."
This is most blessed. Alas, how little is the
spirit of Ezra entered into in our time-serving
age, when almost any means are adopted for
carrying on what is called the work of the Lord,
and any help is greedily sought, even from the
unholy and profane, with no thought of the
awful dishonor done to the name of the Lord
Jesus Christ. Money is begged from all sources;
patronage desired from the ungodly, if they
have but wealth and influence—and this by professed followers of Him who said, "If I were
hungry I would not tell thee;" and whose servants in apostolic days "went forth, for His
name's sake taking nothing of the Gentiles."
Ezra's faith and godliness might well put all
such to shame. His stand contrasts with the
dreadful lowering of the standard so prevalent
throughout Christendom.

Having borne faithful testimony to the king,
he and his company turned to God in fasting and
prayer, beseeching Him to lead them forth as of
old; and, the record adds, "He was entreated
of us" (ver. 23). And so will He ever be where
there is faith to count upon Him, and holiness to
refuse all that would compromise His glory.

Not only did Ezra thus honor God's name before the powers of the world, but he was equally
careful in caring for what belonged to the house
of God, the treasure committed to him, "that

good deposit " consisting of the gold and silver given by his brethren as an offering unto the Lord's house, and the vessels entrusted to him by the king. All were carefully weighed and tabulated, and delivered for safe-keeping to twelve of the priests, who were especially separated for this particular trust. To them Ezra gave a solemn charge, reminding us of Paul's charge to his son in the faith, Timothy, in the first chapter of his second epistle. "Ye are holy unto the Lord," Ezra says to them, "the vessels are holy also; and the silver and the gold are a free-will offering unto the Lord God of your fathers. Watch ye, and keep them, until ye weigh them before the chief of the priests and the Levites, and chief of the fathers of Israel, at Jerusalem, in the chambers of the house of the Lord " (vers. 28, 29). These were earnest and serious words, and must have made each of the twelve feel intensely the sacredness of the trust committed to them. So to us has a deposit of holy things been entrusted, even the truth of which God has seen fit to make us stewards. We are to safe-guard this holy treasure all through our journey, until we reach the place of manifestation, when all will be weighed once more in the balances of the sanctuary. Well will it be for us then if we have lost nothing on the way, but have held fast, like the beloved apostle Paul, all that has been committed unto us.

The priests and the Levites duly witnessed and tabulated the amount of gold and silver and the weight of the vessels, and the appointed guardians took all in their charge, after which the journey was begun.

On the twelfth day of the first month the caravan left the river of Ahava, seven days after Ezra's first start (chap. 7 : 9), a week having passed in needful preparation. All along the journey the hand of God was upon them, and Ezra testifies, " He delivered us from the hand of the enemy and of all such as lay in wait by the way " (ver. 31). What indeed had they to fear from the hand of the enemy when under the protecting care of the hand of God. And what has any saint to fear when that same almighty, yet infinitely tender Hand is ever upon him for good. It has well been said that God is all that we take Him for. The great trouble with many of us is we are so straitened in ourselves, and thus we limit the Holy One of Israel. "Able to do exceeding abundantly above all that we ask or think " is the unlimited resource available to faith.

At last Jerusalem was reached, and for three days the pilgrims rested after their long and arduous journey. Then came the day of reckoning, when account was to be made of the treasure conveyed by the twelve appointed priests. The gold and silver and the vessels were all weighed in the house of God by Meremoth, Eleazar, Jozabad and Noadiah, four men, upon the fourth day. The number in each case is significant, for throughout Scripture four speaks of testing. "By number and by weight of every one," the test is made, and all recorded in the priestly record, and found intact. The twelve had fulfilled their trust in a way that you and I, my reader, will be glad indeed to have done, if the day of reckoning give us as clean a sheet as they obtained.

The accounting rendered in a rightful manner, the newly arrived company now flock about the altar of God as a band of worshipers, with a great number of burnt offerings; and, as at the dedication of the temple, with "twelve he-goats as a sin offering for all Israel." They take their stand with their brethren as part of a failed people, acknowledging their iniquity and the iniquity of their fathers, but counting on the covenant-mercy of their faithful God (ver. 35).

It was a scene of great moral beauty, and must have deeply affected the whole company, as once more they were permitted to approach God at the appointed place, and sing the Lord's song about His altar and in His house. Often had they longed for this hour when "by the rivers of Babylon they sat down and wept when they remembered Zion" (Ps. 137). There they had cried, "If I forget thee, O Jerusalem, let my

tongue cleave to the roof of my mouth; if I prefer not Jerusalem above my chief joy." Now
they were actually in the place where Jehovah
had caused His name to dwell of old, and the
sweet savor of a multitude of burnt offerings
ascended to His throne to testify to the gladness
of their hearts; while the sin offering, burned to
ashes, told how fully they recognized the evil of
having departed from Him who should ever have
been the joy of their souls; the God of their fathers, now fully recognized as their God, despite
their feeble condition.

It has been supposed by many, on the authority
of Jewish tradition, that the "Songs of degrees"
(Ps. 120 to 134) were sung by Ezra and his company at various stages of the way, until at last
they stood in the house of the Lord and could
lift up their hands in the sanctuary and bless
Jehovah. These psalms, read in this connection,
are, at least, very suggestive, and lead the soul
along the way from the tents of darkness to the
house of God most blessedly.

The last verse of our chapter tells us that the
king's commissions were duly delivered to the
authorities beyond the river, as a consequence
of which they dared no longer hinder; but in
accordance with their instructions "they fur-
thered the people and the house of God." So
had the wrath of man been made to praise Him,
and the remainder been restrained.

## CHAPTER IX

## The Break-down by Amalgamation

THERE is perhaps no greater trial a man can be called upon to face, than to take, through grace, a position he has seen from the word of God to be scriptural, and then to be rudely awakened to the realization that the people who were in that position before him, are not what he had hoped to find them. Yea, that they are even less spiritual, less devoted, less zealous for God, than some he has left behind him in systems where quasi-darkness prevailed. Then indeed one needs to be firmly held by the truth, or he is likely to be altogether overcome and completely disheartened. Many an unstable soul has, by such a test, been utterly swept away from his moorings. Such often go back in despair to the unscriptural positions they had abandoned, and give out a bad report of the land, thus hindering others from following the light vouchsafed to them. While some, with too much conscience to build again the things they had destroyed, become what one might call spiritual free lances—and sometimes, alas, spiritual Ishmaelites, their hand against every man, and every man's hand against them; criticizing, fault-finding, restless and unhappy; occupied with evil, lamenting the conditions of the times; bewailing the unfaithfulness of anybody and everybody but themselves; and so falling into a spirit of Pharisaism that is helpful to no one, and a hindrance to all they come in contact with.

Now all this results from occupation with persons instead of with Christ. It is supposed that because people occupy a position of peculiar favor, and have been blessed with special light, they must needs be personally more to be relied on than the generality of Christians, and that the flesh is less likely to act in them than in others. Often one hears of people "coming out to certain brethren," or "joining" this or that company of saints. All this is bound to result in disaster.

It is to Christ alone we are called to go forth, without the camp, bearing His reproach. *He*, blessed be God, never disappoints. If the eye be fixed on Him—if the heart be occupied with Him—if He be recognized as the one only Centre —then, let saints be what they may as to their spiritual state, there can be no lasting disappointment, for Christ abides.

If I see it to be according to Scripture to gather with fellow-believers to the name of the Lord Jesus, owning that "there is one body, and one Spirit," the behaviour of those already so gathered cannot alter the truth for one moment.

Rather does it call for exercise of soul on my part that I may be a help to them, stirring them up to fresh devotedness and renewed zeal in self-judgment.

It is far easier to stand aside and point out the low state of the rest—even to withdraw altogether from their company—than to emulate Ezra who, by his personal faithfulness, lifted the whole company to a higher plane. There will be less trouble, less perplexity, less concern, if one simply turns away and leaves the rest to go on as they will; but God is not thereby glorified nor are failing saints recovered.

The position of gathering to the name of the Lord in simplicity as members of the one body, is not one in which there is no trouble. Far from it. But it is a place where all trouble can be set right and every difficulty met *by the word of God alone;* and this is what cannot be said of any sect in Christendom. There human ingenuity, man-made regulations, carnal laws and ordinances are relied on to keep things in order and to settle disputes. But those who turn, in faith, from all this to Christ alone as Centre and the Word alone for guide and disciplinary instruction, find that Word all-sufficient if there be but obedience to its principles. Of all this the present and the last chapters furnish us with a most blessed illustration.

The first burst of praise and worship over, for

Ezra there came this rude awakening to which I have referred above. One can imagine the awful disappointment, the poignant grief that were his when the sad state of affairs that had developed among the separated Jews was revealed to him. No description can bring it before us more vividly than his own words.

"Now when these things were done, the princes came to me, saying, The people of Israel and the priests and the Levites have not separated themselves from the peoples of the lands, doing according to their abominations, even of the Canaanites, the Hittites, the Perizzites, the Jebusites, the Ammonites, the Moabites, the Egyptians and the Amorites. For they have taken of their daughters for themselves, and for their sons; so that the holy seed have mingled themselves with the peoples of those lands: yea, the hand of the princes and rulers hath been chief in this trespass: and when I heard this thing, I rent my garment and my mantle and plucked off the hair of my head and of my beard, and sat down astonied " (vers. 1–3).

Devoted and faithful steward of God! How our hearts are moved by his bitter grief when he is thus brought to realize the low condition of the people who are in the only right position. Could one be astonished if he had turned heart-sick away from them all, and in lofty seclusion of spirit endeavored to go on alone with God, giving up all hope of corporate testimony?

But this he does not do. In faithfulness to God he cannot forego the position, and he loves the people of the Lord too much to give them up.

One thing is encouraging to begin with. While, alas, "the nobles and princes were chief in this trespass," yet there *were* princes who were, clearly, not of the mind of the rest, but "who sought and cried because of the abominations done in their midst." The very fact that these men sought Ezra out to lay the true condition of affairs before him, was evidence of their desire to help and deliver the rest.

It is pitiable indeed when among those outwardly separated, links are formed and maintained that deny the integrity of that separation; and it is unspeakably sad when the leaders fail in this very thing and thus encourage the simple in departure from God. More than once have we seen people who would not tolerate an ecclesiastical yoke with unbelievers, yet uniting with the world in business, even in marriage, and in kindred ways. This is similar to what we have here in Ezra.

The people were out of Babylon as to their bodies, but the spirit of Babylon possessed them still. This it was led to amalgamation with the uncircumcised nations of the land. The same evil principle frequently works in a directly op-

posite way.  Often have we seen those who were
supposed to have judged the sin of sectarianism
and left human systems, yet maintain as sectarian a spirit when gathered out as any could
possibly have who contended for the most rigid
denominationalism.   It is related of Luther that
he said in the beginning he had spent much time
in denouncing the people of Rome, until he
found "every man had a greater pope in his own
heart than ever sat in the papal chair."   This is
the fruit of legality; while what we have in our
chapter is rather an unholy license—a "turning
the grace of God into lasciviousness"—an utter
misuse of that grace.

Almost heart-broken, Ezra manifested all the
signs of deepest distress of spirit, and sat down
in bitter astonishment.  That such things prevailed in Babylon would not have amazed him.
That they could be tolerated among those gathered to the place of the Name, dumbfounded
him.

But at once the news of his grief spread among
the people with a blessed and soul-cheering result.  That all were not in sympathy with the
looseness that had come in soon became evident.
"Then were assembled unto me," he tells us,
"every one that trembled at the words of the
God of Israel, because of the transgression of
those that had been carried away; and I sat
astonied until the evening sacrifice " (ver. 4).

God had said, long before, by Isaiah, " To this
man will I look; to him that is humble and of a
contrite spirit, and that trembleth at My word "
(Isa. 66: 2). Such there were still among the
remnant, and upon them the Lord could look in
blessing. These men and Ezra, acting with God,
would be a majority, however few in number.
Such men are likely to be regarded by the un-
spiritual as troublers and "old fogies ;" but
where there is real exercise of soul, God can be
depended on to show whom He recognizes, in due
time.

It was "at the evening sacrifice" that Ezra
arose from his heaviness and was uplifted in
spirit above the depressing circumstances that
had so bowed him with grief. The evening sacrifice speaks of the cross. It was "the continual
burnt offering "—Christ the holy One doing the
will of God even unto death—"a sacrifice of a
sweet smelling savor." As this blessed odor
greets Ezra's nostrils, he is delivered from his
speechless anguish and enabled to pour out his
soul in confession and prayer.

And is it not ever thus ? As Christ and His
cross are before the soul one is raised above
occupation with evil and depression of spirit because of failure on the part of one's brethren.

Falling upon his knees, and spreading out his
hands—" holy hands, without wrath and doubt-
ing "—before God, he opened his mouth in a

petition that is most affecting in its humility, its regard for God's holiness and truth, and the wonderfully blessed way in which he, personally pure (as Daniel, in *his* ninth chapter, and Nehemiah's companions in *his*), identifies himself with the people in all their failure and sin.

The balance of the chapter is entirely devoted to this prayer; it will repay the closest study and meditation: "O my God, I am ashamed and blush to lift up my face to Thee, my God: for our iniquities are increased over our head, and our trespass is grown up unto the heavens. Since the days of our fathers have we been in a great trespass unto this day; and for our iniquities have we, our kings, and our priests, been delivered into the hand of the kings of the lands, to the sword, to captivity, and to a spoil, and to confusion of face, as it is this day " (vers. 6, 7). In these words, observe, how far back Ezra goes in tracing the present evil to its source. It was the sin that had resulted in the captivity which had never been really judged, and had been the parent sin of all the rest. The low state of the whole nation affected even the returned remnant. And so it is in Christendom. We have sinned since the days of our fathers. First love was left at the very beginning and true recovery there has never been. Who has really felt the sin of the Church in turning from her glorified Head and linking herself with the world? Here and there the Spirit of God produces contrition and some sense of the failure, but who has fully fathomed it? Yet ever and anon God works in revival, drawing a few back in heart to Christ; but declension almost invariably follows. It has been said that "eternal vigilance is the price of liberty," and it is as true in spiritual things as·in carnal.

Ezra details before God the work His grace had wrought; only the more to emphasize the insubordination that had misused that grace so sadly. "And now for a little space grace hath been showed from the Lord our God, to leave us a remnant to escape, and to give us a nail in His holy place, that our God may lighten our eyes, and give us a little reviving in our bondage. For we are [not were] bondmen; yet our God hath not forsaken us in our bondage, but hath extended mercy unto us in the sight of the kings of Persia, to give us a reviving, to set up the house of our God, and to repair the desolations thereof, and to give us a wall in Judah and Jerusalem" (vers. 8, 9). The reference to the "nail" is doubtless a recognition of Isaiah's prophecy of the "nail in a sure place," upon which Jehovah's glory was to hang, which is, in the full sense, Christ Himself (Isa. 22: 21–25). A partial fulfilment had already been given; God had acted in great grace in thus giving a "little reviving," though they were still bondmen; for they share

in the failure of the whole nation. It was no
time for fleshly exultation, no time for pride of
position; but only for lowliness of spirit and humiliation of soul because of the dark record of
evil in which all had their share.

Ezra next recalls the special sin of the remnant,
and here again he confesses all as his sin. "And
now, O our God, what shall we say after this?
for we have forsaken Thy commandments" (yet
he who so speaks had possibly been less than a
week among them. What an example for any
who would walk with God to-day, and what a rebuke to the Pharisaism that would coldly point
out the failure of others, while professing to
have no part in it oneself!)—"we have forsaken
Thy commandments, which Thou hast commanded by Thy servants the prophets, saying, The
land unto which ye go to possess it, is an unclean
land with the filthiness of the peoples of the
lands, with their abominations, which have filled
it from one end to another with their uncleanness. Now, therefore, give not your daughters
unto their sons, nor seek their peace or their
wealth forever; that ye may be strong, and eat
the good of the land, and leave it for an inheritance to your children forever" (vers. 10–12).
Thus had God spoken. Alas, how had this word
been forgotten by those who had in other re-
spects honored His truth, by returning to the
divinely-appointed Centre. Separation would

have been their strength. Amalgamation was likely to be but their ruin; unless, indeed, the evil were judged and put away from their midst. And this snare of amalgamation with the ungodly is ever a lurking danger to the children of God. I do not for a moment speak of the coming together of believers, who have been kept apart by dissension and unscriptural judgments, as amalgamation. God forbid! When that which is of the same nature flows together, it is not amalgamation but unity. Things different in character are amalgamated to form a union which can never be a true unity. It is against such amalgamation we are warned in 2 Cor. 6: "Be ye not unequally yoked together with unbelievers : for what fellowship hath righteousness with unrighteousness ? and what communion hath light with darkness ? and what concord hath Christ with Belial ? or what part hath a believer with an unbeliever ? and what agreement hath the temple of God with idols ? For ye are the temple of the living God, as God hath said: I will dwell in them, and walk in them; and I will be their God and they shall be My people " (vers. 14–16). In the beginning "God divided the light from the darkness," and it has been the business of the devil ever since to seek to link the twain together.

Feeling in his soul the seriousness of so unholy a union, Ezra goes on to own God's justice in visiting them with His displeasure. "And after all that is come upon us for our evil deeds, and for our great trespass, seeing that Thou, our God, hast punished us less than our iniquities deserve, and hast given us such deliverance as this, should we again break Thy commandments, and join in affinity with the peoples of these abominations, wouldst not Thou be angry with us till Thou hadst consumed us, so that there should be no remnant nor escaping?" (vers. 13, 14). Light obeyed, results in greater light; but "if the light that is in thee become darkness how great is that darkness." God must visit those in chastisement who trifle with His truth. The more truth, the greater the responsibility, and the more severe the displeasure of the Lord if it be set at naught or spurned.

Feeling all this deeply, Ezra can only conclude with a fuller expression of confession than ever, and a throwing himself and the people, in all their wretched condition, right into the arms of the God they have sinned against. "O Lord God of Israel, Thou art righteous: for we remain yet escaped, as it is this day: behold we are before Thee in our trespasses: for we cannot stand before Thee because of this" (ver. 15). And so he concludes his prayer and leaves the case in the hands of God, who, though Ezra knew it not, had even then begun to work, as the concluding chapter gives abundant witness.

How much greater might be the blessing in many a similar time of distress, were there more of such dealing with God and less of appeal to man; more humiliation and confession and less pnblishing the sorrows abroad; more spreading out the hands unto the Lord and less pamphlet-eering.    Oh for grace to hearken unto the lesson here given for our learning!

## CHAPTER X

# Humiliation and Lifting Up

MIGHTILY wrought the Spirit of God in the hearts and consciences of the guilty people, while Ezra was praying and speaking of their fallen condition to the Lord. So much so, that the work of recovery was already well under way, for when he "had prayed, and when he had confessed, weeping and casting himself down before the house of God, there assembled unto him out of Israel a very great congregation of men and women and children: for the people wept very sore" (ver. 1). These were gracious tears indeed, and told of stirrings of soul that could only lead to blessing. How different might the after-history of these people have been had Ezra turned coldly away from them in disgust or despair, and left them to go on in their low estate. Such conduct could not have helped, and might only have provoked the flesh in them; but the sight of this newly-arrived man of God on his face in agony of spirit over their carelessness and unscriptural ways, brought them to their senses, giving them to realize, perhaps for the first time, something of the gravity of their sin.

Shechaniah, one of the sons of Elam, became the mouthpiece of the now repentant wrongdoers, confessing unreservedly the failure, and, in a manner beautiful in its season, seeking to comfort the heart of Ezra. " We have trespassed against our God," is his frank acknowledgment, 'and have taken strange wives of the people of the land.   This was in direct violation of the prohibition in the law of Moses. They had not consulted in this grave matter "that which was written;" hence a grievous error had been committed which now bore sorrowful fruit indeed; for there must be many a heartbreak ere matters were put right; and, in fact, against the poor ignorant heathen women, wrong had been done that could never be righted on earth.   But Shechaniah dares to count on God's mercy and adds: " Yet now there is hope in Israel concerning this thing " (ver. 2).   But this hope of future blessing is based on one condition only, and that, complete judgment of the evil, manifested in putting away all the strange wives. He calls on all who have sinned to enter into covenant with God to be obedient in this matter, and bids Ezra be of good courage and act as a judge in each case that shall arise (vers. 3, 4). The latter exacted an immediate pledge of the chief priests, the Levites and all Israel, that they would do as Shechaniah had said; and hard as it must have been for many of them, they sware to be obedient.

Refusing all physical refreshment because of

the travail of his soul, "Ezra rose up from before the house of God, and went into the chamber of Johanan the son of Eliashib," there to mourn in secret over the sin that now made such drastic and heart-rending action necessary if the people would be right with God (ver. 6).

Word was immediately sent to all the children of the captivity that they should gather together at Jerusalem within three days; otherwise, any refusing so to do would be cut off, or "separated from the congregation of those that had been carried away," and all his substance forfeited (ver. 8). To refuse now to obey the Word would show a hardness of conscience that could not be tolerated and a wilfulness of spirit that proved the culprit altogether unfit to go on with his brethren.

At the appointed time all the men of Judah and Benjamin gathered themselves together to Jerusalem. It was the twentieth day of the ninth month, in the rainy season, and "all the people sat in the street of the house of God, trembling because of this matter and for the great rain" (ver. 9). A dismal company surely, but a determined one, ready to carry out the word of the Lord at all costs.

Faithfully Ezra the priest placed their sin before them, abating nothing of their guilt, and commanding them how to act if truly repentant. They had transgressed. There had been a direct

violation of God's revealed will, in taking strange
wives to add to the already heavy load of Israel's
trespass.    He, therefore, called on them to
"make confession unto the Lord God of your
fathers, and do His pleasure: and separate yourselves from the peoples of the land, and from
the strange wives" (vers. 10, 11).

The wrenchings of heart this would occasion
can be better imagined than described, but
firmly the whole congregation answered, "As
thou hast said, so must we do" (ver. 12). There
was no caviling, no trying to avoid the result of
their unequal yokes, but a whole-hearted determination to obey the word of God at all costs.
Had conscience only been active a few years before, what pangs of anguish might now have
been avoided! Thus it ever is, when men attempt to play fast and loose with the will of the
Lord.

But all must be done in an orderly and lawful
way, so they asked for time to arrange every
thing as humanely as possible.  "But the people
are many, and it is a time of much rain, and we
are not able to stand without, neither is this a
work of one day, or two; for we are many that
have transgressed in this thing.  Let now our
rulers of all the congregation stand, and let all
them that have taken strange wives in our cities
come at appointed times, and with them the
elders of every city, and the judges thereof,

until the fierce wrath of our God for this matter be turned from us" (vers. 13, 14). This was no mere carnal expedient to gain time, but expressed the earnest desire of the people that, in the sad puttings-away that must ensue, all things should be done decently and in order. Doubtless there also entered into it the wish to avoid any wrong being done to any lawful wife who was really of the seed of Israel.

Chief priests and Levites assisted Ezra in the matter, and in the space of three months the iniquity had been dealt with throughout the land, all the heathen women and their offspring being set aside (vers. 15–17). Heart-rending must some of the experiences have been; but all were the fruit of departure from God and acting in self-will.

The chapter closes with a third list of names—this time of most solemn import. It is the record of those who "had taken strange wives; and some of them had wives by whom they had children" (ver. 44). God, who before had noted the faithfulness of many of these very men in coming up from Babylon, now took cognizance of the failure of each one just as particularly. For this they must suffer loss at the day of Christ.

On the part of those so near to God as the priests, this sin was especially obnoxious, and we are therefore definitely informed that "they gave their hands that they would put away their wives; and being guilty, they offered a ram of the flock for their trespass " (ver. 19). Thus the breach was made up, and they were restored to their forfeited privileges.

With this record the book of Ezra ends. He had been used of God to bring His separated people to a realization of the way they had failed in regard to maintaining the trust committed to them; self-judgment had resulted, and now the way was open for happy fellowship and helpful ministry. In using the word *fellowship* in this instance, I am not forgetful of the fact that it is a word that belongs entirely to the New Testament. I use it here rather as ideal and expressive of what was typified than that the thing itself was then truly known and enjoyed.

Fellowship is the result of the Holy Spirit's descent to earth and His indwelling of all believers. He thus brings us into the fellowship of God's Son. Where separation from evil is maintained and saints hold the Head, there is communion one with another in the Spirit's power. This is characteristic of the present dispensation of the mystery, and is an advance on anything known in Old Testament times.

Where Christians do not thus go on with God, walking in the Spirit, there may be a certain kind of fairly agreeable, and even enjoyable companionship, but genuine fellowship will be unknown.

With this remark we close, for the present, the instructive and searching book of Ezra. For further information of an equally important character as to the returned remnant and their priestly minister, we must turn to the following book in our Bibles, written by another equally devoted servant, though a man of more soldier-like character, Nehemiah; while in the book of Esther we find recorded God's care over those who remained in Babylon when they might have gone to Jerusalem, and with whom He does not openly connect His name.

"Now unto Him that is able to guard you from stumbling, and to present you faultless before the presence of His glory with exceeding joy, to the only wise God our Saviour, through Jesus Christ our Lord, be glory and majesty, dominion and power, both now and ever, Amen! (Jude 24, 25—1911 Version).

# Nehemiah

# NOTES

## ON THE

# BOOK of NEHEMIAH

---

## INTRODUCTION

IN the book of Ezra, we see a remnant people gathered back to the place where the
Lord had set His name, after a long period of
bondage and exile in Babylon, the centre of the
false religious system of that day. Nehemiah
pursues the further history of this company for
some years afterwards, but is especially devoted
to the work of guarding the place of privilege,
as indicated in the large space given to the narration of events in connection with the building
of the wall of Jerusalem. This was a wall both
of protection and exclusion, and doubtless speaks
to us to-day of principles which may easily be
abused where self-judgment and spirituality are
lacking, but which are nevertheless of supreme
importance if any scriptural testimony is to be

maintained in a day of declension. It is considered a mark of liberality and brotherly kindness with many, to declaim against all exclusiveness on the part of believers in the Lord Jesus Christ. But it is to be feared numbers object to a term they neither understand nor see the reason for.

A word in the book of Deuteronomy might help as to this. In chapter 22: 8 we read: "When thou buildest a new house, then thou shalt make a battlement for thy roof, that thou bring not blood upon thy house if any man fall from thence." The battlement surrounding the flat roof of the Israelite's dwelling conveys much the same thought as the wall enclosing Jerusalem. The roof was to the oriental the place of communion and retirement (1 Sam. 9: 25; Prov. 21: 9), of prayer (Acts 10: 9), and of testimony (Matt. 10: 27). It was commonly used very much as both the parlor and the study of the occidental. There the family would commune together, and there they would entertain friends. But if there were no protecting wall about this favored place, it would be one of danger to the young and to any inclined to be careless. Therefore the divine instruction that a battlement be built to completely surround the house-top; otherwise the owner of the house was held responsible if any one fell from thence, and so was slain.

The house-top is a fitting picture of assembly privilege. For, as gathered to the name of the

Lord Jesus, believers are in the place of retirement from the distracting things of the world, of communion with the Father and the Son, and with one another, in the Spirit's power, and this is likewise the place of prayer and of testimony. But hallowed as such a place is, there are always the young in Christ and those weak in the faith to be considered. Pre-eminently for their sakes it is imperative that the wall of separation (not only from the world, but from worldly Christianity) be maintained, otherwise many of these little ones will fall from this hallowed sphere of privilege into which grace has brought them.

And here I desire to quote the words of a brother beloved, written in a private letter some time since, but which I feel are of value for all believers desiring so to walk as to please God, not only individually, but in corporate testimony: "By some an attempt is being made to pull down the barriers of truth and make us give up what we have. If the younger men among us, who are soon to take the lead, if the Lord tarry yet a while, are not true in practice to the truth, not only of the gospel but also of the Church of God, the truth itself will slip away from them. As I see the developments all around, I burn with jealousy for the truth we have. It makes us, in its practice, a people rejected by all, but who have the bread that *all need*. If we keep separated from every movement which leaves out what hurts in the truth; if we just live out in practice what the truth is, we will remain no doubt a small, unpopular people, but we will be to the end God's vessel of truth to His whole Church on earth; and that will be ten thousand times better throughout eternity than to have been on popular lines for greater access to men.

"Our assemblies, if kept truly pure, are little fortresses for the defence and sallying out of truth. Let us build them up strong, solid and faithful...Principles of independency *annul the constitution* of the Church of God as laid down in Ephesians, and make it impossible for us therefore to carry out its by-laws, as I may call them, given us in Corinthians."*

These are sound and seasonable words, and form a fitting introduction to the special lines of divine truth emphasized in this instructive portion of the word of God, the book of Nehemiah.

The years that have passed since they were written have witnessed the rapid development of apostasy in the form of Modernism, making it more imperative than ever that real believers should walk in separation from those who deny every fundamental truth of Scripture.

---

* Extracted from a letter by P. J. Loizeaux.

# CHAPTER I

## An Exercised Man

IN the twentieth year of Artaxerxes, king of Persia, his cup-bearer, Nehemiah, the son of Hachaliah, was in deep exercise of soul concerning the condition of the re-gathered remnant, whose history we have been studying, as related by Ezra the Scribe.* Nehemiah means *comfort* or *consolation of Jehovah,* and he is one whose name expresses his character, as is so often the case in Scripture, when names were not given by any means so carelessly as now. Like Paul, he was to comfort others with the comfort wherewith he himself was comforted of God (2 Cor. 1: 4). This is a weighty principle in God's ways with His servants. Many a saint is permitted to go through deep waters, to pass through severe trial both of body and mind, not only for his own profit, but that he may be the better fitted to be a channel of blessing to his brethren when cast down and in distress. Happy is the saint who is thus subject to the will of God and enabled to be His agent in consoling his discouraged fellows and restoring them, through a ministry received in times of sorrow, when they are backslidden and disheartened.

---

* See "Notes on the Book of Ezra," by the same.

The station of Nehemiah was one of worldly prosperity. It is true he was a servant; probably a bondman, but so were all his people; and he dwelt in a royal palace, and seems to have been a favorite with the king. But, like Moses, his heart was with his lowly brethren, and his spirit was zealous for the testimony of the Lord.

To him, Hanani, one of his brethren, and other Jews came, whom he questioned closely concerning the remnant who had gone up to Jerusalem. The report was not encouraging. They replied: "The remnant that are left of the captivity there in the province are in great affliction and reproach; the wall of Jerusalem also is broken down, and the gates thereof are burned with fire" (ver. 3). That Hanani felt this keenly there can be no doubt, but that he, or his companions were before God about it, as was Nehemiah, seems scarcely probable. It is one thing to shake the head and sigh over the vicissitudes of the congregation of the Lord, it is quite another to look up to Him to give deliverance, and to put His truth and testimony above every other interest. This latter Nehemiah did.

His brethren's unhappy report caused him deepest searching of heart and contrition of spirit, so that he gave himself to fasting and prayer with many tears; for, like Paul in a brighter dispensation, he knew much of what it was to weep over the failures of the people of God. To Him who had forsaken His city and given His people up to captivity, but who had granted a little reviving in their bondage, Nehemiah turned in prayer. He uses the same title so frequently found in the record of Ezra, "the God of heaven." This indicated the removal of God's throne from earth to heaven. In deepest humiliation he joins with Ezra and Daniel in confessing his sin and the sin of his people. "We have sinned," he cries ; and again, "Both I and my father's house have sinned;" and once more, "We have dealt very corruptly." Genuine confession like this reaches the ear of God. It indicates a soul able to look at matters from God's standpoint. Nehemiah is no carping critic, no self-satisfied Pharisaic looker-on upon the failure of others. "I thank Thee that I am not as other men" would never come from his lips. Instead, he bows his head in common confession with his brethren, and brokenly cries, "We have sinned."

But he is a man of faith as well as a man of prayer, and so he at once proceeds to remind God, as it were, of His own word; how He had declared in Lev. 26 : 40-45 and Deut. 4 : 23 ; 30 : 1-6 that even though He might scatter His people because of their transgression, yet if in the stranger's land they would turn unto Him, keep His commandments, and do them, He would gather them again, though it were from the uttermost parts of the earth, and bring them back to the place He had chosen, "to set His name there." This promise Nehemiah pleads, and touchingly cries: "Now these are Thy servants and Thy people, whom Thou hast redeemed by Thy great power and by Thy strong hand. O Lord, I beseech Thee, let now Thine ear be attentive to the prayer of Thy servant, and to the prayer of Thy servants who desire to fear Thy name: and prosper, I pray Thee, Thy servant this day, and grant him mercy in the sight of this man" (vers. 10, 11). "This man" was none other than the great Artaxerxes himself; but to Nehemiah he was just a man, and he desired that his heart might be controlled by God for the furtherance of His purpose of grace towards His people.

In other circumstances he could and did give honor to whom honor was due. But in the presence of the great King of kings this puissant monarch was but a man, and such is he in Nehemiah's reckoning. He had, in large measure, learned to put not his trust in princes, but to cease from man whose breath is in his nostrils. To the living God he looked; on His compassion and omnipotence he reckoned; and the sequel shows that he was not disappointed.

# CHAPTER II

## The Failed Testimony

IT pleased the God of heaven, in bringing about
an answer to His servant's petition, to attract
the attention of the Persian ruler to the grief-
stricken face of Nehemiah. Kindly the monarch
inquires after the cause of this change of countenance, for the son of Hachaliah had been wont to
exhibit a cheerful mien, as became one whose
confidence was in the Lord. "Why is thy countenance sad," asks the king, "seeing thou art not
sick? This is nothing else but sorrow of heart."
Fearful of his sovereign's displeasure, his cup-
bearer replies, "Let the king live forever: why
should not my countenance be sad, when the city,
the place of my father's sepulchres, lieth waste,
and the gates thereof are consumed with fire?"
(ver. 23). Nehemiah could not be indifferent to
a matter of this kind. He was no misanthropical
pessimist—rather indeed the very opposite—but
he could not be unmoved by the terrible breakdown on the part of his loved people and the de-
solate condition of that city that should have been
the glory of the whole earth.

But, observe, he did not stand aside and write
pamphlets on the failure of his brethren or simply
denounce them for their backslidings while doing
nothing to help them reach a better state; nor

did he wash his hands of the whole matter and
conclude that because the failure had indeed come
in, he was justified in giving up all concern about
the testimony committed to Judah. Not at all.
His was a grief deep and genuine; but it was one
that led to exercise before God, and an earnest
desire to be an instrument in the hand of the Lord
for the establishment of the truth, and the recovery and encouragement of the feeble few who
had broken down so sadly in the very place where
Jehovah had set His name.

And so when the king inquired, "For what dost
thou make request?" he did not answer till he had
"prayed to the God of heaven." What an atmo-
sphere of prayer surrounds this man! It is his
constant resource throughout all his varied experiences. He walked with God because he talked
with God. Now, assured of the Lord's mind, he
made request for permission to visit the land of
Judah and the city of Jerusalem, that he might
"build it." This was morally very lovely. He
desired to build, to edify. Any one with a small
measure of discernment can stand off and either
bewail or criticize the failures of others, but one
must needs be in touch with God to be a true
builder. Such an one was Paul, "a wise master-
builder," and he, by the Spirit, directs that "all
things be done unto edifying." "Knowledge," he
tells us, "puffeth up, but love edifieth" (or, buildeth up). This is an all-important truth.

Many there are who entered on the path of

separation with high hopes and fond expectations; eagerly they drank in the precious truths the Holy Spirit of God was making known in the place where He had liberty to work as He would. But to-day, alas, alas! many of these have turned away disheartened, and that because of breakdown on the part of brethren whom these others deem less clear of sight, less devoted and less intelligent than themselves. So they stand off and bewail the divided condition, the worldliness, the cold-heartedness that has come in among those who sought to walk together in separation from the prevailing apostasy. But to what end? Such a course profits neither those who so judge, nor those judged. Better, a thousand times better, to rise up in the spirit of Nehemiah, and throw oneself in the breach as a builder. The heart may be grieved and the countenance sad, but there will be a deep-toned joy in seeking thus to enlighten, instruct, and edify weaker brethren: endeavoring in the fear of God to keep the Spirit's unity in the bond of peace, and occupy saints with the blessed Gatherer Himself instead of the failure of those gathered.

Yes, as the days darken and the dispensation fast hastens to its close, it is men of the Nehemiah stamp who will be of real value to the people of God, and who shall thus save themselves and those who hear them.

In the presence of his consort, Artaxerxes gave the desired permission, stipulating a defined leave of absence, in which Nehemiah would be free to carry out the desire of his heart, and go to his brethren as a true prophet to speak words of exhortation, edification and encouragement (ver. 6). All that may be needed for the work of building is granted by the king, even as the King of kings, who is also head of His body, the Church, delights to supply His willing workers with all things that pertain to the ministry committed to them. And here we note that Ezra and Nehemiah were men of like mind in tracing every blessing to the good hand of God (ver. 8).

The intervening journey soon completed (for a burning love urged him on), Nehemiah crosses the river and presents the king's letters to the governors of the mixed Samaritan people, who had been settled in the land of the ten tribes since the days of Esar-haddon. At once we read of two men who are grieved and displeased; they were Sanballat the Horonite and Tobiah the Ammonite, called contemptuously, Tobiah the *servant*. When they heard of his arrival, "it grieved them exceedingly that there was come a man to seek the welfare of the children of Israel" (ver. 10). As these men caused Nehemiah much trouble and concern later on, it will be well to inquire here as to who or what they might represent, and to ask if any such adversaries are likely to be encountered to-day in connection with the defence of the "present truth."

Sanballat is called a Horonite, generally supposed to mean a native of Horonaim, a city of Moab. Of Tobiah's ancestry we are left in no doubt. We have therefore in these two foes representatives of those hostile races of whom it was written, "The Moabite and the Ammonite should not come into the congregation of God forever," as we are reminded later in chapter 13: 1. The prohibition in Deut. 23: 3-6 gives the reason for this: "An Ammonite or Moabite shall not enter into the congregation of the Lord; even to their tenth generation shall they not enter into the congregation of the Lord forever: because they met you not with bread and water in the way, when ye came forth out of Egypt; and because they hired against thee Balaam the son of Beor of Pethor of Mesopotamia, to curse thee. Nevertheless...the Lord thy God turned the curse into a blessing unto thee, because the Lord thy God loved thee. Thou shalt not seek their peace nor their prosperity all thy days forever."

Reading such a command, we naturally ask why such a doom upon Moab and Ammon for refusing aid to Israel when about to enter the land of promise? Why should it have been expected of them and not of others? The answer is very simple. There were ties of blood that gave Israel right to expect their assistance, but these ties were utterly repudiated. Moab and Ammon were the natural sons of Lot, but by his own daughters! They were really then "bastards, and not sons"

(Heb. 12 : 8). They surely speak to us of those professing to be children of God, but not born of the Spirit. And so they ever, as born only of the flesh, persecuted the spiritual seed. They are the representatives of fleshly religion, of carnal profession, and as such they detest reality, and hate the truth that, "Except a man be born again he cannot see the kingdom of God." They feel they have as much right to the ordinances of God, and as much liberty to participate in His service and worship as any; but they are only natural men with a veneer of religiousness, and such have ever been the bitterest opponents of what really honors Christ and glorifies God. They abound to-day as they have abounded all down the centuries, and their object is still, as ever, to corrupt if they can, and to destroy if they cannot corrupt.

Leaving Sanballat and Tobiah for the present, gnashing their teeth in their rage and vexation, we follow Nehemiah to the city of God. Reaching Jerusalem, he rested three days. Then, conferring not with flesh and blood, but taking a few men with him, though telling none what God had put in his heart, he arose in the night and went out to view in silence the ruin that had come in. This night journey around the walls of the city is deeply pathetic. Who that has any real care for the people of God has not known something of it? The nobles and rulers and all the people are wrapt in slumber, but this lonely man, whose heart God has touched, keeps his midnight vigil, and

goes from gate to gate and tower to tower, noting
with deepest sorrow and concern the breaches sin
has made. "I went out by night," he says, "by
the gate of the valley, even before the dragon
well, and to the dung port, and viewed the walls
of Jerusalem, which were broken down, and the
gates thereof were consumed with fire. Then I
went on to the gate of the fountain, and to the
king's pool: but there was no place for the beast
that was under me to pass. Then went I up in the
night by the brook, and viewed the wall, and
turned back and entered by the gate of the valley,
and so returned" (vers. 13-15). It was no carping
critic viewing with indifferent feelings the de-
fencelessness of his brethren; but a man of purpose and prayer, beholding what stirred his soul
to its depths, with the desire to build up what
carnal ease and self-seeking had permitted to fall
into ruin.

It was not till after this night view that he
called the people, with their rulers and the priests
of the Lord together, to give them cognizance of
his mission. He does so most delicately. There
are no reproaches, no Pharisaic and odious com-
parisons or contrasts, but he identifies himself
fully with them and says: "Ye see the distress
that we are in; how Jerusalem lieth waste, and
the gates thereof are burned with fire: come, and
let us build up the wall of Jerusalem, that we be
no more a reproach" (ver. 17). Such an one is a
God-sent and Spirit-qualified leader. He does not

say, "You are in distress;" but "We are." He does not command, "Go, and build," but he entreats, "Let us build." He does not say, "You are a reproach," but he pleads, "Let us be no more a reproach." And then he tells of the good hand of his God upon him, and of the king's commission.

The people are aroused and encouraged, and cry at once, "Let us rise up and build;" and so they join hands with God's dear servant for the work he has planned. No doubt there was not the exercise of soul in all that conditions called for; but the work must be done nevertheless, and there will be more exercise as they go on.

And now we hear of Sanballat and Tobiah again; and with them a third adversary, Geshem the Arabian. This man is either an Edomite or an Ishmaelite, more probably the latter; but in either case he speaks of the flesh warring against the Spirit. Both Ishmael and Esau were types of the natural man—hence of the flesh—and were opposed to Isaac and Jacob, the seed of promise. Geshem is elsewhere in this book called Gashmu. When this unworthy trio hear of the work contemplated at the place of the Name, they indulge in sarcastic merriment. Nehemiah noted that, "They laughed us to scorn, and despised us, and said, What is this thing that ye do? will ye rebel against the king?" (ver. 19).

Heretofore the line of demarcation between the outwardly separated Israelites and these mixed nations had been almost obliterated; hence there was peace and quietness. But now a man has come who contemplates rearing afresh the wall of exclusion, and this is bitterly resented, though at first they attempt but to laugh down the determination of the remnant. To all their sneers Nehemiah calmly replies: "The God of heaven, He will prosper us; and therefore we His servants will arise and build: but ye have no portion, nor right, nor memorial, in Jerusalem!" (ver. 20). He has thrown down the gauntlet and declares his uncompromising attitude in a manner not to be misunderstood. Henceforth he will be hated as only those can hate who resent having their false religious claims made nothing of!

The out-and-out worldling does not hate what is truly of God so bitterly as the Christless professor who has a name that he lives but is dead. Such an one cannot bear spiritual realities; for when confronted with them the hollowness of his profession is exposed, like Dagon when the ark of Jehovah was set down before it. This explains the bitterness with which these adversaries opposed the work of God going on at Jerusalem.

# CHAPTER III

## THE GATES OF JERUSALEM

THE work at once began, and it is to be noted what a thoroughly individual thing it was. Nehemiah is the servant used to stir up the rest; but they *are* stirred up, and "To every man his work" is the motto that might well describe the busy scene. This chapter is like a page from the books of God's record of service, and will doubtless be opened at the judgment seat of Christ, when each will be rewarded for his own work— and some who shirked, alas, will then suffer loss. For both the workers and the shirkers are here mentioned, and here their names shall stand till the Lord Himself has pronounced His judgment upon all. Such records are deeply instructive, and deserve to be pondered with care that they may stir up our minds by way of remembrance.

In the New Jerusalem there are to be twelve gates (Rev. 21: 12), and each several gate of one pearl; so that, look upon the city from whichever standpoint one may, he will be reminded of the precious truth that Christ "loved the Church, and gave Himself for it" (Eph. 5: 25). He came from heaven as a merchantman seeking goodly pearls; and having found one pearl of great price, He bought it, at the cost of all that He had; "though He was rich, for our sakes He became poor," that we might be rich. And that heavenly city, of which Christ is the centre and the lamp for the display of God's glory, has "a wall great and high," speaking, as did the wall of the earthly city, of security and exclusion.

Jerusalem in Nehemiah's day seems to have had twelve gates also, though only ten are mentioned in this chapter: but in chapter 8:16 we read of "the gate of Ephraim," and in 12:39 of "the prison gate." The ten mentioned in the present portion remind us of the number that, it has been well said, sets forth responsibility towards God and man, of which the ten words in the law were the measure; while the twelve of the heavenly city (and note how many twelves there are in Rev. 21), as some have suggested, would set forth perfect administration, or governmental completeness, only to be known in the day that the kings of the earth bring the glory and the honor of the nations unto it.

I have thought there might be divine lessons for us in the names and order of these gates. That there is danger always of being fanciful, I realize. An insubject imagination is only "evil continually" (Gen. 6:5), in the things of the Lord as well as in all else, and one would therefore seek to avoid it. But, in looking at these gates, it is not so much my thought to seek to give the interpretation of them as to make a practical application of truth which, I am convinced, is much needed in this Laodicean day. We shall therefore take them in their order, as we go through the chapter, noting likewise the interesting and instructive points brought out in connection with service as we go from port to port.

We begin, then, with

### THE SHEEP GATE,

of which we read in the first verse: "Eliashib the high priest rose up with his brethren the priests, and they builded the sheep gate; they sanctified it, and set up the doors of it; even unto the tower of Meah they sanctified it, unto the tower of Hananeel."

This was priestly work indeed, for through this gate the beasts were led whose death and blood-shedding were to picture the one Offering of the ninth of Hebrews. They pointed on to the perfect sacrifice of that unnamed One of Isaiah 53, who was "led as a lamb to the slaughter, and as a sheep before her shearers is dumb, so He openeth not His mouth."

Thankful we are that for us it is not necessary to ask, as did the eunuch, "Of whom speaketh the prophet this? of himself, or of some other man?" (Acts 8: 34). The other Man is well known indeed to those of us who have been brought to trust the Man Christ Jesus, who gave Himself a ransom for all. In Him we have beheld the Lamb of God who taketh away the sin of the world (John 1: 29).

The Sheep Gate clearly speaks to us, then, of the Cross. It was at the Sheep Gate the Lord met the palsied man and healed him, as recorded in John 5, as it is at the Cross the helpless sinner finds life and peace. Here the remnant of old began to build the wall, priestly hands piling stone upon stone, and setting up the beams and bars. And here every one must begin who has really to do with God, other than in judgment. The wall, we have already seen, speaks of holiness, which must shut out evil; but what evil is, we can never rightly know until we have understood in some measure the meaning of the Cross. It was there that all the iniquity of man's heart was fully revealed; there too that the absolute holiness of God's character was declared in an even more marked way than it will be made known in the lake of fire. In the Cross it was that mercy and truth met together, and that righteousness and peace kissed each other (Ps. 85: 10).

> " 'Tis in the cross of Christ we see
> How God can save, yet righteous be."

The most important truth of Scripture is, that on the cross the judgment of a holy God against sin fell upon His spotless Son, when He "suffered, the Just for the unjust, that He might bring us to God" (1 Pet. 3: 18). There is nothing like the apprehension of this to give peace to a troubled soul. I have been awakened to see myself a lost, guilty sinner. Perhaps for years I have been go-

ing about to establish my own righteousness, and
trusting that all would surely be well with me
because of fancied merit in myself. I have de-
luded myself with the notion that God, who is
love, must therefore allow sin to pass unpun-
ished, or that my sin was, at any rate, of weight
so light it would never sink me down to the pit
of woe. But now all is changed. I have learned
that I am a lost man! My sins, which once
seemed like trifles, insignificant as molehills, now
rise before my terrified vision as dark, shapeless
mountains, which I fear will bury me beneath
their awful weight in the nethermost depths of
the abyss of divine wrath. I look on my right
hand, but I find no helper. Refuge fails me. In
my despair I cry out, "No man cares for my soul!"
(Ps. 142: 4) ; and in the hour of my deepest distress there comes to me One with feet beautiful
upon the mountains, a messenger, one among a
thousand, who tells me the good news that God,
the God whom I have so grievously sinned against
and so flagrantly dishonored, has found a ransom,
and can thus deliver me from going down into the
pit (Job 33: 24). My sins and guilt have all been
laid on Jesus. My judgment has fallen upon His
holy head, and thus I can go righteously free.

Well does such a message deserve the name of
"gospel!" Good news indeed! More welcome than
cold water to a thirsty soul!

As of old, when Noah took of every clean beast
and of every clean fowl, and offered burnt-offer-

ings upon the altar (Gen. 8:20), so now Jehovah has looked upon the work of His beloved Son and "smelled a sweet savor," which is truly a "savor of rest" (*margin*); for sin is thus canceled, and God can be just and the Justifier of him that believeth in Jesus. Christ thus becomes the Door of the sheep, as He said: "I am the door; by Me if any man enter in, he shall be saved, and shall go in and out, and find pasture" (John 10:9).

Of all this, and more also, may the Sheep Gate remind us. A gate of judgment it is too; for of judgment, in Scripture, the gate often speaks, as in Oriental cities it was there that justice was administered. But here it is judgment falling, not upon the guilty, but upon the guiltless One who voluntarily stood in the place of the sinner. "He was delivered for our offences, and raised again for our justification; therefore being justified by faith, we have peace with God through our Lord Jesus Christ" (Rom. 4:25; 5:1).

All thus justified are now the sheep of the Good Shepherd who died, the Great Shepherd who lives in glory, the Chief Shepherd who is coming again. As His sheep, they have title to enter in through the gate into the city. It is saved souls, *and they alone*, who here on earth are gathered by the Spirit to the name of the Lord Jesus in separation from the world and its evil, and it is such alone who will be within that wall of jasper gathered around the Lamb in the glory.

Let me press it upon the reader—has all this

been made good to your soul? Is your confidence for eternity based upon the work of Christ? Are you trusting alone in Jesus, who in those solemn hours of deeper than Egyptian darkness, "fought the fight alone," vanquished Satan's power in resurrection, and is now exalted at God's right hand to be a Prince and a Saviour?

Oh, be persuaded! If you are resting on anything short of this, your soul is in peril most grave and fearful; for it is only "the blood of Jesus Christ, God's Son, that cleanses from all sin" (1 Jno. 1: 7). If, however, this is the ground of your confidence, if you are saved and know it, if the lesson of the Sheep Gate has been truly learned in the presence of God, I ask you to pass on with me now to

### THE FISH GATE.

But on the way there is a small portion of the wall being built by the men of Jericho. Jericho was the city of the curse, but "Christ hath redeemed us from the curse of the law, being made a curse for us; as it is written, Cursed is every one that hangeth on a tree." So these happy Jericho men are now in the place of blessing, and serving in newness of spirit. Next to them builds, apparently alone, Zaccur, the son of Imri, but God's eye is upon him, and he shall find his name on the honor roll in the day of Christ. Then we read: "But the Fish Gate did the sons of Hassenaah build, who also laid the beams thereof, and set up the doors thereof, the locks thereof and the bars thereof" (ver. 3).

The name of this port at once brings to mind the word of the Lord addressed to Simon and Andrew when He found them "casting a net into the sea." "He saith unto them, Follow Me, and I will make you fishers of men." Precious it is to learn that, without a word as to delay, they *"straightway* left their nets and followed Him" (Matt. 4: 17-20).

It is a weighty truth, often I fear forgotten in this pushing, restless age, that the great business of those already saved should be to bring others to Christ. Alas, alas, the indifference as to this among many of the people of God is most appalling! The Fish Gate is closed, or fallen in ruins, and there are no devoted "sons of Hassenaah" who are enough in earnest about the condition of the lost to build it up again. Is it not a shame, a crying shame, that it should ever be true of saints going to heaven, that they are unconcerned about sinners going to hell? And God has said, "He that withholdeth corn, the people shall curse him."

Oh, the heartlessness of it! Souls perishing under one's very eyes, and no voice raised to proclaim God's message of love to the lost! Brothers, sisters, be honest with God! Face the question in His presence, *What are you doing for souls?* Will friends, neighbors, relatives, rise up in that day and say: "I lived beside him for years; he knew

I was going to hell; he never warned me, nor told me of a way of escape." I beseech you, don't turn it aside with pious expressions about, "So much fleshly energy," and "the need of building up the saints." Words like these from men who lift not a finger to keep others from going down to eternal ruin, are disgusting indeed; yea, they are worse; they are actually wicked and abhorrent in the ears of Him who saith, "He that is wise winneth souls" (R. V.).

Build up the Fish Gate, brethren; go out after the lost, and bring them inside the wall, where, having been saved, they will be cared for and helped in the things of God.

I know all have not the same gift; all cannot preach to thousands. But surely it is not gift that is lacking so much as grace. It takes no special gift to distribute gospel tracts, or speak a loving word in season to needy souls. If you have "gift" enough to spend hours talking about the weather, or the various questions of domestic, business, or political life, you have all the gift that is needed to drop a tender, warning message in the ear of a careless one, or to point an anxious person to Christ.

Let none shirk this work, for the day of manifestation draws on apace. Then His eyes that are as a flame of fire will pierce into every hidden motive, every unworthy, selfish thought, and bring all to light. In verse 4 we read of three who repaired the stretch of wall adjoining the

Fish Gate, and then we read of the Tekoites; and the Holy Ghost has noted that "their nobles put not their necks to the work of their Lord" (ver. 5). They will have to face this record at the judgment-seat of Christ; and I fear there are some God-made, and many self-made, "nobles" among the people of the Lord to-day who manifest as gross indifference to the work of God.

That, on the other hand, mere fleshly zeal will not be owned of God, I quite admit; and this brings before us the need of enforcing the lessons suggested by the next five gates.

### THE OLD GATE.

"Moreover the old gate repaired Jehoiada the son of Paseah, and Meshullam the son of Besodeiah; they laid the beams thereof, and set up the doors thereof, and the locks thereof, and the bars thereof."

One would not try to be too insistent on the special meaning of this gate. I had thought of it as the old used in the new, the place of nature in the economy of grace; for our bodies, with all their marvelous members, belong to the old creation still; but He who will glorify them by and by finds use for them in His own service even now in the day of their humiliation.

But the suggestion of another that the old gate would be the port of entry for the old path seems a clearer and higher thought. It is in Jeremiah 6: 16 that we read: "Thus saith the Lord, Stand ye in the ways, and see, and ask for the old paths, where is the good way, and walk therein, and ye shall find rest to your souls." And so the Old Gate might speak of subjection to the revealed will of God—abiding in that which was from the beginning. This still impresses upon us the great truth that we are called to recognize in all things the Lordship of Christ, and to hold every power we possess at His command, serving with grace in the heart.

> "Naught that I have mine own I call,
>   I hold it for the Giver;
> My heart, my strength, my life, my all,
>   Are His and His forever."

Evil is not in natural things themselves, but is in the abuse of them. Every talent we have is to be used for His glory. Woe to the man who hides one of them away, under pretence that nature, in this sense, is opposed to grace!

This is what the Holy Spirit presses upon us when He says: "I beseech you therefore, brethren, by the mercies of God, that you present your bodies a living sacrifice, holy, acceptable unto God, which is your reasonable service" (Rom. 12: 1). The child of God should remember that he has been bought with a price. His body is purchased with the blood of Christ. He is not merely called to "consecrate" himself, as people put it to-day, but to gladly own that he is already consecrated by the death of the Lord Jesus. The blood and the oil have been placed on the ear, the hand and the foot—he belongs to Christ. The ear, to listen for His commandment; the hand, to do His bidding; the foot, to run in His ways (see Lev. 14: 14-18, 25, 28, 29).

Can anyone truly enter into this, and yet be careless in regard to service? Impossible. You are not only saved from hell, but purchased to be the bondman of Jesus Christ.

There is a depth of meaning in that word "present," as noted above. Your body is His already. He might simply demand His own; but in grace He says, "I beseech you...present your body." Have you done so? Have you, in other words, owned His claims upon you? If not, will you longer delay? O beloved, yield yourself unto Him, that thus you may bring forth fruit unto God. "Herein is My Father glorified, that ye bear much fruit" (John 15: 8).

I do not press it that the Old Gate was meant to teach this special truth, and I trust none will find fault over an application.

Whatever the meaning one more spiritually-minded may discern, the fact remains that "Ye are not your own; ye are bought with a price." It is this I seek to emphasize, for it is with many, well-nigh forgotten. Vast numbers of Christians live as though their only thought was to enjoy the present scene, "on the east of Jordan;" pampering every whim of their blood-purchased bodies, and looking forward to going to heaven at last without having ever known the toil and conflict—yet the deep, hidden joy—of the servant's path.

Especially is this often so of those in comfortable and easy circumstances. The willing workers of verse 8 might well rebuke such. "Next unto him repaired Uzziel the son of Harhaiah of the goldsmiths. Next unto him also repaired Hananiah the son of one of the apothecaries." I question if goldsmiths' and apothecaries' sons had known much of downright hard labor, but here we see them hard at work helping to fortify Jerusalem. God has not forgotten that their soft white hands became hardened and sun-burned as they used trowel and mortar on the walls of the holy city.

Nor would I pass over the Gibeonites, Melatiah and the men of Gibeon (ver. 7), whether by these we are to understand descendants of the once wily deceivers who entrapped Joshua into disobedience, or Israelites indeed, dwelling in the ancient city. In either case, we may be reminded of what we once were, and what grace has made us.

After the goldsmiths and the apothecaries, repaired Rephaiah, the son of Hur, ruler of half of Jerusalem. He did not hire a servant to do the work for him, but though a man of wealth and power, he labored with his hands, and the Lord took note of his devotedness.

In verse 10 we read of a man whose sphere of labor was very circumscribed but very necessary. Jedaiah repaired "over against his house." This is noteworthy. Many of God's people can do little in a public way in His service, but they can each be concerned about maintaining the wall over against their own houses. And this is tremendously important. It is useless to talk of separation in the assembly, if there be not separation maintained at home. If the children are allowed to go into the world, or to bring the world into the home, depend upon it, the public testimony will avail for little. Godly words in the meeting and worldly ways in the house, will soon disgust neighbors and friends, and prove the undoing of the household.

Another edifying spectacle is afforded us in verse 12: "Next unto him repaired Shallum the son of Halohesh, the ruler of the half part of Jerusalem, *he and his daughters.*" It must have been a grand sight to behold this ruler and his daughters so zealously affected in a good thing. Our sisters have here a bright example of devotedness to the Lord. Would that it might be followed by thousands more!

Oft-times, one fears, where the truth is known that women are called upon to be in subjection, and not to lead in public work (after the fashion of the day), there is a settling down on the part of many sisters to a life of inaction and spiritual desuetude. But all work is not of a public character, as we have already had occasion to observe. There are many ways and abundant opportunities afforded godly women to labor, both in the

gospel and in building up the wall of protection
and exclusion of evil, without appearing on the
platform and usurping authority over the man.
Let there be but a willing mind, and it will not
be necessary to bewail the lack of opportunities
for women's service in a scriptural way.

But if any are to be used of God, there must
be not only this recognizing of His claims upon
us, but also that lowliness of spirit that ever com-
mends a servant.  So we pass on to

### THE VALLEY GATE.

"The valley gate repaired Hanun, and the inhabitants of Zanoah" (ver. 13).

This surely suggests humility—a willingness
to take a lowly place that thus the Lord may be
exalted.  One fears it is a gate little used by many
of us nowadays.

Pride is ever characteristic of fallen creatures,
who have nothing to be proud of; for "what hast
thou that thou hast not received?"  Even in connection with service for the Lord, how this unholy thing creeps in, leading one servant to be
jealous of another, instead of catching the Master's voice as He says, "What is that to thee?
Follow *thou* Me!"

What Cowper says of sin in general may be
predicated of pride in particular:

> "It twines itself about my thoughts,
> And slides into my prayer."

It is indeed the root-sin of all. By it Satan himself fell, and one "being lifted up with pride, falls into the condemnation of the devil."

God has said, "To this man will I look; to him that is humble, and of a contrite spirit, and that trembleth at My word." It is perhaps merely a truism to write that only as one walks humbly before Him, is he in a condition of soul to be safely used in service. I do not mean that God cannot overrule all things, and in a sense use even the basest of men. The devil himself has to serve. God used Balaam, and others equally ungodly. But in such cases it is to the condemnation of the very one used.

To go on preaching and handling the truth of God while the heart is lifted up and the eyes lofty is one of the most dangerous courses one can take, and certain to end in ruin and disaster.

We have much cause, as we contemplate our coldness and indifference, and the appalling power of the world over us, to be on our faces before God, instead of walking in pride, only to learn eventually that He "is able to abase" us, as in the case of Babylon's haughty king. If we humble not ourselves, He must humble us in His own way, for it is part of His purpose to "hide pride from man."

Keeping this, then, before our minds, we pass on to the solemn and much-needed lesson of

### THE DUNG GATE.

"But the dung gate repaired Malchiah the son of Rechab, the ruler of part of Beth-haccerem" (ver. 14). Humbling work this, for a ruler, but necessary labor surely.

The Dung Gate was the port whence they carried forth the filth, that the city might not be defiled. And so we read, "Having therefore these promises, dearly beloved, let us cleanse ourselves from all filthiness of the flesh and spirit, perfecting holiness in the fear of God" (2 Cor. 7: 1).

Real blessing there cannot be if this is forgotten; but if we have truly learned the lesson of the Valley Gate, that of the Dung Gate will be no difficulty. As saints and servants we are called, not to uncleanness, but to holiness. We are to cleanse ourselves; that is, to judge, in the presence of God, and turn away from, all filthiness—let its form be the grosser one of the flesh, or the less objectionable (in the eyes of men) of the spirit.

In the first three chapters of Romans we have sharply delineated the naked hideousness of the filthiness of the flesh. In the first three chapters of 1st Corinthians and in the 2nd of Colossians, we have unveiled the filthiness of the spirit: a mind exalting itself against God and His Christ —a wisdom that is earthly, sensual, devilish. So we read elsewhere of the "desires of the flesh and of the mind," in which we *once* walked.    (See Eph. 2.)

From all these things we are now called to cleanse ourselves.    Body and mind alike are to be preserved free from impurity, for the glory of God.

"Flee also youthful lusts" is a much-needed word.    In the world about us, men live to pander to the lust of the flesh, and the lust of the eyes, and the pride of life.    It should be otherwise with the Christian, and must be otherwise if he is to be a vessel unto honor, sanctified and meet for the Master's use, and prepared unto every good work.    Down with the bars of the Dung Gate, brethren; out with the filth!    "Be ye clean that bear the vessels of the Lord."

Thus we pass on our journey round the walls, and come next to

### THE GATE OF THE FOUNTAIN.

"The gate of the fountain repaired Shallun the son of Col-hozeh, the ruler of part of Mizpah" (ver. 15).

To the woman at the well, the Lord Jesus spoke of a fountain (not merely a well) of living water. Again in John 7 He cried, "He that believeth on Me...out of his inward parts shall flow rivers of living water."    The fountain of living water is a type, or symbol of the Holy Spirit who indwells all believers.

It has been asserted by many that until the

Christian surrenders himself fully to God, he does not receive the gift of the Holy Ghost. This is a mistake. "If any man have not the Spirit of Christ, he is none of His" (Rom. 8: 9) ; "After that ye believed, ye were sealed with that Holy Spirit of promise" (Eph.1:13)—sealed, too, "until the day of redemption" (Eph. 4: 30) ; "Because ye are sons, God hath sent forth the Spirit of His Son into your hearts" (Gal. 4: 6).

But that there is often in the experience of many what looks, indeed, like a "second blessing," no observant believer can deny. What is really meant by it? Simply this: that though the Holy Spirit indwells all children of God in this dispensation, yet, in many, worldliness and self-pleasing are so characteristic, that He who should control us for Christ, and fill us with freshness and power as He ministers Christ to our souls, is become like a fountain choked with stones and rubbish, and thus the life is barren and the testimony powerless. Awakened at last to see the folly of such a life of uselessness to God and reproach to Christ, the saint humbles himself in self-judgment, the filth is put away, and now the once-choked fountain is running over, and the Spirit of God in power takes control of the believer to use him for the Lord's glory, and to make him a vessel of refreshment to others. There is a fountain of living water within, and out of his inward parts flow rivers of living water for others (John 7: 38).

"Be ye filled with the Spirit" is a word the importance of which cannot be over-estimated. May every child of grace go on to know more of it in power as he walks in obedience to the word of God! For there are two things that in Scripture are practically inseparable—I refer to the Spirit and the Word. A Spirit-filled Christian will be a Scripture-filled Christian.

In verses 16 to 25 we read of many persons who repaired that portion of the wall extending from the fountain gate to the water gate. There are fine shades and significant expressions used in several instances that we do well to notice. Of one and another we only read that they repaired such and such a portion. In verse 20, of Baruch we are told that he *"earnestly* repaired the other piece, from the turning of the wall," etc It is not for nothing God inserted that adverb. Three are mentioned in verse 23 who repaired over against their houses, and we can be sure every detail was precious to God. But passing on to verse 26 we reach

THE WATER GATE.

"Moreover the Nethinim dwelt in Ophel, unto the place over against the water gate toward the east, and the tower that lieth out."

The Nethinim were servants, and it is meet that they should have the care of this gate, for water is very generally a type of the word of God. "Wherewithal shall a young man cleanse his way?

By taking heed thereto according to Thy word"
(Ps. 119: 9).

We do not read of any repairs being made
here, only that the Nethinim dwelt over against
the water gate. Possibly this port needed none.
At any rate, we know that of which it speaks
needs not to be repaired, for the word of God
liveth and abideth forever. All vain man's as-
saults upon it have left it uninjured and un-
changed. We are called upon to defend it, con-
tending earnestly for the faith once for all delivered to the people of God, but it would be impiety to attempt to patch or improve it.

The water of the Word it is that Christ uses
to wash His disciples' feet and to keep them free
from defilement (Jno. 13:1-16; 15:3). It is written: "Christ also loved the Church and gave Himself for it, that He might sanctify and cleanse it
by the washing of water by the Word," etc. (Eph.
5: 25, 26.)

It is remarkable that what in Ephesians is connected with the Spirit, is in Colossians linked with
the Word. Compare Eph. 5: 18-20 with Col. 3:
16. Both alike are a source of joy and blessing.
And we need not wonder at this similarity in
effect, for of the Word it is said, "Holy men of
God spake as they were moved by the Holy
Ghost."

In chapter 8 of this book (Nehemiah) we see all
the people gathered together "as one man into the
street that was before the water gate," there to

listen to the reading of the word of God. The result is joy and blessing.

O fellow-believer, I beseech you, "meditate on these things, give thyself wholly to them," and thus shall your profiting appear to all, as you "let the word of Christ dwell in you richly," for, "All Scripture is given by inspiration of God, and is profitable for doctrine, for reproof, for correction, for instruction in righteousness, that the man of God may be perfect, thoroughly furnished unto all good works" (2 Tim. 3: 16, 17). This, then, is the servant's furnishing. He is to study to show himself "approved unto God, a workman that needeth not to be ashamed, rightly dividing the word of truth."

And this means far more than reading books, however helpful, written on the Bible. It necessitates diligent, painstaking study of the sacred Word itself. Other books may help, often, to lead out the mind on certain broad lines, but *the* Book must supersede them all if there is to be real growth in the knowledge of God.

By this alone will you overcome the wicked one, if "the word of God abideth in you" (1 John 2: 14).

Another company of Tekoites repaired between the water gate and that which next claims our attention, namely:

### THE HORSE GATE.

"From above the horse gate repaired the

priests, every one over against his house" (ver. 28).

The horse is used with striking frequency in Scripture as a figure of the warrior.

It is so described in Job 39: 19-25, where, "He saith among the trumpets, Ha, ha! and he smelleth the battle afar off." In Zechariah 1: 8, and in Rev. 6, we read of four symbolic horses, which speak of warrior powers; and when the eternal Word of God, clad in blood-dipped vesture, descends from heaven to the battle preceding the awful supper of the great God, at the beginning of the Millennium, He is seen in vision riding on a white horse, and the saints are seen similarly mounted.

The ass is the symbol of peace; the horse, of war. When the Prince of Peace rode into Jerusalem of old, it was on the ass. When He comes to judgment, it is on the horse.

The Horse Gate may speak, then, of soldier-service in a world opposed to God and His truth. It bids us "earnestly contend for the faith once for all delivered to the saints" (Jude 3, R. V.).

The truth has been given to us at great cost, not only to the One who is Himself "the Truth," but for its preservation, and recovery when lost at times, myriads of warrior-saints have suffered and died.

Alas that we, children of such glorious sires, should so lightly value what to them was dearer than life! We live in a day not of open persecution, but of laxity and latitudinarianism. We are affected much by the spirit of the times; hence there are few among us who, like that mighty man of old, grasp the sword of the Spirit to defend the truth of God, and fight till the hand cleaves to the very weapon it holds. (See 2 Sam. 23:9, 10.) But God's Eleazars will have rich reward in the day when many, we fear, will be saved but so as by fire.

Let me quote here the words of another, which might well be written in letters of living fire:

"Renounce all the policy of the age. Trample upon Saul's armor. Grasp the Book of God. Trust the Spirit who wrote its pages. Fight with this weapon only and always. Cease to amuse, and seek to arouse. Shun the clap of a delighted audience, and listen for the sobs of a convicted one. Give up trying to *please* men who have only the thickness of their ribs between their souls and hell; and warn, and plead, and entreat, as those who feel the waters of eternity creeping upon them."*

And remember, beloved, as you fight, that the day of testimony for God is fast passing away. It will soon be too late to stand for the truth, and too late to minister Christ to needy souls. "The night cometh when no man can work" (John 9:4).

---

*Archibald Brown, of London.

Of this we are reminded as we pass on to

## THE EAST GATE.

"After him repaired also Shemaiah the son of Shechaniah, the keeper of the east gate" (ver. 29).

The gate of the sunrising points on—does it not?—to the morning without clouds, when He shall come down like rain upon the mown grass, and as clear shining after rain.

Having shone forth as the Bright and Morning Star, and as such gathered His redeemed to Himself in the clouds, He will be manifested to Israel and the nations that are spared as the all-glorious Sun of Righteousness, with healing in His wings. This is the special character in which He is presented to Israel and the earth, but the two are only different aspects of His one coming again.

For that glad morning weary saints all along have waited and longed, straining their eyes to catch the first glimpse of the Bright and Morning Star. Wicked servants have said, "My Lord delayeth His coming;" but He "is not slack, as some men count slackness, but is long-suffering to usward, not willing that any should perish" (2 Pet. 3:9). "The night is far spent, the day is at hand." It is high time to be aroused from our lethargy, for already the long-expected midnight cry is ringing through the world, "Behold, the Bridegroom cometh; go ye out to meet Him!" The shout of the Lord, the voice of the archangel, and the trump of God, will soon resound through the vaulted heavens, announcing the return of the long-absent One, and ushering in the morning. But for many it will be the beginning of the darkest night earth has ever known.

Oh, let us be up and doing while it is called to-day, that we may not be ashamed before Him at His coming. "Even so, come, Lord Jesus."

Only a small part of the wall remains to be noticed, but among the workers upon it there is one we must not cursorily pass by. Meshullam the son of Berechiah repaired, we learn, "over against his chamber" (ver. 30). Here was a man who probably had no house, no real home. He was but a lodger; but even so, he was faithful to Him who appointed him to glorify God in that narrow place. He went to work with energy and repaired over against his one little room. And thus he becomes a bright example for every one in like circumstances, bidding such remember that "he that is faithful in that which is least, is faithful also in much."

### THE GATE MIPHKAD

is the last in order. "After him repaired Malchiah the goldsmith's son unto the place of the Nethinim, and of the merchants, over against the gate Miphkad, and to the going up of the corner" (ver. 31).

The word Miphkad, according to the dictionaries, means review, or appointment (for judg-

ment).  It was doubtless the gate where contro-
versies were tried, after the Eastern fashion. How
solemn is this!  For it is when the Lord comes
that "we must all appear before the judgment-
seat of Christ."  That will be the Gate Miphkad
for the believer.  There will be the last great
review.  Every detail of the saint's life will come
up for inspection.  It may be then that,

> "Deeds of merit, as we thought them,
>   He will show us were but sin;
> Little acts we had forgotten,
>   He will tell us were for Him."

Oh, the unspeakable solemnity of it!  All our
ease-loving and self-seeking brought to light then!
All our pride and vanity manifested!  Everything
put on its own proper level.  All our works in-
spected by Him who seeth not as man seeth. How
many of us will wish we had been more true and
real in our work down here.  Things we valued
highly on earth, how lightly will they weigh up
there!—as the very small dust of the balance; yea,
lighter even than that—altogether, lighter than
vanity!

And those things we have neglected and fool-
ishly ignored in the days of our pilgrimage, how
much more precious than gold will they appear
in the light of that judgment-seat!

O beloved, shall we not seek to be *now* what
we shall then wish we had been?  Let us do now
what we shall then wish we had done; turn now

from what we shall then wish we had judged.
The Lord grant that His people be awakened to
the reality of these things, and the importance of
living for eternity!

And thus we have traveled round the wall from
one part to another, and have, I trust, been blessed
in doing so. We might close our meditations here,
only that God does not end in this way, for in the
last verse we come back again, having made the
circuit, to that with which we began—

### THE SHEEP GATE.

"And between the going up of the corner unto
the Sheep Gate repaired the goldsmiths and the
merchants."

It is as though God would not have us turn
away without reminding us that the Cross with
which we began will be before our souls for eternity. After all has been gone into at the judgment-seat, we shall turn from it to the Judge Himself, who is our Redeemer and Bridegroom. We
shall see Him as a Lamb that had been slain. At
His once-pierced feet we shall fall in adoration,
and forever sing praises "unto Him that loveth
us, and hath washed us from our sins in His own
blood."

We shall never get beyond the Cross. It will
be the theme of our praises throughout all the
ages to come. Oh, to ever live in the light of it
now! It speaks of sins forever put away, and

also of a world under judgment for the rejection of God's Son. Our place, then, is outside of it all. "Let us go forth therefore unto Him outside the camp, bearing His reproach. For here have we no continuing city, but we seek one to come" (Heb. 13: 13, 14).

# CHAPTER IV

## SOLDIER-SERVANTS

THE work which was so precious in the eyes of the Lord was but a theme for mockery and scorn in the mind of the mixed people, whose overtures of participation on common ground had been refused. Sanballat's rage is stirred; but for the present it takes outwardly the form of contemptuous sneering: "What do these feeble Jews?" he asks his Samaritan brethren. "Will they fortify themselves? will they sacrifice? will they make an end in a day? will they revive the stones out of the heaps of rubbish which are burned?" And Tobiah the Ammonite joins in the mockery, exclaiming with a lightness he evidently did not feel, "Even that which they build, if a fox go up, he shall even break down their stone wall" (vers. 1-3). Yet he and all his ilk were to prove later that, when guarded by Jehovah's subject servants, it was too strong a wall for such foxes as they to break through.

In the name of the Lord, Nehemiah and his companions built steadily on, and that Name was to prove a strong tower into which the righteous might safely retreat from the malignity of their foes. When the people of God cleave to His Word and exalt His name, they need fear no enemy, human or supernatural. It is *themselves* who are responsible for any breaches made in the wall. It is unbelief and self-will in the people of God that weaken or destroy those battlements against which the enemies outside might batter in vain.

Realizing this in some measure, the people of Judah lift up their hearts to the One whose they were and whom they served. "Hear, O our God; for we are despised," they cry; "and turn their reproach upon their own head, and give them for a prey in the land of captivity; and cover not their iniquity, and let not their sin be blotted out from before Thee; for they have provoked Thee to anger before the builders" (vers. 4, 5). If any feel the difference between this prayer and such as are suited to the Christian in this dispensation of grace, the explanation is involved in the question. That was not the time when grace and sufferance were enjoined. The dispensation of law was still in force, and we must view these utterances from that standpoint. The important thing for us to observe is the way in which the remnant cast themselves wholly upon God. Sanballat, Tobiah, and the rest are *His* enemies, not merely theirs, and they count on Him to deal with them.

And so they prayed and builded, for such is the force of "*So* built we the wall," in verse 6.

Thus with the help of God the breaches were repaired, for willing hands made light work, and "the people had a mind to work."

But soon the opposition took a different form. When the united nations (notice the lengthened list — Sanballat, Tobiah, the Arabians and the Ammonites, and the Ashdodites) heard that the work was actually nearing completion, and that the wall was being repaired in a substantial manner, their indignation became greater than ever. They had hoped the rubbish would impede the progress of the work to such an extent as to completely dishearten the Jews; but bit by bit this had been cleared away, and the stones uncovered and set in their places. Hence these enemies of what is of God realize something more than mockery is required if they would not soon be effectually shut out of the holy city.

As one reads such a record, it is almost impossible not to observe how accurately the history of old fits a later work of God—even that of the present time. As a result of centuries of darkness and superstition, practically every precious truth of the Scriptures was overwhelmed by the ecclesiastical rubbish gradually accumulated. When at last the reformers were raised up to recall God's people to God's own Word, they found themselves confronted by just such a task as that which Nehemiah had to face; and ever since, when there has been a settling down on the part of God's people, the rubbish has accumulated again at an alarming rate, human tradition soon swamping what was of God; and so the need of persistent, devoted, prayerful toil, to separate the precious from the vile has been ever manifest. Carnal professors will mock, so-called liberals will demonstrate their bitter hatred of everything holy, but they who wait upon the Lord shall renew their strength, and find all needed grace to stand in the evil day, and to distinguish between what is really divine and what is but of man in the great mounds of mingled truth and error, lying all about the ruined wall that once separated Church and world. Every fresh attempt to "try the things that differ" will provoke the ire of the worldly-religious mass; but what is of God is of too much value to be surrendered at the behest of fleshly foes.

The adversaries of Judah determined upon a sudden onslaught on the remnant, and so "conspired all of them together to come and fight against Jerusalem, and to hinder it" (ver. 8). This was but a call to "watch and pray," and so it was recognized by Nehemiah and his fellow-laborers. The language of verse 9 is most instructive: "Nevertheless we made our prayer unto our God, and set a watch against them day and night, because of them." This was holding things in the right proportion. Prayer alone would have been presumption. But they watch against the enemy at the same time that they call upon God.

In verse 10 we have the first note of discouragement from within. Constant toil and watching have worn upon the spirits of the Jews, and so the report comes to Nehemiah: "The strength of the bearers of burdens is decayed, and there is much rubbish; so that we are not able to build the wall." But to these disheartening words Nehemiah vouchsafes no reply, save to labor on. The adversaries continue their plotting without and the people grow faint within, but the Tirshatha continues to look up and count upon the living God.

The third trial is mentioned in verse 12. There were scattered Jews living among the Samaritans. They "came unto us ten times," says Nehemiah, warning of the preparations for an assault, and declaring the utter inability of the remnant to stand against such powerful foes.

It was certainly discouraging to one who relied on a fleshly arm, but the man of faith could count on God through it all. Heretofore the people had labored, prayed, and watched. Now they must be prepared for conflict. So the governor set the people after their families in the vantage-places upon the wall, armed with swords, spears and bows. But he would not have them put their confidence in the weapons, but in the living God: "Be ye not afraid of them; *remember the Lord,* which is great and terrible, and fight for your brethren, your sons, and your daughters, your wives and your houses" (ver. 14). This was to be their battle-cry, "Remember the Lord!"

Many a merely human conflict has been won by the inspiration of a watch-word recalling some past great event. In our own day, again and again,

Spanish troops were repulsed as the American soldiery drove all before them with the cry, "Remember the Maine!" So Napoleon often inspirited his troops by causing them to remember some former victory. But what could stir the soul of an Israelite indeed more than such a cry as this, *"Remember the Lord!"* Similarly when pressing upon Timothy the need of devotedness in the Christian warfare, Paul cries, "Remember Jesus Christ!" (2 Tim. 2 : 8).*

This is faith's resource. The God who gave His Son for our redemption, who raised Him from the dead and set Him at His own right hand in highest glory, can be counted on in every time of trial to supply all needed grace for seasonable help.

When Nehemiah's enemies knew that their plans were known, and the citizens of Jerusalem armed and watchful, they gave up all hope of hindering by open warfare; while the remnant rejoiced that "God had brought their counsel to nought;" and so they returned every one with confidence to the work.

But this deliverance did not cause them to be any the less careful. Henceforth Nehemiah divided his own servants into two companies, one of which wrought in the work and the other stood guard heavily armed; while the builders and burden-

---

* The verse is really an exclamatory rather than a declarative sentence: "Remember Jesus Christ, of the seed of David, raised from the dead according to my gospel!"

bearers themselves labored, each with his sword girded by his side, or with a trowel in one hand and a weapon in the other. Both alike speak of the Word. The trowel is the Word used for edification, the sword is the Word used to contend earnestly for the faith once for all delivered to the saints. Significant are the words that close verse 18, after this vivid description of soldier-laborers: "And he that sounded the trumpet was by me." The trumpet stands for the ministry of the Word, and it was meet that the trumpeter should abide with the ruler and get his instructions directly from him. So does the servant of Christ need to abide in Him that he may speak as the oracles of God, and then the trumpet gives no uncertain sound.

Scattered as the workers and soldiers were upon the whole length of the wall, it was important that all should be subject to one voice, the voice of Nehemiah, and this was expressed by the trumpet. Wherever the loud blast was heard, there all were to gather, counting upon God to fight for them (vers. 19, 20).

"*So,*"* continues the inspired record, "we labored in the work: and half of them held the spears from the rising of the morning till the stars appeared."

There was much work to be done and time was

---

* This little word "so" is quite characteristic of Nehemiah. It is found about twenty times.

pressing, so they dared not take their ease while there was light enough to labor. And at night all lodged within the wall, that they might be a defence to their brethren, though many had homes outside the city.

In all this devoted service, Nehemiah and his guard were ensamples to the rest, for so continuously were they on duty that they did not so much as remove their clothes, save for washing. It was a time to try men's souls, but the testing only proved how zealously affected in a good thing were the governor and his helpers. In this they shine as examples for us, bidding us hold fast what God has committed to us, and hold forth the word of life to others, while refusing all compromise with the unholy spirit of the age in which we live.

# CHAPTER V

## INTERNAL STRIFE

OUTSIDE foes may rage, but they cannot really injure the people of God if there be love and harmony within. "Only," writes the apostle, "let your conversation (the conduct) be as it becometh the gospel of Christ; that whether I come and see you, or else be absent, I may hear of your affairs, that ye stand fast in one spirit, with one mind striving together for the faith of the gospel; and in nothing terrified by your adversaries: which is to them an evident token of perdition, but to you of salvation, and that of God" (Phil. 1: 27, 28). The contrary is involved in the warning given by James: "Where envying and strife is, there is confusion and every evil work" (James 3: 16). And this Paul also set before the Galatians, when he wrote: "If ye bite and devour one another, take heed that ye be not consumed one of another" (Gal. 5: 15). The sheep of the Lord's flock need to keep close to the Shepherd and to one another if they would be guarded from the prowling wolves who ever seek their destruction. But how sad, and what shame it is when they fall to devouring one another, thus giving place to the devil. Of this we are warned in the happenings narrated for our instruction in this chapter.

The opening verses are like Acts 6:1: "There was a great cry of the people and of their wives against their brethren the Jews. For there were that said, We, our sons and daughters, are many, and we must procure corn for them that we may eat, and live. Some also there were that said, We have mortgaged our lands, vineyards and houses, that we might buy corn in the dearth. There were also that said, We have borrowed money for the king's tribute, and that upon our lands and vineyards. Yet now our flesh is as the flesh of our brethren, our children as their children; and, lo, we bring into bondage our sons and our daughters to be servants, and some of our daughters are brought into bondage already; neither is it in our power to redeem them; for other men have our lands and vineyards" (vers. 1-5).

What a pitiable state of affairs is portrayed here by the simple narrative of the complaints of the people against their own brethren! The worst of it all was, that the accusations were true; and the demands of the usurers were, so far as business principles are concerned, such as all nations recognize as legitimate. But God's people were not to be guided by such principles. From the beginning He had told them not to exact usury of their brethren, but rather to make provision for the poor, as giving unto Him. They had all been in poverty once, and He had enriched them according to the grace of His heart, not according to their deserts. Alas, how soon had they forgotten this when it came to dealing with one another.

And what sorrows have come upon the children of God in all dispensations because of this very thing! The full manifestation of grace in the present age nas not hindered the same mercenary spirit often appearing among those who owe all to the mercy of God. We have already referred to Acts 6; and the conditions prevailing in the assembly at Corinth, long after, were the fruit of a similar state. Brother dragged brother to law, and that before the unjust—men who, whatever their reputation in the world, were not suited to deal with things in the Church. How incongruous are such conditions with the grace of Christianity!

Nor is it only in connection with temporal things that such a spirit has been manifested, but, alas, in fancied zeal for the holy things of God how often has the same evil principle of exaction prevailed. Questions have arisen in Christian assemblies, often of the most perplexing character, concerning which an almost instantaneous judgment has been demanded; and if tried souls and weak gatherings have not been able to bow to the *ipse dixit* of certain carnal leaders, excision or excommunication have been resorted to, in defiance of the word of God and the Spirit of Christ. What is all this but the same thing prevailing in spiritual matters which wrought so much havoc in these temporal affairs?

Oh for more men who, instead of tacitly acquiescing in these unholy conditions, are stirred to a righteous anger by such un-Christlike ways! Nehemiah's upright and unselfish soul was moved to indignation, and with the assurance that came from knowing he sided with God, he rebuked the nobles and the rulers for thus exacting usury of their brethren. The matter was brought up for open consideration in a "great assembly," and the guilt of the leaders charged home upon their consciences before all the people. "We," he says, "after our ability, have redeemed our brethren the Jews, which were sold unto the heathen; and will ye even sell your *brethren?* or shall they be sold unto us?" They were speechless; what answer could they make?

Apply it to conditions such as I have refered to above. Think of the toil and labor that have been expended by devoted servants of Christ to bring lost sinners to His feet. Think of the ministry exercised afterwards to lead on these young converts and establish them in the truth. Think of the pastoral care exercised by earnest, faithful men who knew them as individual members of the flock of Christ—not as a mass without heart or conscience—and then think of the spirit of exaction that can press some test-question on such saints, and ruthlessly cut off and cast out souls for whose blessing others have labored so persistently — and this by men who profess to act for God and to seek His glory!

Oh, brethren, let us listen to the words of Nehemiah and bow our head in the dust if we have been parties to such unholy ways. "It is *not* good that ye do: ought ye not to walk in the fear of our God because of the heathen our enemies? I likewise, and my brethren, and my servants, might exact of them money and corn: *I pray you, let us leave off this usury.* Restore, I pray you, to them, even this day, their lands, their vineyards, their oliveyards, and their houses, also the hundredth part of the money, and of the corn, the wine, and the oil that ye exact of them" (vers. 9-11).

These are suited words for the present solemn time when God has been exercising many as to the very things of which we have been speaking. It is not a time to demand the uttermost farthing of one another, but rather to heed the word, "I pray you, let us leave off this usury." If we have been guilty of robbing any of our brethren of their blood-bought privileges, let us hasten to restore what we can ere the Lord arise as their champion and we be put to shame. For He has said, "Hear the word of the Lord, ye that tremble at His word; Your brethren that hated you, that cast you out for My name's sake, said, Let the Lord be glorified; but He shall appear to *your joy,* and *they* shall be ashamed" (Isa. 66: 5). Cutting and comforting words are these mingled by the Lord Himself. Oh, for a heart to take heed to them ere it be forever too late!

On the part of the rulers in Judah there was an instant response when the words of Nehemiah had moved them to repentance. "Then said they, We will restore them, and will require nothing of them; so will we do as thou sayest" (ver. 12). And this was sealed with an oath, and further confirmed by a graphic action on the part of the Tirshatha. He shook his lap and said, "So God shake out every man from his house, and from his labor, that performeth not this promise, even thus be he shaken out, and emptied." And this was attested by the solemn "Amen!" of the congregation, who praised the Lord for the mercy shown. It was the same spirit that led the apostle Paul, long afterwards to write: "I would they were even cut off that trouble you!"

In the closing verses, Nehemiah contrasts his own behaviour with that which he had so severely censured. One is again reminded of Paul. It was an occasion where he was compelled to "speak as a fool" that he might close the mouths of any gainsayers. He relates how that from the day of his appointment as governor he had never availed himself of the perquisites of his office, that he might not be burdensome to the people whose blessing he sought.

Former governors had felt free to do this, but the fear of God restrained him from doing the same. Instead, he had kept open house for a hundred and fifty of the Jews and rulers, besides strangers from the surrounding villages. He was one who had learned that "it is more blessed to give than to receive," and he acted accordingly.

The people might forget all this—alas, too often do; but he cries, "Think upon me, my God, for good, according to all that I have done for this people" (ver. 19). This may seem to savor of self-complacency, but who of us would dare judge so devoted a servant? And again we need to remind ourselves that the dispensation of grace had not yet dawned. Law was still in the ascendant, and the spirit shown by Nehemiah is so beyond his age that we can only give thanks for what God had wrought in the soul of His dear servant, while we pray for wisdom and grace to serve His people in our own generation unselfishly, and in the Spirit of Christ, leaving all question of appreciation or reward to be settled at His judgment-seat.

## CHAPTER VI

### PLOTS AND SNARES

A GAIN our attention is directed to the opposition of Sanballat, Tobiah, and Geshem
(or Gashmu) with the rest of Judah's enemies.
Every move within the city was reported to them
without, and no doubt they had felt a sense of
deep satisfaction when the news of internal strife
had reached them. This may account for our
having heard nothing of them in the last chapter.
If God's people get quarrelling among themselves,
the enemy from without can afford to rest in his
tents, but as soon as things get right within he
actively bestirs himself.

Word having reached the adversaries that the
wall was builded and no breach left in it (although
the doors had not yet been set up on the gates),
Sanballat and Geshem sent an apparently friendly message to Nehemiah, saying, "Come, let us
meet together in some one of the villages in the
plain of Ono" (ver. 2). They would lure him
unto neutral ground, outside the wall, as though
to confer on matters of importance; but he recognized the evil purpose of their hearts; he inwardly knew their thought was to do him mischief.

His reply is worthy of the man, and should

have a voice for any in our day who are tempted
to take neutral ground where the truth of Christ
is in question. "I am doing a great work, so
that I cannot come down: why should the work
cease, whilst I leave it, and come down to you?"
He had been entrusted by God with a commission "to restore and build Jerusalem," and he
would brook nothing that would for a moment
turn him aside from this. A separated man, he
would have no part in the surrounding confusion
where the word of God was rejected and His people despised. Notice here: it was no question of
ministering to, or caring for the children of God
scattered abroad that was before him. We may
be sure Nehemiah would have been as ready to
help the dispersed of Israel as those in Jerusalem.
But these Samaritans were the enemies of God's
truth, while pretending to serve Him. "They feared
the Lord, and served their own gods" (2 Kings
17: 33). They represent, as we have seen, unreal
professors, yet presuming to have full title to the
name and place of worshipers. With such the
faithful servant can have no fellowship. He must
maintain and guard what has been committed to
him, and if he attempts to mix with these "deceitful workers" he will only lose what he himself has.

Four times Sanballat and Geshem sent to Nehemiah "after this sort," and four times he returned the same answer.

Then they changed their tactics. They had tried

conciliatory methods and failed to corrupt him.
Now they would use a scandalous report with
intent to intimidate him. There is nothing new
under the sun. Satan's wiles are such that the
man of God must not be ignorant of his devices.

The fifth time Sanballat sends his servant with
"an open letter in his hand." Oh, these "open
letters!" How often, while fairly worded, have
they been penned only to gender strife. This one
contained a covert insinuation to the effect that
all Nehemiah's work had been unauthorized, and
a direct charge that his object was self-aggran-
dizement and rebellion against the king. Themselves in rebellion against God, they charge God's
servant with their own sin. The "open letter"
reads somewhat graciously, but the object of its
writer was to occupy the Jews with his apparently
gracious spirit in order to poison their minds
against Nehemiah. "It is reported among the
nations, and Gashmu saith it, that thou and the
Jews think to rebel: for which cause thou buildest
the wall, that thou mayest be their king, according
to these words. And thou hast also appointed
prophets to preach of thee at Jerusalem, saying,
There is a king in Judah; and now shall it be
reported to the king according to these words.
Come now, therefore, and let us take counsel together" (vers. 6, 7). Such were the contents of
the open letter, and we are not told what impression, if any, it made on the Jews. It was so
worded as to intimate that Sanballat's only de-

sire was to clear Nehemiah of the charges whispered about, and yet so cunningly phrased that any disaffected ones within might readily charge the governor with fearing an investigation if he did not go down to confer with Sanballat.

But Nehemiah is not at all concerned about this. He knows he is personally right with God and he fears not suspicion and idle tales. "There are no such things done as thou sayest," he retorts boldly, "but thou feignest them out of thine own heart."

So was it also when evil workers sought to undermine the apostle Paul's influence, and so has it ever been when the truth was hated. To discredit, by fair means or foul, the messenger, is one of Satan's cunning devices in order to discredit the message. To do this, his tools often affect great humility themselves; and pretending to be zealous for the liberty of the people of God, they cry "Pope!" "Diotrephes!" "Heretic!" when any servant of Christ and the Church seeks to stand steadfastly against iniquity, hoping thereby to throw dust in the eyes of simple believers, in order to gain their own unrighteous ends.

Trials like these are not easy to bear. To have one's good evil-spoken of, to be called a "lord over God's heritage" when trying to serve in lowliness, is painful indeed to any sensitive soul. But it is well not to retaliate, nor even to explain, but just to refuse the cowardly charge and leave results with God.

Nehemiah's conscience was free, so he could throw the accusation back upon the man who made it; and knowing it was only done to weaken their hands from the work, he looks heavenward and cries, "Now therefore, O God, strengthen my hands" (ver. 9).

But Satan has not yet exhausted his ammunition. A man is found *within the city* to act for Sanballat and Tobiah, upon the payment of a bribe. Shemaiah, the son of Delaiah, is said to have been "shut up." This probably means that he was ill, or confined to his house, and unable to take his place among the workers on the wall. Such a man, if not in fellowship with God as to His then present ways, would prove a ready tool for the conspirators. Nehemiah called upon him, and Shemaiah warned him with pretended sincerity of danger to his life, counselling that he should flee to the temple, there to seek security by hiding in the sanctuary. To do so would have at once spread fear and distrust among the people, and this was just what Sanballat desired.

But God's devoted servant again rose, strong in faith, superior to the situation. "Should such a man as I flee?" he asks, "and who is there, that, being as I am, would go into the temple to save his life? I will not go in" (ver. 11). To desert the rest and act as though panic-stricken, would ill become one in his position, one who also had confessed his faith in God so boldly. He realized that he was again face to face with evidence of the plots of his enemies, and that God had not sent Shemaiah with such a message, but that he was hired by Tobiah and Sanballat to give this unworthy counsel. With these were others who shared in the conspiracy; one, a prophetess named Noadiah, and several unnamed men, also in the prophetic office. Sad and solemn it is when those who take the place of speaking for God are found in sympathy with the adversaries of His truth, thus hindering the work He has committed to His loyal servants.

Nehemiah, in his customary way, brings the whole matter at once to God, and puts the case in His hands. "My God," he prays, "think Thou upon Tobiah and Sanballat according to these their works, and on the prophetess Noadiah, and the rest of the prophets, that would have put me in fear" (ver. 14). It is no longer a matter between Nehemiah and the conspirators but it is now an affair between God and these unholy plotters. And in His own time He can be depended upon to settle all righteously.

At last, despite every effort to frustrate the work, "the wall was finished" in fifty-two days from the time they began to labor. When this was manifest to the surrounding nations "they were much cast down in their own eyes: for they perceived that this work was wrought of our God" (ver. 16). With what different feelings would the Jewish remnant contemplate the completed wall! Praise and thanksgiving would well up in their breasts, that Jerusalem was once more a protected city.

No doubt the enemy hated such "narrow exclusiveness," and would search eagerly for some small breach whereby to force an entrance, or pass in by night. Judah's exclusiveness was their security. So long as the spirit of the people within answered to the strong wall without, they were safe. Their *position* was now clearly defined. The next question was, Would their *condition* answer to it? Alas, the very next verse manifests a bad state. With some at least, the separation was only outward—not of heart and conscience. How often has this been repeated in the history of God's people!

A position may be taken which outwardly is fully in accord with Scripture; yet the heart may not go with it at all. People *talk* of separation, priding themselves on being in a certain ecclesiastical circle, apart from sects of man's devising, while yet in their homes and in business-life going on with the world as though never separated at all. This is of the very essence of Phariseeism—an outward position rigidly maintained, while inwardly corruption holds sway.

Inside the walls of Jerusalem it was far from being in accord with the position taken. "Moreover in those days the nobles of Judah sent many letters unto Tobiah, and the letters of Tobiah came unto them. For there were many in Judah sworn unto him, because he was the son-in-law of Shechaniah the son of Arah; and his son Johanan had taken the daughter of Meshullam the son of Berechiah. Also they reported his good deeds before me, and uttered my words to him. And Tobiah sent letters to put me in fear" (vers. 17-19). It was a complete overturning of divine order. God had said, "The people shall dwell alone, they shall not be reckoned among the nations." And to so abide was to be strong and be under His protecting hand. But the unequal yoke had been entered into. Mixed marriages, despite the bitter lesson in Ezra's day, were still tolerated and excused; and so conscience was broken down and the nobles of Judah lost all power of discrimination. The wall might separate between them and ungodly Tobiah, but there was no separation in spirit, so they easily found means of communication with the haters of God's truth.

To Nehemiah they prated of the good qualities and benevolence of "brother Tobiah," and to the latter they spoke complainingly of the unnecessary strictness of the governor. They were traitors and hinderers, though occupying positions of prominence among the Jews. "Discerning of spirits" is a gift to be coveted; for dullness of sight is becoming increasingly characteristic of many who once were counted upon as able to discern between good and evil.

When the heart goes with the world and worldly religiousness, all kinds of excuses will be made for those who go on with the mixed condition.

Their position and actions—no matter how unscriptural—will be palliated and explained away; while those who truly go on with God will be subjected to the extremes of criticism, and every word and deed viewed as unfavorably as possible. Hence the need of being deeply exercised as to the inward state, as well as carefully walking in the path outlined in the word of God.

The chapter we have been considering is full of warnings for our own times. Happy those who have ears to hear and hearts to understand.

Mere outward separation, with its accompaniment of breaking bread in scriptural simplicity on the first day of each week, will avail for nothing, if there be not heart-detachment from the world and heart-attachment to the Lord Jesus Christ, leading to holiness of life and self-judgment. Only thus can we keep in any measure the unity of the Spirit in the bond of peace.

# CHAPTER VII

## RESTORING ORDER

THE greater part of this chapter from verse 6 to the end, consists of the register of the genealogy, which has already been considered in our study of the book of Ezra (chap. 2), and which we need not again go over here.

This might seem to leave very little that is new for our present concern; but a careful examination of the five opening verses will reveal much on which we may meditate with profit, as being of marked importance at the present serious moment of our history as saints and servants of God and of our Lord Jesus Christ. The more Nehemiah's record is examined, the more it will be seen that every sentence is pregnant with instruction for these closing days of the dispensation of grace. "Written aforetime," they were, nevertheless, "written for our learning;" and we shall be blessed indeed if we carefully appropriate and earnestly practise the lessons they convey to us.

"Now it came to pass, when the wall was built, and I had set up the doors, and the porters and the singers and the Levites were appointed, that I gave my brother Hanani, and Hananiah the ruler of the palace, charge over Jerusalem; for he was a faithful man, and feared God above many" (vers. 1, 2). There are several matters of moment to occupy us in these two verses. The wall, we have seen, speaks of separation—both *from* the world and its evil, and *to* the Lord, the God of Israel. The gates speak, not of unscriptural exclusion that has no heart for those who are of the one family, but of fellowship, admitting to the privileges to be enjoyed within the walls all who have divine title to enter, and barring out all others. And this suggests the importance of Nehemiah's appointment of *porters,* or gate-keepers. He was not indifferent as to who came or went. The business of the porters was to act as watchmen of the gates, permitting only such to come inside as could give evidence of their right so to do.

In applying this to the ordering of the Christian assembly, it is easy to see what an important place the porter occupies. Suppose a company of believers, gathered to the name of the Lord Jesus Christ, in separation from worldly and ecclesiastical evil: how long will its purity and holy character be maintained if people are allowed to come and go as they will without true, godly care as to their new birth, their behavior, the doctrines that they bring, or the associations they go on with? Hence the need of the sometimes unpleasant service of the porter.

I do not mean that certain ones should be appointed as inquisitors of those applying for fellowship; rather, that all should be duly exercised before God as to who are received to the holy and exalted privileges of Christian fellowship. In the breaking and eating of the loaf, and the drinking of the cup, we not only set forth the Lord's death, and fellowship with Him who thus gave Himself for us, but we thereby manifest our communion or fellowship with those participating with us in this solemn observance. And how can there be fellowship if there be not confidence and unity? Therefore the folly of declaring that, "We examine no one: each must judge himself: none are accountable to others."

Such principles are subversive of Christian communion. We are called upon to discern those who, with us, partake at the table of the Lord. "If any man that is called a brother be a fornicator, or covetous, or an idolator, or a railer, or a drunkard, or an extortioner, with such an one" we are commanded "not to eat" (1 Cor. 5: 11). But must we not then examine those called brothers if we are to be obedient to this scripture? And again, "If there come any unto you, and bring not this doctrine" (*i. e.*, the doctrine of Christ), we are told to "receive him not into your house, nor greet him, for he that greeteth him is partaker of his evil deeds" (2 John 10, 11, N.T.). But if the gates be left wide open, and the porter asleep, or off duty, who shall hinder persons—either themselves bringing the evil teaching, or contaminated by known association with it—forcing their way in, to the defilement of the whole company? Hence the need of godly care in receiving to Christian fellowship.

It is sometimes said, "We receive all who are Christ's." But do any really mean this? Who dares pronounce as to those who are Christ's? "The Lord knoweth them that are His" (2 Tim. 2: 19). We make a great mistake when we attempt to give oracular decisions as to so momentous a matter. We are only called upon to examine the profession, the life, the doctrine, and, as a matter of course, the associations of the applicant for fellowship. Even then, when all due care has been exercised, a self-deceived one, or a deceiver, may be unwittingly permitted to creep in (Jude 4), to cause serious trouble later; but if there were no porter-service at all, who can conceive the state of things that would soon exist! The world itself is not so foolish as to leave its ports of entry unguarded. It is certainly far easier to allow any who desire to come in unchallenged; but it is neither for their blessing nor the peace of the assembly, not to speak of the glory of the Lord. So it would have been easier in Nehemiah's day to have opened the gates at dawn and left them open till nightfall, with no watchful porter to question persons desiring to enter; but in that case how much of the work we have been considering would have gone for nothing!

The porter at the gate was therefore a person

of great importance in Jerusalem, and only dis-
creet and cautious men should have performed
this service. And what answers to this in the
Christian assembly is the exercise of godly,
thoughtful care as to who are permitted to share
in the holy things committed to the people of
God. Fellowship is worth too much to be frittered
away by mere sentimentality. It has been said,
"Eternal vigilance is the price of liberty"—and
we might say it of Christian fellowship also,
which is soon dissipated if the porter's service is
overlooked.

The second order established by Nehemiah was
that of the *singers*. And they too may give occasion for fruitful meditation. The spirit of
praise is the spirit of power. A rejoicing assembly will be one where God is free to work, and
will become a channel of blessing to those without. In Israel the singers were a distinct company, separated from the body of the people. But
the New Testament contemplates no such incongruity as a choir—surpliced or otherwise—to lead
the praises of the assembly. The Lord Jesus
Himself is the Leader, and all believers are exhorted to "sing with the spirit and with the understanding also." "Speaking to yourselves in
psalms, and hymns, and spiritual songs, singing
and making melody in your heart unto the Lord;
giving thanks always for all things unto God and
the Father in the name of our Lord Jesus Christ"
(Eph. 5: 19, 20). "Let the word of Christ dwell

in you richly in all wisdom; teaching and admonishing one another; in psalms and hymns and spiritual songs, singing with grace in your hearts unto the Lord" (Col. 3:16). In these verses we have clearly set forth the singers, the song, and the accompaniment. All believers are the choristers. The accompaniment is not the grand pipe organ or the delightsome orchestra, but something sweeter far in the ears of God—the melody that rises from a heart filled with His grace.

We may distinguish psalms from hymns. The former would more properly be expressions of praise. To praise is to psalm. (See Ps. 105:2, *margin*). A hymn is rather an ascription of the perfections of Deity ; it expresses the highest point of worship, magnifying God, not because of His works in our behalf, but of His matchless perfections. A spiritual song would be different from either of these. It might be a recital of God's ways or of the believer's experience.*

When gathered in assembly we come together as singers. There the Lord takes His place in the midst to lead our worship and praise, as it is written, "In the midst of the assembly will I sing praise unto Thee" (Heb. 2:12). Thus, as occupied with Him, His death and the fruit resulting therefrom, praise well becomes each saint.

---

* Those who are accustomed to the "Little Flock Hymn Book" might see in No. 235 a typical psalm; in No. 150, an almost matchless hymn; while No. 139 is a good example of a spiritual song.

This is not to legislate against every other spiritual exercise, but it is surely what is characteristic.

And now we turn to consider the third class mentioned in the first verse. These are the Levites, or ministering servants of God. Of old one tribe alone were Levites. But in this dispensation, just as all gathered saints have porter-responsibility upon them, and all are to be singers, so all are servants. "To every man his work" is the Lord's word for each. But Levite-service may also speak of public ministry, and this of course is not general, but a special responsibility placed upon those who have been gifted accordingly— yea, who are themselves gifts given to the assembly for the edification of the body of Christ.

Such service must be exercised in direct responsibility to the Lord. The Church does not appoint ministers of the Word. Christ as Head alone appoints, and by the Spirit qualifies. The Church tests those who come as ministers by the message they bring, comparing it with the word of God. If it be according to what is there revealed it must be accepted. If contrary to the teaching of Scripture, both teacher and doctrine are to be refused.

There is room in every scripturally-gathered company of saints for all divinely-given ministry. The true Levite will find a welcome there. But, after all is said and done, there is no infallible court on earth that can decide whether or no a man is a gift to the assembly. The only rule is that of Prov. 18: 16: "A man's gift maketh room for him." Hence, if one fancies he is called to expound the Word, and his ministry is not appreciated, he need not abuse the saints, but should rather consider that among them at least his gift has not made room. He may be a minister to others, but not to them. If assured of his divine call, let him patiently go elsewhere; but let him also carefully consider whether he may not be boasting himself of a false gift, and so cause shame at last, because of the emptiness of his ministry (Prov. 25: 14). To serve as a Levite in this special sense, one must be in living touch with God, speaking from a full heart of what has stirred his own soul; otherwise his ministry will be barren and profitless. We shall see the Levites doing their God-appointed service in the interesting scenes of the next chapter.

In the second verse now before us we read of two men placed over Jerusalem. We may be assured it was not nepotism that led Nehemiah to appoint his own brother Hanani as one of these. To have done this because of relationship would have been most offensive. On the other hand relationship must not hinder when spiritual qualification is evident. Of Hananiah, his coadjutor in this service, it is said that "he was a faithful man, and one that feared God above many." Blessed words of commendation are these! Would that they might be rightfully applied to many more of us! What honor could be greater than to be designated faithful by the Lord Himself on His judgment-seat.

These last-mentioned men had authority over the porters, and to them Nehemiah commands: "Let not the gates of Jerusalem be opened until the sun be hot; and while they stand by, let them shut the doors, and bar them; and appoint watches of the inhabitants of Jerusalem, every one in his watch, and every one over against his house" (ver. 3).

Two things concern us here. First:—Entrance into the city was to be in broad daylight. People were not to be permitted to slip in, in the dark. This may have a voice for us. Let all assembly matters especially as concerning reception and excision be open and above-board: nothing underhanded or hidden should be tolerated. Second:—Watchfulness was still required of all. It was not enough to have official porters. All were to be watchmen for the good of all. "What I say unto you, I say unto all: Watch!" As long as we have anything to maintain for God down here we need to be on the watch—never off guard for a moment, lest our wily foe introduce what will cause lasting sorrow and disaster.

The city was large and great, we are told—that is, the space enclosed by the walls; but the people were few, and the houses were not builded. The wall enclosed all that had originally been marked off as the city of God. But the remnant were feeble, and care would be needed to maintain the place taken. In view of giving each one his proper portion Nehemiah now investigates the registry made when the first company came up. It was no new work he was engaged in. He is but carrying on what had been commenced some years before. The original record is therefore examined, and all ratified by the governor. As we have already gone over this register we need only refer the reader to the remarks made in the notes on the 2nd chapter of Ezra.

Its appearance here shows how completely Nehemiah had identified himself with the work which the Spirit of God had wrought through Zerubbabel and Joshua. He was one with them, and together they sought the glory of the God of Israel. Let this have a voice for all who have ears to hear.

# CHAPTER VIII

## THE GREAT BIBLE-READING

IN every genuine revival among God's people the revealed Word of the Lord has had a large place. It was so in Josiah's day, and in the awakening under Hezekiah. It has been so throughout the Church period. It was the recovery of the Word that brought about the Reformation of the 16th century, and every true awakening since has been based upon Bible study and Bible practice. Of no spiritual movement in history could this more truthfully be said than of that special work of God which began almost simultaneously in many parts of Great Britain and Ireland in the first half of the 19th century. Here and there little companies of devoted believers were found gathering together to search the Scriptures, seeking a right way for themselves and their children in the midst of the existing ecclesiastical confusion and dead formality. To them was revealed from the Word that Christ Jesus is the one Centre of gathering, that the Church is one body in which the Holy Spirit dwells and which He is to guide. Thus disowning everything for which they could find neither a plain "Thus saith the Lord" nor a simple divine principle exemplified in Scripture, they turned away from all sects and systems to be known only as brethren in Christ, members of His body, seeking to walk in subjection to the Holy Spirit. For such, these remnant books are full of important and much-needed instruction. They have failed—failed grievously and openly— as did the restored Jews of old; but the same resource remains for these as for those—the abiding, unerring word of God. And it is this that is so strikingly set forth in our chapter. There are seven things here brought to our notice, and I desire to write of them in order.

First, it is a united people waiting on God. This is what verse 1 suggests. "All the people gathered themselves together as one man into the open place that was before the Water Gate." We have already observed that the Water Gate intimates something of the cleansing, refreshing, reviving power of the word of God. What more fitting place for a company of people to be in who are seeking divine instruction than "the open place before the Water Gate?" Depend upon it, God will never disappoint His saints when thus before Him. Of old He said to Moses, "Gather the people *together,* and I will give them water" (Num. 21: 16). And in a higher sense will that word ever be fulfilled when His people are with one mind and one heart gathered together to learn His will from His all-sufficient Word.

In the second place we hear the cry, "Bring the Book!" Verse 1 goes on to say, "And they spake unto Ezra the scribe to *bring the book* of

the law of Moses, which the Lord had commanded to Israel." People may sneer and call this
*bibliolatry* if they will. Worship of the book it
is *not*. It is rather the acknowledgement that
the Author of the Book is the all-wise and all-
sufficient One who has so given His Word as to
make it a safe guide in every time of confusion.
What was it that freed the people of the Lord in
the middle ages and overthrew the power of
Rome? It was the response to this same cry,
"Bring the Book!" And whenever or wherever
God's children are thus ready to hear His Word
and do it, there must be blessing and divine il-
lumination.

Mark, they did not seek Ezra's opinion, nor the
ideas of Nehemiah, nor yet those of Zerubbabel.
They honored these servants of God, and rightfully so; they would have despised the Master if
they had not reverenced His sent ones; but the
servants were to be ministers of the Word—not
of science or philosophy, nor yet of theology—
but of the word of the living God; hence the cry,
"Bring the Book!"

It is a grievous thing when merely human writings or words are put upon a level with the
Book of books. One dreads the use often made
of esteemed brethren's writings. Something is
called in question, and at once there is a great
effort made to show that Mr. So-and-So taught
thus, or Mr. Somebody else has written this or
the other. In this way the authority of the word

of God is weakened in men's souls, and people
are content if they think they hold what Mr. A.
or Mr. B. held, even though they are quite unable
to find authority for it in the book of God. This
is a snare of which we need to be watchful lest
we find ourselves once more teaching for doctrines
the commandments of men.

Thirdly, we learn that when Ezra brought the
book, "He read therein before the street that was
before the Water Gate from the morning until
midday, before the men and the women, and those
that could understand; and the ears of all the
people were attentive unto the book of the law"
(ver. 3). This is most blessed—an attentive people solemnized by the word of God. So great was
the company that a pulpit of wood was erected
for Ezra, and on his right and left were companies of devoted Levites waiting to hear the
Word and explain it to the people. It was a day
when books were not easily multiplied. Perhaps
Ezra had the only Bible there was in all the land;
but in the manner indicated it was made the common property of all the people.

Subjection to the Word is the fourth point
that comes prominently before us in verses 5 to 8.
"Ezra opened the book in the sight of all the people (for he was above all the people); and when
he opened it, all the people stood up: and Ezra
blessed the Lord, the great God. And all the
people answered, Amen, Amen, with lifting up
their hands; and they bowed their heads, and wor-

shiped the Lord with their faces to the ground."
Who that has any conscience at all can fail to be
touched by the reverence thus shown for the word
of God? Such a Bible-reading was no free and
easy, carnal coming together to argue over certain
doctrines or debate intricate questions to the be-
wilderment of the simple, and the spiritual harm
of the more advanced. Neither was it a place for
some leader to shine, and to have his interpre-
tations received without question as the mind of
the Lord. This great Bible-reading was marked
by a holy subjection to God and a hallowed reverence for His Word that contrasts strikingly with
modern flippancy and irreverence in handling holy
things.

To minister the Word to such a company must
have been both a great joy and a solemn responsibility for Ezra and the Levites as they "caused
the people to understand the law, and the people
stood in their place. So they read in the book in
the law of God distinctly, and gave the sense,
and caused them to understand the reading" (vers.
7, 8). It needs to be borne in mind that, after
the captivity, Hebrew, as a spoken language, had
largely been displaced by Aramaic, hence the need
of carefully explaining the Hebrew words to the
waiting people.

Fifthly, the word of God as a source of joy and
refreshment. This is what is suggested in the
next section, verses 9 to 12: "And Nehemiah,
that is the Tirshatha [or, governor], and Ezra

the priest the scribe, and the Levites that taught
the people, said unto all the people, This day is
holy unto the Lord your God: mourn not, nor
weep. For all the people wept when they heard
the words of the law." Their awakened consciences told them how guilty they and their fathers had been in refusing to obey the word of
God; but their tears of penitence testified to the
self-judgment that was going on; and, with God,
sin judged is sin put away. Hence the cheering
words of verse 10. "Then he said unto them, Go
your way, eat the fat, and drink the sweet, and
send portions unto them for whom nothing is prepared; for this day is holy unto our Lord: neither
be ye sorry; for the joy of the Lord is your
strength." God loves to surround Himself with a
holy, happy people; but the two things of necessity go together. Holiness and happiness are inseparable. Who can fail to see in what is here
before us a striking picture, often fulfilled, when
God has visited His people in giving them bread?
Refreshed and edified themselves, they become
channels of blessing to others, sharing gladly with
those "for whom nothing is prepared."

"So the Levites stilled all the people, saying,
Hold your peace, for the day is holy, neither be
ye grieved. And all the people went their way
to eat and to drink, and to send portions, and to
make great mirth, because they had understood
the words that were declared unto them" (vers.
11, 12). How much deeper the joy to-day, in the

light of a full gospel, when saints gather about a risen Christ, and His word is brought home to each heart in the Spirit's power, leading to similar exercises and lifting-up before God.

It is of *obedience* to the Word that the sixth section speaks. On the second day the chiefs of the people came together again, and the reading of the Word was continued. On this occasion a notable discovery was made: "They found written...that the children of Israel should dwell in booths in the feast of the seventh month" (ver. 14). Now this was at once recognized as a challenge to obedience. Here was something which had been *unobserved for a thousand years*—and still it was in the Book! Verse 17 shows us that in the palmiest days of David and Solomon no attention had been paid to this particular precept. "Since the days of Joshua the son of Nun unto that day had not the children of Israel done so." To obey it required considerable inconvenience; they might have argued that what Samuel, David, Solomon and others had overlooked was surely non-essential; but "they found it written," and that settled it for an obedient people. So the whole company went out to the mountains, and brought olive, pine, myrtle and palm branches and made booths, "as it is written," and in these they dwelt, thus calling to mind the days of God's care for His pilgrim people in the wilderness: "And there was very great gladness." What a lovely example of unquestioning obedience to the Word!

And so we come to the seventh thought, in closing our somewhat rapid survey of the chapter: The word of God is all-sufficient for every experience of life. "Also day by day, from the first day unto the last day, he read in the book of the law of God. And they kept the feast seven days; and on the eighth day was a solemn assembly, according to the manner" (ver. 18). Those seven days looked on to the Kingdom, when the Lord shall be surrounded by a happy, redeemed people, the *eighth* day bringing an outlook into eternity. Throughout Time the word of God contains all His people need for spiritual food and daily guidance.

Oh, for grace ever to hide that Word in our hearts, thus to be kept from sin, and to have our steps ordered accordingly, and every thought brought into captivity to the obedience of Christ!

# CHAPTER IX

THE relations of the word of God and prayer come out vividly in this portion. The seven days' ministry of the Word had had a most blessed effect so that "in the twenty and fourth day of this month (the same month that was ushered in by the great Bible-reading) the children of Israel were assembled with fasting, and with sack-clothes, and earth upon them. And the seed of Israel separated themselves from all strangers, and stood and confessed their sins, and the iniquities of their fathers. And they stood up in their place, and read in the book of the law of the Lord their God one fourth part of the day; and another fourth part they confessed, and worshiped the Lord their God" (vers. 1-3).

The order here is most instructive. It was *first* the Word, then prayer, confession, and worship. The Word had been having its effect in a wonderfully real way since the seven days' feast. What that Word judged, they had been judging. What that Word commanded they had sought to do. Hence we have as a result the remnant reaching what was probably the highest moral state they ever occupied from the Babylonian captivity to the coming of Messiah. Their separation was complete. "They separated themselves from *all* strangers." It was now for the first time that position and condition seemed to coalesce.

And so they come together again desiring to learn more of the mind of God that it might lead to increased devotedness. So the Bible-reading is again prominent. The first quarter of the day is spent in hearing the Word. Then the next quarter is given up to prayer: "They confessed and worshiped the Lord their God." It is unwise, and may be hurtful, to reverse this order. The Word and prayer should ever go together— but it should be the Word first; then prayer follows intelligently. The believer should be a man holding the even balance of learning from the Word and cultivating the spirit of prayer. We need to hear God speaking to us that we may speak rightly to God.

One who gives himself pre-eminently to the Word, neglecting prayer, will become heady and doctrinal—likely to quarrel about "points," and be occupied with theoretical Christianity to the hurt of his soul and the irritation of his brethren. On the other hand, one who gives himself much to prayer while neglecting the Word is likely to become exceedingly introspective, mystical, and sometimes fanatical. But he who reads the word of God reverently and humbly, seeking to know the will of God, and then gives himself to prayer, confessing and judging what the Scriptures have condemned in his ways, and words, and thoughts, will have his soul drawn out in worship also, and thus grow both in grace and in knowledge, becoming a well-rounded follower of Christ. Apart from a knowledge of the Word, prayer will lack exceedingly in intelligence; for the objective must ever precede the subjective, but not be divorced therefrom.

Here, in Nehemiah 9 (which as we have elsewhere noticed is linked, in confession, with Daniel 9 and Ezra 9), the Levites lead the people in their prayer and praise, standing "on the stairs," as though going up to the heavenly sanctuary. And in the prayer that follows—the longest in the Bible (Solomon's dedicatory prayer being considerably shorter)—there is much blessed instruction as we listen to the rehearsal of God's ways with their fathers and the confession of their own failure and sin.

The opening words remind us of the beginning of what is generally called the Lord's prayer—and of what should occupy a pre-eminent place in *all prayer*—"Hallowed be Thy Name." The Levites called on all the people to stand up and bless the Eternal One, their God, whose glorious name is exalted above all blessing and praise. To Him alone creation is ascribed and, as though testifying against the idolatry all about them that led the nations to worship and serve the creature rather than the Creator, they acknowledge that "all the host of heaven worship Him." He it was who had chosen Abram, bringing him out of the Chaldees, making him in very deed to answer to his new name Abraham—"the father of a multitude." To him the promise of the land of Canaan was given which in due course was fulfilled in his seed—multitudinous as the sand of the sea, brought out of Egyptian bondage, led through the sea and the wilderness by the cloudy pillar, first to the mount of God and then to the land of promise (vers. 4-12).    The Levites celebrated the giving of the law at Sinai; and it is of moment to notice that they declare it was then —and not before — that the holy Sabbath was made known to them (ver. 14). This would seem conclusive evidence that whereas God sanctified the seventh day at the completion of His work, as recorded in the second chapter of Genesis, He did not give it to man by command until He had a redeemed people gathered about Himself in the wilderness.  It was a sign, or reminder, not alone of God's rest after the creative days, but of the deliverance of Israel from Egyptian bondage, and the pledge of a rest yet to come.

After celebrating the mighty acts of the Lord, the Levites go on to confess the fearful breakdown of the people, and that from the very first. Their fathers dealt proudly, and in place of recognizing their dependence on this mighty Deliverer who had wrought so wondrously on their behalf, they hardened their necks and harkened not to His commandments—in their rebellion desiring even to return to the very land of bondage from which He had taken them.  Their wilderness history was a most humbling record, full of evidences of their folly, and yet abounding with testimonies of Jehovah's faithfulness, who sustained them through all those forty years "so that they lacked nothing; their clothes waxed not old, and their feet swelled not" (vers. 13-21). And when at last they reached the land given by covenant to Abraham, the nations therein were rooted out before them and they themselves planted in their place; there they multiplied and grew, rejoicing in the abundance of the fruitful fields of Canaan, and delighting themselves in the great goodness of their covenant-keeping God (vers. 22-25).

But disobedience and rebellion characterized them almost from the days of Joshua, and God's holy law they cast behind their back, despising His precepts and slaying His prophets, when such were sent to show them their sin and call them back to subjection to His word. When, in their distresses, they cried to Him He granted them deliverance—not for their deserts, but for His own name's sake, according to His mercies; thus again and again manifesting His tender love and care.

Yet scarcely had He interposed on their behalf than they turned aside as before, sinning against His judgments (that is, the testimonies rendered), "which if a man do he shall live in them," thus fighting against His Holy Spirit who spake in the prophets; until, at last, the kings of Assyria and Babylonia were permitted to root them out of their inheritance, carrying them captive to the land of the stranger.

The Levites own the justice of all God's dealings with the nation. "Thou hast done right, but we have done wickedly," is their humble acknowledgment. And they go on to confess how their kings, princes, priests and fathers had not kept the law, nor harkened to His commandments, nor turned from their wicked works; and so they remained bondmen to that very day, subject to the kings of Persia; even though a little reviving had been granted them, and they had been gathered once more at God's centre. Now, bearing in mind all the evil consequences of disobedience in the past, they made a "sure covenant" (alas, again to be soon broken!) and, putting it in writing, signed and sealed it; pledging themselves to cleave to the Lord, to separate from all strangers, and faithfully to do His will (vers. 33-38).

That they were truly in earnest none can doubt, but the future would show once more, as the past so often had done, that man is not to be trusted, and that were God's covenant based on human faithfulness, instead of divine grace, all hope for man's lasting blessing would be vain.

Yet it is well to have such seasons of exercise as this which we have been contemplating. Undoubtedly, it was for many a step forward, which they never retraced, although for the nation, as such, there could be no full restoration till the advent of God's Anointed.

# CHAPTER X

## THE NEW START

I T is both true and false (according to the thought one has in mind) that God never restores a failed testimony. If by this expression, frequently heard at the present time, it be meant that failure having once blighted a movement that originally was of God, it will never again reach its pristine glory, the statement is undoubtedly true. But if it be meant that, ruin having come in, God will not answer the cry of repentance with revival and restoration when His face is earnestly sought, it is utterly false. It is to be feared that it is spiritual lethargy and an unwillingness to bestir oneself and seriously face existing conditions, which are the real causes why many once gathered to the name of Jesus now go on in isolation, blaming the divisions and lack of spirituality evidenced by others as the reason for their having left the path of subjection to God's revealed will as to the corporate testimony of His people.

To such, what we have just been considering ought to speak loudly. Things had got indeed very low among the remnant. Their actual condition had become most dishonoring to God. Nevertheless their position was a right one, and nothing could be gained by forsaking it. The important thing was to remain where they were, and seek to put away all that hindered their enjoyment of the Lord's favor, that thus their state individually and corporately might be approved of Him.

So we have seen them turning unitedly to the Word, earnestly inquiring as to what God had said, and when "they found it written," acting upon it, though it meant, as in many instances it did, bitter sorrow and painful humiliation.

Having pledged themselves (in accord with the spirit of the legal dispensation) to put away all strangers and to walk obediently before God, they drew up a written declaration, signing and sealing it, from Nehemiah the Governor down to the lowest in rank of the common people, "all they that had separated themselves from the people of the lands unto the law of God, their wives, their sons, and their daughters, every one having knowledge, and having understanding" (vers. 1-28).

It was a serious, solemn and definite thing they had undertaken, and it would require purpose of heart to carry it out. "They clave to their brethren, their nobles, and entered into a curse, and into an oath, to walk in God's law, which was given by Moses the servant of God, and to observe and do all the commandments of Jehovah our Lord, and His judgments and His statutes; and that we would not give our daughters unto the peoples of the land, nor take their daughters for our sons: and if the peoples of the land bring ware or any victuals on the Sabbath day to sell, that we would not buy it of them on the Sabbath, or on the holy day: and that we would leave the seventh year, and the exaction of every debt" (vers. 29-31).

Notice carefully what it was they had covenanted to do—

First: To walk in God's law; or, in other words, to be subject to the Holy Scriptures. Second (and of course all that followed was involved in the first) : To maintain separation from the peoples of the land that there be no unequal yoke. Third: To honor God by a careful observance of the Sabbath day, not permitting greed or lust for strangers' dainties to lead them to violate its sacredness. Fourth: To let the land lie fallow every seventh year, for disobedience to which command they had of old been carried to Babylon, while for seventy years the land kept Sabbath. Fifth: To deal graciously with each other as brethren, leaving the exaction of every debt, not acting in the spirit of the usurer.

Are there not weighty lessons for us in these pledges? I mean for those who have sought to give Christ His place as Head, and to act on the truth of the oneness of the body of Christ, but who have so miserably failed to keep the Spirit's unity in the bond of peace. Wherein have we missed our way? Has it not been in what is here set forth in Old Testament language? Must we not confess that we have not been obedient to the word of our God? We prided ourselves on having taken a right position—directed thereto by the Word—but we have not been careful to be individually subject to that Word. Is it not a fact that to many the "voice of the assembly" has been louder than the voice of God in Holy Scripture? Is it not a fact that the traditions of the elders have, in critical times, been more relied on than "Thus saith the Lord?" Is it not time then that, as individuals and as gathered companies of saints, we go back to the simplicity of early days, and seek to be guided henceforth alone by the word of the Lord which abideth forever?

And have we not, likewise, greatly missed the truth of separation? Have we not often been quite satisfied in that we were separated ecclesiastically from the world-church, while socially and in our business relations we were linked up with the world to an even greater extent than many not outwardly separated as we? Has not the spirit of the world come into our homes and assemblies? Is it not manifest in the books we enjoy, the clothing we wear, the company we frequent, the language we use? What is mere ecclesiastical separation if we are otherwise so much linked with the world?

And is it not true that, when we have been somewhat aroused as to this, we have enjoined strictest separation from saints often more godly than ourselves, instead of from the spirit of the present age of evil? Has it not often happened that saints of God have been passed by or coldly greeted because of some difference in judgment as to a disciplinary question difficult to determine righteously, while utter worldlings have been given every evidence of affection? These are serious questions that had better be faced now than at the judgment-seat of Christ.

We know that, as we are not under law but under grace, the Sabbath of a past dispensation is now for us fulfilled in Christ, but are we then giving Christ His place, and not permitting our greed for gain or our lust after earth's pleasant things to break in upon that Sabbath-rest we should ever enjoy in Him? Can our business affairs always bear the test of His eyes that are as a flame of fire? Have we one weight for testing sacred things and another for what we call secular affairs? May there not be cause for exercise as to these matters? And may it not be that right here is one reason for our leanness?

And what of the seventh year? It was this "leaving the seventh year" that really showed that Israel were a people confiding in the living God. "To live by faith" is often spoken of as though it were the calling or prerogative of those separated to the ministry of the Word. But are not *all* believers called to live by faith—to hold things here with a loose grasp, but lay hold on eternal life as the one thing needful? And have we been largely forgetting this, and contenting ourselves with "gathering on divine ground," "scripturally breaking bread," "maintaining the testimony," and all the rest of what is merely outward and ecclesiastical, while losing our grip on eternal realities and living as though this world were by far the more important of the two? Is it any wonder then that when matters arise among us calling for the exercise of spiritual discernment and godly judgment we are found wanting, and what should be for the unifying of the saints becomes the means of their scattering?

And this brings us to the fifth pledge: What about the exaction of every debt? Have we not been hard and exacting and over-much righteous with one another, alienating those we ought to have drawn with cords of love, and demanding of each other what subjects of grace should be ashamed to press? Surely, as before intimated, it is high time to "leave off this usury."

The end of the dispensation is fast approaching. The Judge is standing at the door. The Lord is looking on, close at hand. The word of God is being given up and its truth denied on every hand. It is high time that those who love that Word cease their exactions one of another, and all alike judging everything that has hindered fellowship, put away for ever the evil things that have wrought such havoc, and so stand shoulder to shoulder, heart to heart, and hand in hand, for God and His truth with all who seek to be loyal to Him and His Word in the little time that remains ere "the coming of our Lord Jesus Christ and our gathering together unto Him."

On the rest of the chapter I have few remarks to offer. Judging the evil, the remnant sought, so far as they might, to put things in order in regard to providing for and maintaining the service of the house of God, giving of their firstfruits and tithes that there might be abundance to carry on the ministry and to support the ministers. Depend upon it, if the Lord's people get right individually, that which is corporate will flourish, and there will be abundant provision for maintaining a visible testimony. Lack of spirituality closes up hearts and purses. Godliness opens both. The poverty of the people was no barrier when their consciences were in exercise, and they determined "not to forsake the house of their God" (vers. 32-39). And so will it ever be where the love of Christ reigns.

Apart from this all must degenerate more and more until all testimony for God is gone. One who knew and suffered much as standing for "the present truth" left behind seasonable words of warning with which I bring this portion to a close.

"What is important is not 'The Brethren,' but the truth they have...God could set them aside, and spread His truth by others—would, I believe, though full of gracious patience, if they be not faithful. Their place is to remain in obscurity and devotedness, not to think of Brethren (it is always wrong to think of ourselves), but of souls, in Christ's name and love, and of His glory.

"Let them walk in love, in the truth, humble, as little (and content to be little) as when they began, and God will bless them. If not, their candlestick may go as that of others—and oh, what sorrow and confusion of face it would be after such grace!...

"As regards also the activity outside them, it is one of the signs of the times, and they should rejoice in it ...But it does not give their testimony at all...I do not believe attacks on anything to be our path. Self-defence is every way to be avoided. The Lord will answer for us if we do His will...God has no need of us, but He has need of a people who walk in the truth, in love, and holiness. 'I will leave in the midst of thee an afflicted and poor people, and they shall trust in the name of Jehovah' (Zeph. 3: 12).

"The gospel we may, and must, rejoice in; yet it only makes the testimony of Brethren outside the camp more necessary than ever; but it must be real...If brethren fall in with the current Christianity inside the camp, they would be but another sect with certain truths"— *J. N. D.*

In the light of much that has transpired one can almost hear the voice of prophecy in such words. Beloved brethren, let us one and all heed their serious message.

# CHAPTER XI

T HE Bridegroom in the Canticles says: "I went down into the garden of nuts to see the fruits of the valley, and to see whether the vine flourished, and the pomegranates budded. Or ever I was aware, my soul set me among the chariots of my willing people" (Song 6: 11, 12; 1911 *Version*) ; and in psalm 110: 3 we read, "Thy people shall be willing (or, a free-will offering) in the day of Thy power, in the beauties of holiness from the womb of the morning: thou hast the dew of thy youth."

Words like these form a fitting introduction to the chapter now soliciting our thoughtful consideration—a passage that seems to be filled only with hard names and meagre details if the important truth be passed over that it is God's own inspired honor-roll, never to be forgotten, of His willing people. Then indeed we recognize in it such a delightful valley as that described in the Song, where the vine is flourishing and the fragrant pomegranates budding for the delectation of Him who rejoices to dwell among His willing-hearted saints — made willing by His power working among them, manifested in holiness of heart and life, engendered and refreshed by the precious dews of the Holy Spirit.

A free-will offering was made, not now of money or other means, but of men devoted to the Lord, to dwell in Jerusalem, that the holy city might be furnished and defended. "And the rulers of the people dwelt at Jerusalem: the rest of the people also cast lots, to bring one of ten to dwell in Jerusalem the holy city, and nine parts to dwell in other cities. And the people blessed all the men that willingly offered themselves to dwell at Jerusalem" (vers. 1, 2). As before they had tithed their produce and possessions, so now they tithed themselves. But it was not conscription; for each one chosen responded with a free heart, glad thus to be especially linked with the defence and up-building of the city of the Name. They loved the place where God's honor dwelt, and they were pleased to be at home there.

Of old, in the wilderness, it was the "willing-hearted and the wise-hearted" who built the sanctuary of the Lord; and may we not say that the willing-hearted *are* the wise-hearted? For surely it is the evidence of wisdom abiding in the heart when the whole life is freely devoted to the service of the Lord. And so when the evil had been put away from among the remnant of the Jews, and the interests of Jehovah had been made paramount to every other interest it was the free and loyal service of His willing people that gave joy to the heart of God.

To most of us, perhaps, the details that follow in the balance of the chapter can, in the very nature of things, possess very little interest. It is a mere tabulation of families and individuals whose names to us are often well-nigh unpronounceable, and usually, forgotten almost as soon as read. But in the sight of God it is a tabulation of great importance, and, like other lists we have noticed in these post-captivity books, will be consulted at the judgment-seat of Christ. For these willing offerers shall then learn how good was their choice when they accepted loss in this world that they might the better care for the city of God's choice. Very little is said of these members of the tribes of Judah and Benjamin (vers. 4-9), and of Levi also who dwelt in Jerusalem (vers. 10-18), but every one is well known to the Lord, and every word and act that told their devotedness of heart to Himself will be manifested in that day. And, even now, where scholarship enables one to read something of the significance of these names, there are doubtless helpful lessons which for the present most of us fail to see.

The porters and servants (the "Nethinim"), yea, and the singers too—true sons of Asaph set "over the business of the house of God" who had their special portion by the king's commandment (vers. 19-23)—will all be called by name when Messiah sits upon His throne to reward every one who in every dispensation had respect unto the coming recompense. For it was just as truly a service for some to till the fields and dwell in the restored villages, thus holding all the land for

God, so far as strength and numbers permitted, as it was for their willing-hearted brethren to abide in the city of the coming King (vers. 25-36). He valued all according to the intention of the heart, and He does the same to-day.

We would not therefore pass carelessly over what some might call so "dry" a chapter as this, but reading it thoughtfully and prayerfully let us challenge our own hearts as to how far we have been and are now characterized by the spirit of willing, joyous obedience to all that God has been pleased to make known to us concerning His holy desires. Words need not be multiplied on such a theme; but exercise may well be real and deep, lest in that day, when the record of *our* service is opened on high, there be only a blotted story of slothful, almost forced obedience, contrasting unfavorably indeed with the willing offering of these men of old.

In view of this may we be stirred up to heed the Christian poet's words:

> "Go on; go on; there's all eternity to rest in,
>     And far too few are on the *active service list;*
> No labor for the Lord is risky to invest in;
>     But nothing will make up should His 'Well
>     done' be missed."

# CHAPTER XII

## THE DEDICATION OF THE WALL

I T will be remembered that in the duplicate lists of those who first came up to Jerusalem under Zerubbabel and Joshua the high priest (or Jeshua, as he is here called), the families only of the priests were mentioned, not the names of the chief priests themselves. That lack is supplied in the opening verses of the present chapter (vers. 1-7). God would have these men in everlasting remembrance, who so efficiently fulfilled their service with true-hearted devotion. The chief of the Levites are also mentioned, though of these we have read before in chapters 8: 7 and 9: 4, 5. A later generation of priests, serving doubtless in the latter days of Nehemiah, is given in verses 12 to 21, the sons of those referred to above, faithful men walking in their fathers' footsteps, and ensamples to the people.

But in the intervening verses (10 and 11) we have a short genealogical list carrying down the line of Jeshua for five generations to Jaddua, the great and justly-celebrated high priest who held this supreme office in the days when the Persian dominion was overthrown by Alexander the Great.

There can, I think, be no question as to this table having been added by a later hand, which the Holy Spirit was pleased to use to preserve the record of Jaddua's descent. Verse 22 must have been added at the same time, declaring that a faithful record of the heads of the Levites had been kept to the days of Darius the Persian, whom I take to be Darius Codomanus, overthrown by the great Macedonian conqueror. It is possible indeed that the book of Malachi may have been written about that time, and that he may have added to the list, or the list itself. His solemn message shows us the sad condition into which the children of the remnant degenerated after the fathers had died.

Simple souls will not be confused or perplexed at the suggestion we have made above, if they bear in mind that the entire Old Testament was in the hands of the Jewish doctors in the days of our Lord's sojourn upon earth, and that concerning it all He declared, "The Scripture cannot be broken." It is not necessary therefore to know in each instance the human author of a book or part of a book. We know that "holy men of God spake as they were moved by the Holy Ghost," and thus we have in every part a "God-breathed" record, and that is enough.

It is evident from the next table (vers. 23-26) that both Nehemiah and Ezra lived through "the days of Joiakim the son of Jeshua," as well as in the days of the father, who accompanied Zerubbabel in the first emigration from Babylon. During their life-time the people clung to the word of God, and, with occasional individual lapses, such as we read of in the next chapter, maintained, on the whole, a testimony for the Lord who had brought them back, though in feebleness, to the place where He had set His name. Of the chief of the Levites (ver. 24) it is distinctly said that they were appointed both "to praise and to give thanks, according to the commandment of David the man of God, ward over against ward." The temple might be poor indeed as compared with Solomon's building, "exceeding magnifical," and the people themselves a small and afflicted remnant, but they sought to act on the divine instruction as to the service of the house of God which had been communicated by David to Solomon at the beginning. Likewise, whatever the feebleness to-day, it is the part of faithfulness to go back to "that which was from the beginning," and to endeavor, though in weakness, to carry out that which is written in the word of God.

The present chapter is divided into two almost equal parts, the first twenty-six verses belonging properly to chapter eleven, as being entirely composed of genealogical tables similar to those of the previous chapter. The second division continues the course of the history, and contains the account of the feast of the dedication of the now completed wall of Jerusalem. This was turned into a great occasion of rejoicing and thanksgiving to God, who had not only brought the people back from the strangers' land but had permitted them to surround His house and His holy city with a separating wall, testifying both to friends and enemies alike that they were under His care who had once scattered their nation because of unjudged sin.

From every quarter the Levites gathered "to keep the dedication with gladness, both with thanksgivings, and with singing, with cymbals, psalteries, and with harps" (ver. 27). It was a gladsome occasion indeed, and worthy of being joyously commemorated in coming years.

"The sons of the singers" were gathered together all about the city to participate in the general rejoicing. Jerusalem's wall was a symbol of salvation and her gates of praise.

After the priests and Levites had concluded a ceremony of purification, dedicating the people, the gates, and the wall to the Lord, Nehemiah brought up the princes of Judah upon the wall and divided all into two great companies, stretching out on the right and the left "toward the Dung Gate." With trumpets pealing out their notes of gladness and voices lifted up in songs of praise, the Levites and priests answered one another in antiphonal chants, after the manner of the 24th psalm, Nehemiah leading one company and Ezra the scribe the other. Thank-offerings were offered upon the altar, and "God made them rejoice with great joy"—as He always does when His people walk before Him in holiness and truth (vers. 31-43).

Nor were the servants of the Lord forgotten, for the people brought their tithes into the storehouse, and out of willing hearts gave abundantly for the maintenance of the sons of Aaron, in accordance with the Word (vers. 44-47).

One is reminded of the two-fold offering of Heb. 13 : 15, 16 : "By Him therefore let us offer the sacrifice of praise to God continually, that is, the fruit of our lips, giving thanks to His name. But to do good and to communicate, forget not: for with such sacrifices God is well pleased." These two offerings should never be divorced—thanksgiving going up to God from grateful hearts, and benevolence flowing forth toward men, the practical expression of that gratitude.

There is no surer indication of a low state in God's people than to find the poor among them left to suffer want, and the Lord's servants permitted to endure privation. These last are called to a path of trial, and must needs learn to be abased as well as to abound, to be full and to be empty; but whatever blessing they may find as they thus share Christ's sufferings, it is to the shame of the people of God, whose debtors they are. Were there more conscientious concern about this matter in many places, there would be richer and fuller ministry vouchsafed by God to His people, and more blessing in the assemblies of His saints, who often need to be reminded that:

> "It never was loving that emptied a heart,
> Nor giving that emptied a purse."

Let God be honored with the first-fruits of our substance, and He will soon prove that He will be no man's debtor, but will abundantly confirm the word spoken by Malachi the prophet: "Bring ye all the tithes into the storehouse, that there may be meat in my house, and prove Me now herewith, saith the Lord of hosts, if I will not open you the windows of heaven, and pour you out a blessing that there shall not be room enough to receive it. And I will rebuke the devourer for your sakes, and he shall not destroy the fruits of your ground; neither shall your vine cast her fruit before the time in the field, saith the Lord of hosts" (Mal. 3: 10, 11). That this illustrates a great spiritual truth is certain. That many have proven it to be intensely literal is equally sure. And it has been to the eternal loss of greater numbers who have failed in this very thing, and forgotten that they were only the stewards, not the owners, of wealth entrusted to them, to be used in view of the everlasting habitations.

# CHAPTER XIII

## VIGILANCE *versus* DECLENSION

THE striking contrast between the praise-worthy vigilance of Nehemiah in detecting and dealing with various phases of declension, and the continual tendency to drift away from obedience to the written Word, on the part of many of the people, is most marked in this closing chapter.

That serious evils soon developed is well known to the student of Jewish history. These were of two characters. On the one hand the separation truth of Nehemiah's day was soon held in a one-sided manner, so that position was everything and condition quite ignored. This resulted in Phariseeism—doctrinally correct in the main, but cold, rigid, and heartless—glorying in separation while ignoring the weightier matters of true piety and godly benevolence. On the other hand there was a re-action against all that savored of the puritanism of those days, so that the mass of the people became careless and indifferent, and, save that idolatry was never reinstated, became as impious as their fathers whose sins had brought the captivity. In all this we may well read a solemn warning, bidding us never separate condition from position, nor piety toward God from grace toward needy men.

Sanctification in its practical aspect is by the truth. Hence it is ever gradual—as the truth is learned in the fear of God. Of this we have a splendid example in the first nine verses. On the very day of the dedication of the wall (for so I understand the opening phrase), that portion of the book of Deuteronomy (chap. 23 : 3, 4) was read, which we have already quoted in our notes on chapter two, and which commanded that the Ammonite and the Moabite should be excluded from the congregation of the Lord forever because of their iniquitous course towards Israel in the wilderness. This at once led to a closer application of the truth of separation than before. They had previously separated from all strangers; now they "separated from Israel all the mixed multitude" (ver. 3).

Of Tobiah the Ammonite, who had so bitterly resented the building of the wall in the beginning, and whose wiles had failed to turn Nehemiah aside from his purpose, we have not heard for a long time. Now we get the startling information that Eliashib the priest, who had the oversight of the dwellings of the priests at the house of God, had made a secret alliance with Tobiah during a hitherto unnoticed absence of Nehemiah, in which time he had returned to wait upon the king. The vigilant governor's eye being no longer upon him, Eliashib abused his liberty by preparing "a great chamber" for the ungodly Ammonite, which had been formerly used as a

storehouse for the tithes and offerings. Probably
this apartment was never occupied by Tobiah, for,
ere Eliashib's plan could be fully carried out, Nehemiah returned. Hearing "of the evil that
Eliashib did for Tobiah in preparing him a chamber in the courts of the house of God," he was
sorely grieved, but acted with his accustomed energy, thwarting the unholy purpose by casting the
stuff of Tobiah out of the room and cleansing the
chambers, into which he again brought the hallowed vessels with the offerings. What an example for the people; nor do we again read of
any effort on the part of Tobiah to get a foothold
in Jerusalem.

But another evil soon claimed the returned
governor's attention. God's servants were being
neglected by a self-seeking people, and unable to
support those dependent upon them, the Levites
and the singers, who a little before had willingly
offered themselves for the service of the house
of God, had gone back to their fields, toiling for
daily bread. The test, doubtless, revealed a weakness in these men themselves, but it also showed
the declining state of the people in neglecting the
temporalities of the house of the Lord; so Nehemiah contends with the rulers, and stirs them
up to attend to the gathering of the unpaid tithes.
This being accomplished, the Levites could attend
on their service (vers. 10-14).

A third sign of declension, encroaching upon
the former determination to be faithful to God,

was evidenced in the laxity of some as to the sanctity of the Sabbath, the Lord's holy day, concerning which there had been such particular pledges made. Nehemiah saw some treading winepresses and engaged in other secular occupations on the Sabbath, even buying and selling and carrying burdens on the day of rest. In vain at first he testified against them. Strangers from Tyre brought fish and other kinds of produce which they offered for sale, and for which they found ready buyers on the Sabbath. Thoroughly aroused, Nehemiah contended with the nobles, the rulers of the people, charging this profanation of the holy day upon them, and reminding them that it was for sin such as this that all the past evil had befallen the Jews and the city of Jerusalem. "Yet," he cries, indignantly, "ye bring more wrath upon Israel by profaning the Sabbath" (vers. 13-18).

So, with his accustomed energy, he commanded the gates to be shut at sundown, as the Sabbath drew on, and not to be opened till it was past, while guards were set to see that no burden of any kind was brought into the city on that day. Once or twice the merchants and hucksters lodged all night and all day outside Jerusalem, vainly pleading for admission, but Nehemiah's orders were carried out to the letter. Finally, he threatened them with arrest if they came again with their wares on the Sabbath. Seeing the orders were meant to be carried out, they came no more on that day.

As polluted, the Levites were then commanded to cleanse themselves, and henceforth maintain a guard over the gates "to sanctify the Sabbath day." Thus for the time the evil was again judged and the declension stayed (vers. 17-22).

But not yet could vigilance be relaxed. The flesh was still at work. In spite of all that they had heard and seen, some had been marrying women of Ashdod, Ammon and Moab. They may have excused themselves, as many do now, on the plea that they might lead these women to know and worship the one true God and learn the ways of Israel. But it was all a delusion. Children had been born of these unions, and these children were witness to the corruption that had been brought in. They "spake half in the speech of Ashdod, and could not speak in the Jews' language, but according to the language of each people" (vers. 23, 24). This is ever the fruit of such a yoke in marriage. The children soon follow the ways of the unregenerate parent and use the language of the flesh. Too late is the error realized. Too readily they follow the example and speech of the parent who knows not God.

Again Nehemiah's righteous anger burst forth. He contended with these unfaithful Jews and invoked the solemn judgments of the law upon them, even smiting some, and demanded of all that they swear by God no longer to countenance in any way these mixed marriages, from which only evil fruit could come. He reminded them how Solomon himself had failed so miserably because of this very thing, and besought them to harken unto the law and not expect others to condone their offences (vers. 25-27). No doubt some would speak of his ways as hard and bitter; but *sin* is hard and bitter; and persistency in it often requires severe measures to put things right. It is often not a sign of spirituality to be placid and sentimentally affectionate. Such behavior frequently tells of a conscience asleep and a soul unexercised. There was a time when the Lord Jesus made a scourge of small cords—a bitter whip—to drive out the traders from God's house (John 2: 15). Paul's language too was cutting and denunciatory when Satan's emissaries were seeking to overthrow divine truth; and God's wrath too shall be poured out without mixture in the cup of His indignation.

Another instance of declension closes both the chapter and the book. The grandson of Eliashib, the high priest, having married a daughter of Sanballat, the man of God, Nehemiah, drives him away from his presence. His grandfather's failure is brought again to mind in the descendant's defection.* Remembering Eliashib's intriguing with Tobiah, we are not surprised to read of his grandson's association with the family of Sanballat. In defiance of all that Nehemiah had been

---

*It is not certain, though probable, that Eliashib the high priest is the same as Eliashib the chief priest of verse 4.

insisting on, this youth had married the guileful Horonite's daughter. He was the last with whom the governor had to deal, and he graphically declares, "Therefore I chased him from me." We can almost see the indignant countenance of the now aged Nehemiah as he learns of the perfidiousness of the son of Joiada, and we cannot but admire the energy with which the doughty old warrior drives the culprit from his presence— even making intercession in the spirit of Elijah *against* those who had defiled the priesthood and violated the covenant. Only by such stern measures could they be cleansed from all strangers.

Consistent to the last, Nehemiah appointed "the wards of the priests and the Levites, every one in his business; and for the wood-offering, at times appointed, and for the first-fruits." Nothing was too great for his faith, and nothing was too insignificant for his consideration if it concerned the house, the people, or the honor of the Lord his God. This was indeed "a faithful man, and one that feared God above many"—just such an one as the times demanded, and he held on his way unflinchingly to the end, neither cajoled by flattery nor intimidated by opposition, for to him the approbation of the God of Israel was infinitely more than the good opinion of carnal or natural men.

And so with the prayer, "Remember me, O my God, for good!" the record comes to an abrupt termination, and Nehemiah passes from our view, only to appear again at the manifestation of the sons of God.

If we would learn something of the after-state of the Jews we must turn, as previously intimated, to the last book of the Old Testament, where we learn through Malachi's stern charges the low state into which the remnant had fallen; while the Gospels and the Acts give us the solemn sequel and show the children of those returned from the captivity rejecting both the Son of God come in flesh to them, and the Holy Spirit also!

Well will it be for Christians who may read these lines, to lay all to heart, that similar declension may be through the mercy of God averted in the present age of grace. May He grant it for His name's sake and the glory of His beloved Son. Amen!

# Esther

# INTRODUCTION

NO attentive reader can fail to note the great distinguishing characteristic of the book of Esther: the name of God is not found in it. No divine title whatever, nor any pronoun referring to God is there in its ten stirring chapters. Neither is there any reference to prayer which involves the thought of God as the hearer and answerer. At first glance it might seem that the book of Esther is not unique in this, as the Song of Solomon apparently keeps company with it in the omission of any title of the Deity. But it is not really so; for the name "Jah" (the Eternal) is, in the original, found in the last clause of chap. viii. 6. "Jealousy is as cruel as the grave; the coals thereof are coals of fire which hath a *most vehement flame;*" (literally as noted in the margin, "a flame of Jah"). And even if this were not the case, still the bridegroom is so evidently Jehovah, whose bride Israel was and shall yet be manifested to be, that almost every masculine pronoun may be said to refer to Him. The Song of Songs therefore is really a perfect contrast with the book of Esther, being from end to end full of Jehovah as the Bridegroom of Israel.

In Esther it is quite different. Neither His name, nor any reference to Him, even veiled, is found. At least so it is on the page of the English version. Whether there may be any divine purpose in the reputed fact that the name of Jehovah (Hebrew I H V H) is found there in acrostics four times I do not pretend to say. The passages in which they are said to occur are chap. i. 20, "all the wives shall give;" v. 4, "let the king and Haman come this day;" and v. 13, "all this availeth me nothing;" and vii. 7, "that there was evil determined against him." Properly speaking God is entirely unmentioned: but no believer in the plenary inspiration of Scripture would conclude from this that His voice speaks not to us in this writing as in all the rest of the sacred Oracles.

One rather asks: Why has He inspired so strange a book; and what is His reason for omitting His name?

The answer, as the question, may be a double one. First: in this book we have Israel in what was really a self-chosen path, for opportunity had been given to return to the land of their fathers, there to rebuild the city of God, but they preferred to remain where they were rather than endure the hardship of emigrating to Canaan. They were in Persia and Babylon when they might have been in Palestine, gathered around God's centre at Jerusalem. Second: the great subject of Esther is evidently the secret providence—a "particular" providence too—which is ever watching over the scattered nation during all the long-drawn-out "times of the Gentiles."

In Hosea i. 9, we read of the prophet's son: "Then said God; call his name Lo-ammi (not My people) for ye are not My people and I will not be your God." Because of their disobedience, He was about to refuse to own them, and to permit them to be carried into captivity among the nations. In this condition are they found over two hundred years later, in the times of Esther and Mordecai.

He who had borne with their ways for so long had at last given them up in chastisement, and allowed the Gentile oppressor to destroy the city and the temple, and to transport them to Babylon; there to learn in affliction what they would not learn in years of blessing and forbearance.

The Babylonian conqueror had however in his turn been overthrown by the Persian, under whose mild rule the dispersed Jews now were. It had pleased the Lord to give a little reviving in the midst of their bondage, and a few years before the time of the first verse of our book, He had stirred up the spirit of Cyrus to issue a proclamation to the effect that all who had heart for it might return to Jerusalem and "build the house of the Lord God of Israel" (Ezra i. 1-3). As a result there "rose up the chief of the fathers of Judah and

Benjamin, and the priests and the Levites, with all whose spirit God had raised to go to build the house of the Lord which is in Jerusalem" (Ezra i. 5).

With this remnant, feeble indeed, and few in number, the Lord is pleased in grace to connect His name, although the Lo-ammi sentence remains unrepealed; for we find that if the Name is absent in recording His care over those who remained in Babylon, it is abundantly present in the books of Ezra and Nehemiah, which detail the experiences of the remnant to whom the place of the Name was precious, as it could not be to those who abode elsewhere—even in ease and comparative luxury. It is true it is as "the God of heaven" He makes Himself known to them; but what title more suitable when all earthly glory had departed? and to heaven they now looked for the coming Anointed Deliverer.  Among those who went up there was much to grieve and sadden; much failure and sin;— yet they were gathered around Himself in His own appointed place, in accordance with His own Word.  Hence, He raises up ministry suited to their need, and is not ashamed to link His Name with them.

If Ahasuerus, the great king, be Xerxes, as is generally believed, the history of the book of Esther would come in, chronologically, between the sixth and seventh chapters of Ezra; that is, between the

times when the first company returned to Jerusalem,
and that when Ezra and his company went up.    In
that case we can well understand the fervent faith
evidenced by this dear servant of God who "was
ashamed to require of the king (Artaxerxes Longi-
manus, successor to Xerxes) a band of soldiers
and horsemen to keep us against the enemy in the
way: because we had spoken to the king, saying,
The hand of our God is upon all them for good
that seek Him; but his wrath is against all that
forsake Him" (Ezra viii. 22).    How signally had
this been proven but a short time before in the
triumph of Esther!

If, as others contend, Artaxerxes himself be the
Ahasuerus referred to, it might account for the
stirring of heart that led Ezra and this second company to go up in faith to join their brethren in
the city that was now rising slowly from its ashes.
In either case, God Himself had wrought in their
souls, and they went up to the land of their ancient
patrimony because of their desire to glorify Him.

# NOTES ON THE
# BOOK OF ESTHER

## CHAPTER I

### THE ROYAL FEAST, AND DIVORCE OF VASHTI.

IN the opening verses we note the wide extent of the Persian dominion. "Now it came to pass in the days of Ahasuerus, (this is Ahasuerus which reigned from India even unto Ethiopia, over a hundred, seven and twenty provinces,) that in those days, when the king Ahasuerus sat on the throne of his kingdom, which was in Shushan the palace, in the third year of his reign, he made a feast unto all his princes and his servants; the power of Persia and Media, the nobles and princes of the provinces being before him: when he showed the riches of his glorious kingdom and the honor of his excellent majesty many days, even a hundred and fourscore days" (vers. 1-4).

These verses bring before us something of the earthly grandeur and glory of the "silver" kingdom, which had succeeded the "head of gold," depicted in Nebuchadnezzar's dream, as recorded in the second chapter of Daniel. World-wide dominion would be exercised by but four powers till He should come whose right it is to reign, and should set up a kingdom that shall break in pieces all the others, and shall never be destroyed. This was what God had pictured to the king in the dream of the great image whose head was of gold, with breasts of silver, belly and thighs of brass, legs of iron, and feet of mingled iron and clay.

The sphere of lordship is larger in the case of each succeeding empire, and yet the metal ever deteriorates, from gold to the iron mixed with miry clay, or, according to Tregelles, brittle pottery; the reason doubtless consisting in this, that Babylon presents to us an absolutely unlimited monarchy, while in Persia, Greece and Rome the powers of the chief become more or less circumscribed, first, by assistant counselors, and at last by a sort of union of royalty and democracy, which will eventually result in the *election* of the final Roman emperor yet to come, in the days of the ten toes, which will be the last form assumed by the beast (Rev. xiii. 1-9) after the Church has been raptured away to heaven.*

It is certainly a splendid scene to which our

---

*What Nebuchadnezzar saw as a magnificent image was revealed to Daniel, the man of God, as a series of wild and ferocious beasts, the last of which is again made known to John in the Apocalypse (Dan. 7 and Rev. 13 and 17).

chapter introduces us, and in a certain sense, no doubt, a typical one. But it is clear that all is but the glory of this world, though not in the utter independence of God that we find in Dan. v. There is no mention of impiety connected with the feast described in the following verses: "And when these days were expired, the king made a feast unto all the people that were present in Shushan the palace, both unto great and small, seven days, in the court of the garden of the king's palace; where were white, green and blue hangings, fastened with cords of fine linen and purple to silver rings and pillars of marble: the beds (or couches) were of gold and silver, upon a pavement of red, and blue, and white, and black marble. . . . And the drinking was according to the law; none did compel: for so the king had appointed to all the officers of his house, that they should do according to every man's pleasure" (vers. 5,6,8).

If in Israel's subjection to Babylon we get a picture of the days of darkness and bondage through which the Church passed during the ascendency of the papacy, it would seem that in the "liberal slavery" during the Medo-Persian supremacy, we have foreshadowed the present anomalous and outwardly prosperous condition of Protestantism. In other words, Babylon might be said to find its counterpart in Thyatira, when Satan sought to force the children of God to bow the knee to idolatry—to commit spiritual adultery. Sardis answers more to the conditions of Esther's day—great outward prosperity, with a faithful few who have not defiled their garments, but nevertheless, on the part of the vast majority, a complete union between the world and the professing body. Philadelphia corresponds well with the returned remnant, while Laodicea is suggested by the Pharisaic outgrowth of self-righteousness and formality that followed. At least, it is plain that there are many striking similarities, which would seem to be more than mere coincidences.

Looking at it from this standpoint, while in Ezra and Nehemiah we have a people separated to the name of the Lord, gathered around God's centre, and, in measure at least, subject to His Word; in Esther we have a people equally the Lord's, quite content to go on with the world's patronage; and though here and there some are characterized by great devotion, there is in no sense the same liberty, blessing and understanding of the word of God as might have been theirs had they sought His glory more, rather than their own convenience.

This feast, then, is but the general rejoicing in the light and liberty afforded by the spread of knowledge and civilization—something far different from the feasts kept at Jerusalem, where all pointed to the Lord Jesus Christ—His sufferings and His glories.

No doubt the various colors of the hangings and furniture of the banquet hall may all have some typical meaning, but at present scholars are far from agreement as to the meaning of the words employed; so we do not attempt to enter into it. It is noticeable that "the drinking was according to the law: none did compel." What has been called "the right of private judgment" was fully recognized. The harlot of Rev. xvii, had in her hand a *golden** cup (for of *divine* things she professed to speak) full of abomination and filthiness. The language used in verse 2 seems to imply that she practically forced to the lips of the earth-dwellers the wine of her fornication. She would brook no objection. All *must* drink what she provided. This is ever the rule of the papacy. It is otherwise in Protestantism: you may drink or not, as you please. "None did compel;" and if you like not the design of the cup you have, there are plenty of others to choose from, all of gold, all alike professedly of God, and yet diverse one from the other.

Well it is for those who refuse every cup of man's design, and in lowliness and self-judgment are found poring over the word of God in the place where He has caused his name to dwell (Neh. viii. 3; ix. 3).

*Gold in Scripture is evidently typical or symbolical of the divine glory.

The wine is "royal wine" it is true, and it will exhilarate and excite and fill one with goodly thoughts of flesh and of the glory of earth; but it is not the wine that speaks of a Saviour's precious blood shed for guilty sinners, who in His very death upon the tree was telling out the judgment of this world. *That* is seen as you stand by the altar in the ruined city of God, and behold the drink-offering poured out upon the holocaust, ascending as a sweet savor to God (Ezra iii. 3).

The next few verses give us a picture which we find difficult to apply. When the feast had run on for seven days, the king, evidently inflamed by wine, sent for his queen Vashti to appear before the people and princes, to display her beauty. She had been banqueting with the women in the palace, and refused to obey the imperial mandate. Angered by her pertinacity, the king took counsel with his wise men as to what punishment he should mete out to her because she had not heeded his commandment.

At the suggestion of Memucan, she was put away and divorced in order that her example might not incite the women of the empire to act as she had done when their husbands laid any command upon them.

We are told that "the saying pleased the king and the princes; and the king did according to the word of Memucan" (ver. 21), and published broadcast the official edict that Vashti was to come no more into his presence.

They all had agreed that she had proved untrue to her place as the leading woman of the empire, and that it must be given to another. One might suggest this as an illustration of Rom. xi,—the disobedience of the Gentiles giving occasion for the restoration of the Jews to the place of favor. But, shrinking from any interpretation which might not commend itself to the spiritual mind, we introduce our readers at once to the subject of the next chapter.

# CHAPTER II.

## THE CHOICE OF ESTHER AND THE TREASON THWARTED

WHEN the days of feasting and excitement described in our previous chapter had passed away, and the king had opportunity quietly to weigh his hasty action, his heart seems to have relented, as we are told in the first verse of chapter ii, that, "After these things, when the wrath of king Ahasuerus was appeased, he remembered Vashti, and what she had done, and what was decreed against her." Bound by the law of the kingdom, which made it impossible for him to revoke his own imperial decree, he seems to have become a prey to a measure at least of remorse as he reflected on his way towards Vashti, of whom he had been so proud.

His servants, noticing his dejection, make the proposal that another be sought to take the place of the deposed queen. Accordingly they gather together the fairest maidens of all the provinces, and bring them to Shushan the palace (identical with the Susa of profane history). From this company the future queen was to be chosen.

There is some interesting data afforded by profane history on this point, to which we advert for a moment.

In the *third* year of Xerxes' reign, he made a feast to deliberate concerning the invasion of Greece. Four years later he returned discomfited to Susa, where he plunged into all kinds of pleasures and excesses to drive from his mind the bitter memories of his defeats. His favorite queen seems to have been chosen at this time, and her name is given as Amestris—which, it will be seen, bears a close relation to Esther. All this goes far to prove the contention that Xerxes is the great king here referred to. The name Ahasuerus presents no difficulty, as it is simply an imperial title, like Pharaoh, or Agag, which is said to mean, according to Sir Henry Rawlinson, "Venerable King." It is noteworthy that in Ezra iv. 6 Cambyses is called by this name, while in Dan. ix. 1 it is applied, in all probability, to Cyaxares. The fact that Amestris was reported to be cruel and bloodthirsty would not necessarily militate against this view; as it is most unlikely that the Persians would think of Esther in any other way, after the great slaughter which resulted when the enemies of the Jews were routed. She would naturally be blamed for the miscarriage of Haman's plan.

Returning to the Scripture narrative, charming

in its simplicity and straightforwardness, we are
introduced in verse 5 to the stout-hearted Jew
who is to figure so prominently in future chapters,
as well as in verse 7, to his beautiful cousin
Hadassah, or Esther.

"Now in Shushan the palace there was a certain
Jew, whose name was Mordecai, the son of Jair,
the son of Shimei, the son of Kish, a Benjamite;
who had been carried away from Jerusalem with
the captivity which had been carried away with
Jeconiah king of Judah, whom Nebuchadnezzar the
king of Babylon had carried away" (vers. 5, 6).

The Hebrews, and many Christians, have
gathered from this that Mordecai was a lineal
descendant of Kish, the father of Israel's first
king. Josephus so understood it, for he refers
to Esther as being "herself of the royal family
also" (Ant. vi. 1); and as she was cousin to
Mordecai, both were necessarily of the same lin-
eage. Kish was, however, a common Hebrew
name, especially among the Benjamites; but
standing here, as it does, for the father of a family,
the presumption is certainly in favor of the above
view. As we shall see farther on, there would
appear to be a divine fitness in thus bringing forward at so crucial a period a member of the failed
house of Saul. Had that rebellious and obstinate
king (1 Sam. xv. 22, 23) faithfully performed
the commandment of the Lord in regard to the

utter destruction of Amalek, the book of Esther would in all probability never have been written, as Israel would never have been exposed to the danger therein recorded. We shall see why, further on.

The name Mordecai is said to mean "Little man," and was probably given him for the lack of that which made Saul so much admired, namely, greatness of stature.

He must have been very young indeed when carried away to Babylon, as the captivity of Jeconiah, or Jehoiachin, took place B. C. 599, something over eighty years ere our chapter opens. This aged patriarch "brought up Hadassah, that is, Esther, his uncle's daughter: for she had neither father nor mother, and the maid was fair and beautiful: whom Mordecai, when her father and mother were dead, took for his own daughter" (ver. 7). She, by her grace and beauty, attracted the attention of the officers whose business it was to find a bride for the king, and she was given into the custody of the chamberlain Hegai. "And the maiden pleased him, and she obtained kindness of him; and he speedily gave her her things for purification, with such things as belonged to her, and seven maidens, which were meet to be given her, out of the king's house: and he preferred her and her maids unto the best place of the women" (ver. 9).

It was a strange position surely for a Jewish maiden to occupy, in marked contrast with Moses, in whom, however, she no doubt gloried. He, picked up as a waif, to be called the son of Pharaoh's daughter, by faith relinquished this high place, "choosing rather to suffer affliction with the people of God, than to enjoy the pleasures of sin for a season." As one has remarked, "Providence had placed him in Pharaoh's house, but faith took him out of it." With Esther it was otherwise. There can be no question that her position was entirely opposed to the word of God. Providence might seem to favor her, but faith would assuredly have led her at once to declare herself as a despised Jewess, one of the afflicted people of Jehovah. This she does not do, Mordecai having expressly urged her to carefully conceal it. "Esther had not showed her people nor her kindred: for Mordecai had charged her that she should not show it" (ver. 10). Faithful above many, Mordecai yet had not fully entered into God's mind in regard to the complete separation of His people from the nations. The law expressly forbade the giving of the daughters of Israel in marriage to the Gentiles; but it is very evident that both Mordecai and Esther thought they saw in the proposed union a means of blessing to their people. And so, indeed, it proved to be; but this by no means disannulled or made of none effect the word of God.

In the same way people reason concerning much that goes on in our day. It is seldom that Christians are found who will refuse everything that is contrary to the Scriptures, even though it *seem* to be the means of accomplishing much good. But to walk in the truth is of more importance than busy activity.

Take the question of female ministry as an example. We have often been asked concerning the public ministry of women, "If not of God, how is it that He so frequently blesses it to the salvation of souls? Many women occupying the public platform as teachers and preachers are assuredly blessed of God: does He not therefore set the seal of His approval upon their position?" Admitting the premise, which may not always be before God as it appears to man, the conclusion by no means follows. Clearly and unmistakably the Holy Ghost has said, "I suffer not a woman to teach, nor to usurp authority over the man, but to be in silence" (I Tim. ii. 12). And again, "Let your women keep silence in the churches (assemblies); for it is not permitted unto them to speak; but they are commanded to be under obedience, as also saith the law. And if they will learn anything, let them ask their husbands at home: for it is a shame for women to speak in the church" (I Cor. xiv. 34, 35). Then, solemnly, he adds in verse 37, "If any man think himself to be a prophet, or spiritual, let him acknowledge that the things that I write unto you are the commandments of the Lord." Here is the unerring word of God upon the subject. If that Word is violated, and still blessing results, what does it prove? That God has changed His mind, or ignores, and would have us ignore, His own Word? Ah, no! What then? Simply that He is sovereign, and uses His truth wherever proclaimed, and by whomsoever; but the judgment-seat of Christ will manifest all that was contrary to His mind.

We knew of a man saved in a Roman Catholic church while an ungodly priest, as his after-life proved, was reading the gospel for the day from Luke xv. Are we therefore to reason that the Roman priesthood is according to God because He sets the seal of blessing upon His Word used by one of them? Every unprejudiced mind will say, No! We give Him glory that, in spite of all the failure and disorder of Christendom, His love is so great that it breaks every barrier, and reaches men and women in their deep, deep need by any and all means whereby He can make Himself known; but we deprecate all disobedience to Him as sin.

This principle apprehended in the soul will save from much confusion of mind. Had Mordecai apprehended it, he would never have counseled his cousin as he did. The word of God was ignored. That He deigned to use the ignorers of it in blessing to His people was an act of pure grace.

In marked contrast with Esther's course is that of another Israelitish captive—the little maid of 2 Kings v, who waited upon Naaman's wife. Her sphere was much more circumscribed, but how faithfully she glorified God in it! "A word spoken in season, how good is it!" Such was her testimony to her heathen mistress, and so wonderfully did God own and bless it that it brought a proud Syrian captain to confess Israel's God as the only true God, whom alone he would henceforth serve. Oh for grace thus to buy up opportunities and to use them to His glory while ourselves walking in singleness of heart in the path marked out in the Scriptures of truth!

To return to Esther: Daily Mordecai walked before the court of the house of the women to learn if all was well with her. One after another, the maidens were presented to the king, each vying with the other in the effort to add to her natural charms by means of the sweet odors and other preparations given her. Esther—to her credit be it noted—disdained all these things, save what were officially appointed, and when she was presented to the king, "the king loved Esther above all the women, and she obtained grace and favor in his sight more than all the virgins; so that he set the royal crown upon her head, and made her queen instead of Vashti" (ver. 17). A signal honor, doubtless, but how low had she stooped to obtain it! How had she lost that character of holy separation to Jehovah which should ever have been hers! How truly was she degraded in her very exaltation! The favored wife among many, and her lord an uncircumcised Gentile! How low had the nation fallen when Mordecai, one of the noblest of them all, could rejoice in such a dubious honor being accorded her! And how low spiritually must the Church be, to seek, as she does, the patronage of the world! This can only be purchased by the loss of the holiness and separate character enjoined by the word of God. Such is the lesson we would seek to impress upon our reader's conscience. Far better had it been for Esther to have been poor and unknown, yet cleaving to the Lord her God among the returned captives at Jerusalem, than to be thus exalted in the house of the conqueror. And so to-day; far better to be little and despised in the eyes of a haughty world, and an equally haughty Christendom, while seeking to carry out the truth as to the Christian's heavenly calling,

than, through forgetting this, to be made much
of by those "whose glory is in their shame; who
mind earthly things." This is a snare against
which the Lord's separated people need to be
specially warned to-day. The word of Jehovah
to Jeremiah should be often called to mind: "If
thou return, then will I bring thee again, and thou
shalt stand before Me: and if thou take forth the
precious from the vile, thou shalt be as My mouth:
let them return unto thee; but return not thou
unto them" (Jer. xv. 19).

The present is a time of great sweeping-away of
the ancient landmarks. It is a day of marked indifference to evil—of chronic inability to try the
things that differ. Let us not be carried away with
the tide, but faithfully guard the treasure committed
to us, and spurn the patronage of that which is so
obnoxious to God.

The account of Esther's marriage-feast is but
sorrowful reading if one be able to detect the sad departure from the Word which it indicates. "Then
the king made a great feast unto all his princes and
his servants, even Esther's feast; and he made a re-
lease to the provinces, and gave gifts according to
the state of the king" (ver. 18). It would seem
that Mordecai too was advanced to a position of
trust; for in the next verse we learn that "when the
virgins were gathered together the second time, then
Mordecai sat in the king's gate," which implies that

he became a petty judge, according to the Oriental manner of expressing it. One is reminded of "righteous Lot," who sat in the gate of Sodom; and of how many other dear children of God since, who have sought and obtained positions of power and influence in this poor "Christless world," hoping thereby to be used in its improvement, only to be bitterly disappointed at last, besides being degraded themselves.

Significantly, the next verse tells us again that "Esther had not showed her kindred nor her people, as Mordecai had charged her; for Esther did the commandment of Mordecai, like as when she was brought up with him" (ver. 20).

This, no doubt, would be considered good policy on Mordecai's part, and lovely obedience in Esther, but it was real unfaithfulness to God, often duplicated in our own times. What a contrast with Ruth, the converted Moabitess! "Thy people shall be my people, and thy God my God" is her bright confession. How much more honoring to the Lord than the shrewdness of Mordecai and Esther!

In the last three verses of our chapter an event is recorded which becomes of grave importance farther on in the book. "In those days, while Mordecai sat in the king's gate, two of the king's chamberlains, Bigthan and Teresh, of those which kept the door, were wroth, and sought to lay hands on the king Ahasuerus. And the thing was known to Mordecai, who told it unto Esther the queen; and Esther certified the king thereof in Mordecai's name. And when inquisition was made of the matter, it was found out; therefore they were both hanged on a tree: and it was written in the book of the chronicles before the king" (vers. 21-23).

Although in an unscriptural position, God, who knows the heart of His servant, who sees in Mordecai and Esther true lovers of Israel, will use them signally for His own ends of good to His people, whom He truly loved. If they cover their nationality, and shame Him so that He hides His name too, He will make them nevertheless the instruments of His providence. Mordecai becomes the means by which a plot against the life of the king is thwarted. But for the present no notice is taken of him. The conspirators are hanged, the service of Mordecai is recorded in the records of the kingdom, but he himself is, apparently, forgotten. Such is the favor of this world! In a darker hour, however, One, in whose hand is a sleepless night of the king, shall see that the overlooked service shall be brought to the monarch's attention, and turn it to account for deliverance of that people for whose care His eyes never slumber.

It is of all importance that the saint should ever remember that "all things work together for good to them that love God, who are the called according to His purpose." There may be times when God seems to have forgotten; when clouds are dark; when one is allowed to be neglected, unjustly treated, or coldly set at nought. But rest assured all is naked and open before Him with whom we have to do. Every purpose shall be manifested in its season; and all at last shall be cause for eternal thanksgivings.

# CHAPTER III

## THE WRATH OF THE AMALEKITE, AND THE DECREE OF DOOM

HAMAN is now brought upon the scene, who occupies a large place in the book, and who is execrated by all Hebrews to this day: "Haman, the son of Hammedatha the Agagite, the Jews' enemy," is his significant title. When his name is mentioned even now, orthodox Jews spit and curse him, so hateful is his memory.

"After these things did king Ahasuerus promote Haman, the son of Hammedatha the Agagite, and advanced him, and set his seat above all the princes that were with him" (ver. 1). Agag was the name given to the kings of Amalek, the people "against whom the Lord hath indignation forever." Haman, then, is a royal Amalekite—the last of his proud house to occupy a position of influence and power; for with his death, and that of his ten sons, the name of Amalek, according to Jehovah's word, is blotted out from under heaven.

In order to understand the reason for Mordecai's unyielding attitude in regard to Haman, it will be necessary to look into the history of this warlike and impious people.

In Gen. xxxvi. 12 we find the origin of Amalek, the progenitor of the tribe afterwards bearing his name. "And Timna was concubine to Eliphaz, Esau's son; and she bare to Eliphaz Amalek." See also 1 Chron. i. 36.

Amalek, then, sprang from Esau, which is Edom. Esau is ever a type of the flesh. Even ere the birth of the twins Esau and Jacob, they struggled together—picture of the flesh lusting against the Spirit and the Spirit against the flesh. Esau is the first-born, and then Jacob; for "that is not first which is spiritual, but that which is natural; and afterward that which is spiritual" (1 Cor. xv. 46).

This is again and again set forth in Scripture, the first-born being set aside to make room for one who might stand for or set forth the Second Man. Cain is set aside, and Abel, revived in Seth, is given the pre-eminent place. Ishmael must be cast out that Isaac be honored. Manasseh, too, gives way to Ephraim, as Joseph had been given the place of the first-born in preference to Reuben.

The author of the notes in the *Numerical Bible* has pointed out the close similarity in sound and meaning between Adam and Edom. Edom is but old Adam revived, and from him Amalek springs.

What, then, comes from the flesh? Only ungodly lusts and passions. Of these Amalek is the type. "Among whom we all had our conversation in times past in the lusts of our flesh, fulfilling the desires of the flesh and of the mind; and were by nature the children of wrath, even as others" (Eph. ii. 3).

In Gen. xiv. 7 we first read of the land of the Amalekites, the valleys of southern Palestine, involved in the great conflicts of the Elamite ascendancy. Who the inhabitants were at that time we know not, but the land is called by the name of the war-like tribe who occupied it at the time Moses wrote the record.

It is when next mentioned that we see their true character. In the seventeenth chapter of Exodus they appear as the first of Israel's foes, and they proved a most persistent enemy ever after. God had but recently delivered His people from the cruel Egyptian oppressor. Sheltered by blood, they had eaten the passover with holy confidence while the Lord judged the gods of Egypt and smote the first-born of those who despised His word. Redeemed by power, they had been led in triumph through the Red Sea, and on the eastern shore they sang their song of gladness as they beheld the power of the enemy broken, and knew that they were Jehovah's purchased people. He took them under His own care, and made Himself responsible for all their needs. The waters of Marah He sweetened, and refreshed them beneath Elim's shade. He gave them bread from heaven, and quails when they asked for flesh.

But they failed to realize who it was with whom they had to do. When they pitched in Rephidim, "there was no water for the people to drink." They murmured against Moses, and charged him with having brought them out to slay them with thirst. But God, ever acting in pure grace, until, in their self-confidence, they put themselves under law, said unto Moses, "Go on before the people, and take with thee of the elders of Israel; and thy rod, wherewith thou smotest the river, take in thy hand, and go. Behold, I will stand before thee there upon the rock in Horeb; and thou shalt smite the rock, and there shall come water out of it, that the people may drink. And Moses did so in the sight of the elders of Israel" (Ex. xvii. 5, 6).

A lovely picture, surely, and easily understood in the light of two New Testament Scriptures. "That Rock was Christ" (1 Cor. x. 4). "Jesus stood and cried, saying, If any man thirst, let him come unto Me and drink. . . . But this spake He of the Spirit, which they that believe on Him should receive: for the Holy Ghost was not yet given; because that Jesus was not yet glorified" (John vii, 37, 39). The cross had to come in ere He could be glorified as man. That blessed Rock had to be smitten with the rod of judgment before the Holy Spirit could come to satisfy and fill all who would drink. Of this it is that mystic scene at Horeb speaks. Israel in type are drinking of the living

waters. Surely their troubles are over now forever! Ah, it *should* have been; but, alas, it was
not so. It is at this moment that we read, "Then
came Amalek and fought with Israel in Rephidim."
And so the lusts of the flesh would ever hinder
the believer's enjoyment of the refreshing influences
of the Holy Spirit. The Christian is beset by a
tireless and hateful foe who makes it his business to defraud him, if possible, of the blessing
that is rightfully his.

It is to this the word in Gal. v. 16, 17 refers:
"This I say, then, Walk in the Spirit, and ye shall
not fulfill the lust of the flesh. For the flesh lusteth
against the Spirit, and the Spirit against the flesh:
and these are contrary the one to the other; so
that ye might not (literal rendering) do the things
that ye would."

How will the saint thus beset find deliverance
and victory? Only by mortifying his members
that are upon the earth. But this he cannot do in
his own power. And so Moses says to Joshua,
"Choose us out men, and go out, and fight with
Amalek: to-morrow I will stand on the top of the
hill, with the rod of God in my hand." Beautiful
picture, surely, of our great Intercessor above,
"who ever liveth to make intercession for us."
Aaron and Hur had to hold up the hands of Moses,
but our blessed Lord needs none to thus assist Him.
His advocacy is ever going on. His intercessions

for His saints are unfailing, and He is thus able to
save evermore all who come unto God by Him.
"This is the victory that overcometh the world,
even our faith" (1 John v. 4).

It was on this first occasion of Amalek's hatred and attack against His people that "the Lord
said unto Moses, Write this for a memorial in a
book, and rehearse it in the ears of Joshua: for
I will utterly put out the remembrance of Amalek
from under heaven. And Moses built an altar,
and called the name of it Jehovah-nissi: for he
said, Because of the hand upon the throne of Jah,
Jehovah will have war with Amalek from generation
to generation" (Ex. xvii. 14-16—marginal reading). This was Amalek's awful sin. He would,
if possible, tear Jehovah from His throne, and
usurp His authority. So would the fleshly lusts,
which war against the soul, dethrone the Holy One
and reign in His stead.

In Num. xiv. 44, 45 Israel disobeyed the word
of the Lord, and *presumed* to go up unto the
hill-top in their own strength to meet their foes.
"Then the Amalekites came down . . . and discomfited them, even unto Hormah." The moment
a saint gets out of God's order he exposes himself
to the power of the flesh. There is no safety
save in obedience to the Word.

Balaam foretells the doom of this haughty foe
in Num. xxiv. 20. "When he looked on Amalek,

he took up his parable, and said, Amalek was the first of the nations; but his latter end shall be that he perish forever." Moses too, in his last charge to the people, says, "Remember what Amalek did unto thee by the way, when ye were come forth out of Egypt; how he met the hindmost of thee, even all that were feeble behind thee" (it is ever such who are a prey to the lusts of the flesh), "when thou wast weary; and he feared not God. Therefore it shall be . . . that thou shalt blot out the remembrance of Amalek from under heaven; THOU SHALT NOT FORGET IT" (Deut. xxv. 17-19).

We will not refer at any length to the woes brought upon Israel by Amalek in the days of the Judges, only bidding the reader notice that whenever the people rose up in the energy of faith and the lowliness of self-judgment, all Amalek's power was broken. It will be a profitable exercise to read at leisure and carefully study Judges v., vi., and x, on this subject.

In connection with the commission given to king Saul at the mouth of Samuel, in I Sam. xv, we get the inspired account of God's command and Saul's failure to carry it out. It is most instructive, as well as of special interest, in connection with our study of the book of Esther. Saul was commanded to "go and smite Amalek, and utterly destroy all that they have, and spare them not."

But, alas, though the young king gained a wonderful victory, and "utterly destroyed all the *people* with the edge of the sword," he spared Agag; and Haman is witness that he likewise failed to exterminate the rest of the royal family. Had Saul been true to God, and yielded implicit obedience to His Word, Haman could never have appeared on the scene. Saul's unfaithfulness made the plot of "the Jew's enemy" possible, and exposed the chosen nation to destruction. What a triumph for Satan it would have been if, in place of Amalek's "utter destruction," Israel had been rooted out from among the nations!

There is a solemn lesson here. Sin unjudged, evil propensities unmortified, will result in grave trouble later. Is the reader conscious of indulging some fleshly desire—something, perhaps, that it seems hard to put to death, so dear is it to him, and, withal, so insignificant? Rest assured, it will be the cause of serious disaster if unjudged. It may go on unnoticed for years, but the day will come when it, like Haman, will rise in its power; and well it shall be then if it be not the cause of moral and spiritual shipwreck. Is it a young believer who sees these lines? Remember the word of the Holy Spirit to Timothy, "Flee also youthful lusts." Any unholy desire tolerated in the soul must work eventually to the undoing of your discipleship, to the breaking-down of your testimony.

Samuel showed Agag no mercy; but some of his children—perhaps only one, and that one, mayhap, a weak and puny infant—escaped him; and behold, nearly six hundred years later, a royal Amalekite and a descendant of the house of Kish, the father of king Saul, confront each other!

Haman is advanced before all the princes, for well the flesh knows how to work its way to the front. All fall down before him and own his authority, save one unyielding old man, insignificant in stature and unknown among the great. "And all the king's servants, that were in the king's gate, bowed and reverenced Haman: for the king had so commanded concerning him. But Mordecai bowed not, nor did him reverence" (ver. 2).

Never was Mordecai's moral elevation higher than at this moment. He is no longer the crafty, politic man of chapter two. He shines forth as a man who takes his stand upon the word of the Eternal, let the consequences be what they may. There is no longer a tendency to hide his people and his kindred. He lets all know that he is a Jew. As such he cannot bow to the blatant enemy of Jehovah. The Lord hath indignation against Amalek. So also, in substance, says Mordecai. He sides with God. From now on he is a character delightful to contemplate.

"Then the king's servants, which were in the king's gate, said unto Mordecai, Why trans-

gressest thou the king's commandment?" (ver. 3).
To them it seems the essence of foolhardiness and
stubbornness. We read not of any other, even of
his own nation, so unyielding as he. Why not,
at least, incline his head? Why not go with the
crowd? Why make himself so unpleasantly conspicuous by his peculiar obstinacy? Better men than
he, perhaps, bowed to Haman, the king's prime
minister. Why should he be too narrow-minded
to do so? To all this Mordecai might have replied, God has spoken. He declares He will have
indignation against Amalek forever. I side with
Him. It matters not what others do, I have to
go by what I find written in the book.

"Now it came to pass, when they spake daily
unto him, and he harkened not unto them, that
they told Haman, *to see whether Mordecai's matters
would stand; for he had told them that he was a
Jew*" (ver. 4). There is no evasion now: all is
out at last. The judge in the king's gate is one
of the despised captives, and he will risk the loss
of name and station, yea, of life itself, rather than
be unfaithful to the truth of God.

The king's servants desire to see if Mordecai's
matters will *stand*. Of course they will stand, for
does not he stand with and for God, who "is able
to make him stand?" None ever falls who acts
for God. His power is over all. He may permit
testing and trial, but "whatsoever is born of God

overcometh the world." He is in the right who sides with God.

When Haman hears of the slight thus put upon him, he is "full of wrath." He must have his revenge on the impudent Jew who thus refuses to acknowledge his prestige: but "he thought scorn to lay hands on Mordecai alone; for they had showed him the people of Mordecai: wherefore Haman sought to destroy all the Jews that were throughout the whole kingdom of Ahasuerus, even the people of Mordecai" (vers. 5, 6). What a mess had the obstinate little Jew made of it all now! If he must have such strong convictions, why could he not keep them to himself, and, by getting out of Haman's way, refrain from making himself and all his people obnoxious to him? Could not he conform to the customs of the times? Did he not know that things were different now from what they were in the days of Moses, of the Judges, and of Samuel? Is not this the way men reason to-day? And, doubtless, many so reasoned in the times of Mordecai: but to all he could have given the triumphant answer, It is my place to obey God, and to honor His Word. I leave all consequences with Him.

This is what characterizes ever the man of God in all dispensations. It was this spirit that sustained Noah in testimony against a corrupt, sin-loving world as he built his great ship on dry land.

In this energy of faith Moses forsook Egypt;
Caleb cried, "We are well able to overcome"; Gideon
went forth to war with lamps and pitchers; David
fought an armored giant with a shepherd's sling
and stones; Jehoshaphat set singers in the van of
his army where others would have set mounted
troops; Daniel opened his windows to pray to the
God of heaven; and Paul lived his life of devotion
to the crucified, exalted Lord, and refused to conform to the demands of the men of his day and
age. In this spirit, too, of subjection to revealed
truth, Athanasius suffered banishment rather than
bow to the Arianism of the times; Savonarola
defied the licentious, gold-hoarding officials of
church and state; Luther uttered his mighty *"No!"*
in the presence of the emperor, the bishops and
grandees of the empire; Farel tossed venerated images into the river in the midst of furious priests
and populace; Knox caused a queen to tremble;
and the Covenanters chose rather to be hunted as
the beasts of the field than own the spiritual
authority of degenerate kings and bishops; and a
mighty host, "of whom the world was not worthy,"
refused to bow the knee or bend the neck to unscriptural, superstitious, and human legislation,
making of none effect the word of God.

Men of this stamp are certain to be dubbed by
the time-serving trucklers to the present age as
schismatics, separatists, and what not. But let

such be content to know that *God* is pleased, and they fear not the frown, and court not the approval, of flesh and blood.

Haman's colossal scheme for the annihilation of the Jewish race is worthy of its great instigator, that old serpent, which is the devil and Satan. The proud Agagite was but a mere puppet in his hands.    Haman desired to obtain revenge for the slight put upon his dignity: the devil sought to make void the promises of God.    The awful foe of God and man knew well that Jehovah had declared that from David's house should arise the One who was to bruise his head—One who is to "destroy him that had the power of death, that is, the devil, and deliver those who, through fear of death, were all their lifetime subject to bondage." That nation destroyed, the promised Deliverer could not appear, and the word of God would be rendered null and void.    Again and again had he sought to accomplish this.    When the hand of Saul threw the javelin at the youthful David, it was Satan who inspired it, but God who protected the minstrel from the blow, that he might live to be the conservator of the promise.    When the wicked queen Athaliah sought to destroy all the seed royal, it was the devil who put the awful thought in her mind, but God who nourished the infant Joash in the temple courts.

And so it was the same foul spirit now who

would sacrifice a nation to prevent the Redeemer's advent; as in the day when that long-predicted event had actually occurred, he sought, through Herod, to destroy Him in His infancy by slaying the babes of Bethlehem, only to be outwitted once more; for God directed His Son to a distant land.

Some idea of Haman's wealth and influence can be gained from the intimacy manifested betwixt him and the king in verses 8 to 11, as also the immense amount of silver he offered for the accomplishment of his cherished plans: ten thousand talents in that age having about the value of twenty millions of dollars now.

His superstition too is evidenced in verse 7. Like many a tyrant before, and since, he was a great believer in lucky and unlucky days; so he had the wise men—the traffickers in the credulity of ambitious courtiers—to cast lots, called in Hebrew *Pur,* to determine a suited day when all signs would be propitious for the carrying out of his colossal massacre. Armed with what he considered to be the favor of the gods (for it is unlikely that he, like the Persians, was a monotheist), he entered the king's presence, and, affecting concern for the interests of the state, he says, "There is a certain people scattered abroad and dispersed among the people in all the provinces of thy kingdom; and their laws are diverse from all people; neither keep they the king's laws: therefore it is not for the king's profit to suffer them." And, as though in a burst of magnanimity, he offers to pay ten thousand talents of silver to rid the king of subjects so objectionable. Carelessly, without so much as inquiring the name of the race referred to, Ahasuerus, with that disregard of human life so common in Xerxes, "took his ring from his hand, and gave it unto Haman the son of Hammedatha the Agagite, the Jews' enemy," saying, as he did so, "The silver is given to thee, the people also, to do with them as it seemeth good to thee" (vers. 8-11).

Acting on this, Haman loses no time, but immediately summons the king's scribes, and issues a proclamation, sealed with the king's ring, to be "sent by posts into all the king's provinces, to destroy, to kill, and to cause to perish, all Jews, both young and old, little children and women, in one day, even upon the thirteenth day of the twelfth month, which is the month Adar" (the date determined by the lot), "and to take the spoil of the people for a prey" (ver. 13). Thus had the entire nation been devoted to destruction, and under the unalterable laws of the Medes and Persians—the same laws that left Vashti still a lonely widow, and which would brook of no reversal.

To every people the news went forth, urging them to be ready against that day. "And the

King and Haman," as though the massacre of myriads had not just been planned and sealed, "sat down to drink; but the city Shushan was perplexed" (ver. 15).

# CHAPTER IV

"WHEN Mordecai perceived all that was done, Mordecai rent his clothes, and put on sackcloth and ashes, and went out into the midst of the city, and cried with a loud and bitter cry; and came even before the king's gate: for none might enter into the king's gate clothed with sackcloth. And in every province whithersoever the king's commandment and his decree came, there was a great mourning among the Jews, and fasting, and weeping, and wailing; and many lay in sackcloth and ashes" (vers. 1-3).

In such solemn manner was the decree received by the condemned Jews. To Haman, and to the king, the slaughter of a nation for the gratification of a prince's vanity might be a thing indifferent; but to the people thus devoted, it was the cause of heartrending scenes. They *believed* the word of Ahasuerus. The proclamation was sealed with the royal signet. They *knew* they were under sentence of death, and their hearts were filled with grief and anguish. In this, how like the condition of awakened sinners! All unsaved men are under a

far worse condemnation than that which darkened
the sky of every Jew in the Persian dominions.
Yea, more: because "all have sinned and come short
of the glory of God" that condemnation is, unlike
the present instance, an intrinsically righteous one.
Every honest man must side with the dying robber
on the cross, and confess, "We indeed justly!"
"Death passed upon all men, *because* all have
sinned." Therefore "it is appointed unto men
once to die, and after this the judgment."

If this be really true, how is it that men and
women in general are so indifferent to the solemn
fact? Alas, alas! though God has given His
Word, men will not believe it. Wherever that
Word *is* believed the result is prostration of soul
before the offended Majesty in the heavens, as in
the case of the repentant publican, who cried from
the depths of an anguished heart, "O God, be mer-
ciful to me, a sinner!" It is because men do not
believe God they can go on so carelessly with the
dark clouds of doom gathering ever in greater
density directly over their heads.

Is my reader one of this class? If so, I pray
you, receive the testimony of God against yourself
ere the judgment falls. You have grievously
sinned, and righteously fallen under the ban of
the Holy One. He has published broadcast the
proclamation, "Cursed is every one that continueth not in all things that are written in the book

of the law to do them." You have *not* so continued. Therefore you are under the curse! Do not, I beg of you, try to forget it. How foolish would it have been for the Jews in the days of Esther to have instituted a series of games and popular amusements in order to banish from their minds the awful fact that their death-warrant had been signed, and was about to be put into execution! In such manner did the citizens of infidel Paris act in the days of the plague. Dancing, revelling and debauchery held full sway. The gay carnival went on as though all was well; but it was only the effort of a terror-stricken people to forget the presence of the dreaded and insidious foe. Hundreds fell, stricken on the ball-room floor; hundreds more dropped, grotesquely masked, amid the gayety of the romping crowds upon the streets. The fun and the forced merriment did not stay the hand of the destroyer; the death-cart ever followed the carnival parade! And in some such foolish manner do men, over whose heads eternal judgment hangs, act every day. Oh, the folly of it! Better far to join with Mordecai and his weeping countrymen, and wear the sackcloth and ashes of self-condemnation.

> "No room for mirth or trifling here,
> For worldly hope or worldly fear,
> If life so soon is gone:
> If now the Judge is at the door,

> And all mankind must stand before
> The inexorable Throne!"

"Because there is wrath, beware lest He take thee away with His stroke: then a great ransom cannot deliver thee" (Job xxxvi. 18).

There was no levity on the part of the wailing multitude in our chapter. They were in desperate earnestness. They wished to be delivered from the condemnation. Nothing else would satisfy them. Sackcloth and ashes speak of repentance and self-judgment. In this garb Mordecai and the Jews arrayed themselves.

"So Esther's maids and her chamberlains came and told it her. Then was the queen exceedingly grieved; and she sent raiment to clothe Mordecai, and to take away his sackcloth from him: but he received it not" (ver. 4). How little Esther entered into the terrible circumstances! "A physician of no value," she would. fain strip her aged cousin of the coarse and ugly garb of repentance and robe him in some beautiful court attire, as though a change of clothing would assuage his grief. But are there not many who deal in a similar manner with troubled souls to-day? How common is the thought that outward reformation, a change of habits, will give peace to an anxious soul! O be persuaded, dear reader: no religious ceremonies; no ordinances, however scriptural in themselves; no turning-over of new leaves will ever give a sinner peace with God. Something more than an outward change is required. Mordecai might well have cried, Take away your beautiful garments! How can they give peace to a man under the death-sentence? Does one find delight in fine raiment on the gallows? It is deliverance from condemnation I want, not a mere change of attire. And for the sinner to-day there is no true deliverance until he sees the blessed truth that Another has borne the wrath, endured the condemnation, exhausted the judgment of God against his sin,—then, and then only, does he find rest and peace.

"Mordecai received it not;" so the queen, realizing at last that his must be a grief she has failed to fathom, sends Hatach the chamberlain to him, to learn the cause of his strange behavior. "So Hatach went forth to Mordecai unto the street of the city, which was before the king's gate. And Mordecai told him of all that had happened unto him, and of the sum of money that Haman had promised to pay to the king's treasuries for the Jews, to destroy them. Also he gave a copy of the writing of the decree that was given at Shushan to destroy them, to show it unto Esther, and to declare it unto her, and to charge her that she should go in unto the king, to make supplication unto him, and to make request before him for her people. And Hatach came and told Esther the words of Mordecai" (vers. 6-9).

Nothing but the knowledge that he and his people are freed from the ban will satisfy the man into whose soul the iron has so deeply entered. Esther is furnished with the evidence of the direful state of things, and doubtless well understands at last why Mordecai wept so bitterly, and why her fine raiment had no charm for him.

He would have her go in before the king and supplicate his favor for her afflicted people. She is, however, in a dilemma as to this, being herself, although a queen, subject to the iron-clad laws of Persian court etiquette. Doubtless genuinely distressed, but apparently helpless, she returns answer that "All the king's servants, and the people of the king's provinces, do know, that whosoever, whether man or woman, shall come unto the king into the inner court, who is not called, there is one law of his to put him to death, except such to whom the king shall hold out the golden sceptre, that he may live; but I have not been called to come in unto the king these thirty days. And they told to Mordecai Esther's words" (vers. 11, 12).

It has evidently not dawned upon her that the king's proclamation, unwittingly, had included herself. But so the word ran: "All Jews . . . both men and women." She had kept her nationality a secret; therefore, unknown even to Haman, she had been included in the bloody edict so soon to take effect if a means of deliverance is not discov-

ered. She accordingly hesitates about risking her
life, by going into the dread sovereign's presence
uncalled.

Mordecai replies with spirit: "Think not with
thyself that thou shalt escape in the king's house
more than all the Jews." Yet, such is his faith at
this moment in the certainty of God's counsels that
he adds, "For if thou altogether holdest thy peace
at this time, then shall there enlargement and deliverance arise to the Jews from another place; but
thou and thy father's house shall be destroyed: and
who knoweth whether thou art come to the kingdom
for such a time as this?"

It is a stirring message, and one that has the
desired effect upon the queen, for she rises in the
greatness of utter self-abnegation and devotion;
and, with the sentence of death now in herself,
"Esther bade them return Mordecai this answer:
Go, gather together all the Jews that are present
in Shushan, and fast ye for me, and neither eat
nor drink three days, night or day: I also and
my maidens will fast likewise; and so will I go in
unto the king, which is not according to the law:
and *if I perish, I perish*" (vers. 15, 16).

A greater than Esther not only took His life
in His hand, but gave that precious life in order
to deliver all who would confide in Him from
the curse of the law and the just judgment of an
outraged God. But though Esther's action gives

us just the faintest hint of this, it is altogether admirable as showing on her part a growing moral elevation, hitherto unmanifested by her. That her confidence is in the unnamed One is clear, else why the summons to fasting in the city, and her own abstinence in the palace? It is here one is so struck by the absence of all reference to prayer, where one would naturally expect it. It is as though she has a sense in her soul of the unowned condition of herself and her people; so nothing is said about crying to the God of her fathers. Yet surely He heard the unuttered petition of the heart, and answered it, too, in His own way and time.

"So Mordecai went his way, and did according to all that Esther had commanded him." The appeal is to be made to the One they dare not mention. The sequel will show how deep is His concern for the chosen nation.

## CHAPTER V

THE days of fasting past, the queen ventures into the forbidden presence. "Now it came to pass on the third day, that Esther put on her royal apparel, and stood in the inner court of the king's house, over against the king's house: and the king sat upon his royal throne in the royal house, over against the gate of the house" (ver. 1). The die is cast. The queen has practically forfeited her life in order to save her people. If the king give it back to her it shall be well. She and all hers will see in it the evidence of his grace. If not, she can but die, and for that she is prepared.

Her youth and beauty, as well as her confiding trust, draw out her lord's admiration. "And it was so, when the king saw Esther the queen standing in the court, that she obtained favor in his sight: and the king held out to Esther the golden sceptre that was in his hand. So Esther drew near, and touched the top of the sceptre" (ver. 2).

Grace is reigning! Of this the sceptre of gold speaks. "The king's heart is in the hand of the Lord, as the rivers of water: He turneth it whither-

57

soever He will" (Prov. xxi. 1). He it is who
has inclined the proud ruler of the Medes and
Persians to extend the token of his favor to his
trembling queen. "The most high God ruleth in
the kingdom of men" (Dan. iv. 25), whether they
recognize Him or not, and all power is in His
hand. He has heard the mute prayer of Esther
and her people, and from henceforth we are to see
how He worketh all things according to the counsel
of His own will, despite every effort of the enemy
to thwart His purpose.

> "His purposes will ripen fast,
>   Unfolding every hour;
> The bud may have a bitter taste,
>   But sweet will be the flower."

Knowing that nought but some special guerdon
desired could have brought his favorite wife thus
unannounced and unsent for into the throne room,
the king said unto her, "What wilt thou, queen
Esther? and what is thy request? It shall be even
given thee to the half of the kingdom" (ver. 3).
It is as if a blank check signed were handed her,
reminding us of the many precious assurances of
the New Testament: "My God shall supply all your
need according to His riches in glory through Christ
Jesus," for "He is able to do exceeding abundantly above all that we ask or think." He, who
is neither enriched by withholding nor impover-

ished by giving, says to each trusting soul, "What is thy request?" And Omnipotence waits upon the petitions of His feeble people; and to faith He says: "Be it unto thee even as thou wilt." May we have faith to thus enter into and enjoy His wondrous bounty.

Esther is not slow to proffer her request, though at first sight it seems a little thing indeed. "And Esther answered, If it seem good unto the king, let the king and Haman come this day unto the banquet that I have prepared for him" (ver. 4).

There is nothing that so emboldens a soul, burdened with anxiety, and desirous of obtaining help from another, like a season of communion and fellowship. Such a season Esther desires as a prelude to making known her real burden. As though to cover all suspicion, Haman, whose presence must have jarred terribly at such a time, is invited with the king. "So the king and Haman came to the banquet that Esther had prepared" (ver. 5).

In the house of wine the king affirms again his promise to his beloved queen: "And the king said unto Esther at the banquet of wine, What is thy petition? and it shall be granted thee: and what is thy request? even to the half of the kingdom it shall be performed." It is, in its measure, like the word of the Lord to "His own" at the "banquet of wine" in John xiv. 13, 14, after the traitor had

gone out: "And whatsoever ye shall ask in My
name, that will I do, that the Father may be glorified in the Son. If ye shall ask anything in My
name I will do it." The king puts a limit: "even to
the half of the kingdom." Our blessed Lord puts
a limit too: "in My name"—whatever His holy
name may rightly be attached to. This is the
only bound He will put to our asking. This, doubtless, is the secret of many unanswered prayers.
"Ye ask and receive not, because ye ask amiss,
that ye may consume it upon your lusts" (Jas. iv. 3).
Such prayer cannot have the name of the Lord
Jesus attached to it. The expression really means,
by His authority. One says to another, "Do so
and so in my name." All understand he means
as representing, or having the authority of the
speaker behind him. And so it is in approaching
the God of all grace in prayer. There is holy
confidence when the will has been so truly subdued
that the heart's only desire is that the Lord may
be glorified. Then one can ask "in His name,"
and He has pledged His Word to do it.

We do not profess to say that queen Esther's
case is any parallel to this. It but gives us the hint:
and we turn aside from the narrative to press it
upon the reader's attention. because of the great
importance of the subject.

True prayer is perhaps much rarer than many
have any idea of. It can only spring from fel-

lowship with God in a practical sense. "If ye abide in Me and My words abide in you, *ye shall ask what ye will,* and it shall be done unto you" (John xv. 7). It is for lack of this that the prayer-meeting, and the daily season of reading and prayer in the home—not to speak of the sacred moments which should be spent in the closet with closed doors—often degenerate into a mere lifeless form. Souls are conscious of some secret sin indulged; some unscriptural thing in business or family life being persisted in; and of course there cannot be real prayer as long as this is the case. One has no title to expect an answer from God if walking in any forbidden path. May this be deeply impressed upon our souls!

It has been sometimes said that "the prayer-meeting is the pulse of the assembly," and we believe the expression to be a correct one. A sluggish, lifeless prayer-meeting is the indication that, whatever the activity otherwise, things are in a very low state indeed. It is quite possible to carry on gospel and teaching meetings, and to preserve a certain amount of order and decorum at the table of the Lord, which deceives many into the belief that the Holy Spirit is leading; but it is *not* possible truly to pray out of fellowship with God. This is especially true of the secret place. Even in the meeting set apart for waiting on God, a loquacious, self-confident man may be able to deceive himself

and others into the impression that his is really
the prayer of faith; but a few moments spent in
the presence of God, alone, will show how things
really stand.  There is no liberty, no power; all
is a weariness to the flesh if the will is not truly
subject, and the supreme desire of the soul not
expressed in the words, "Thy will be done."

But we return to our narrative.  It would appear that Esther has not yet that liberty that would
lead her to plead her case with assurance; so to
the king's question she replies, "My petition and
my request is, if I have found favor in the sight
of the king, and if it please the king to grant my
petition, and to perform my request, let the king
and Haman come to the banquet that I shall prepare for them, and I will do to-morrow as the king
hath said" (vers. 7, 8).  To this he evidently
agrees; but what momentous consequences would
hang upon that twenty-four hours' delay!  Satan,
knowing that his time is short, and realizing that
if his unholy purpose is to be carried out something
must at once be done, contrives to bring about
if possible the death of Mordecai at least, ere Esther
has the appointed opportunity to ask his life  with
the rest.

"Then went Haman forth that day joyful and
with a glad heart: but when Haman saw Mordecai in the king's gate that he stood not up, nor
moved for him, he was full of indignation against

Mordecai" (ver. 9). The apparently triumphant Amalekite emerges in greater hauteur than ever from the banqueting house. His cup of earthly glory seems filled to the brim. Who so honored as he? He, alone of all the king's favorites, had been admitted to the queen's presence. But there is one bitter ingredient in that so full goblet. Mordecai, the sackcloth-covered Jew, pays him no attention, whatever, as he passes by. The flesh cannot brook being thus despised. He is deeply grieved and filled with wrath against the only man who failed to do him honor. "Nevertheless Haman refrained himself: and when he came home, he sent and called for his friends, and Zeresh his wife, and Haman told them of the glory of his riches, and the multitude of his children, and all the things wherein the king had promoted him, and how he had advanced him above the princes and servants of the king" (vers. 10, 11). What a disgusting exhibition of vanity and pride! Surely Haman is now "set in slippery places." Even the heathen, noting how soon, in the moral government of the universe, disaster followed on unbounded self-sufficiency and inordinate self-esteem, had coined the proverb, "Whom the gods would destroy they first make mad." And the one true God had, long ere Haman's day, inspired a man to write, "Pride goeth before destruction, and a haughty spirit before a fall;" and "when pride cometh, then cometh shame:

but with the lowly is wisdom" (Prov. xvi. 18 and xi. 2).

With characteristic conceit the vainglorious premier keeps what he considers the choicest morsel to the last. "Haman said moreover, Yea, Esther the queen did let no man come in with the king unto the banquet that she had prepared, but myself; and to-morrow am I invited unto her also with the king." But he cannot conceal his wounded vanity in connection with the incident at the gate, for he adds bitterly, "Yet all this availeth me nothing, so long as I see Mordecai the Jew sitting at the king's gate" (vers. 12, 13).

In the eyes of his satellites and his equally proud and vindictive wife, this is a matter that can readily be disposed of. Why should he wait the appointed time for the destruction of Mordecai with the rest of the Jews? Has he not just shown that none have such influence with the king as he? Why not, on some trumped-up pretext, despatch the insolent Hebrew at once? "Then said Zeresh his wife, and all his friends unto him, Let a gallows be made fifty cubits high, and to-morrow speak thou unto the king that Mordecai may be hanged thereon: then go thou in merrily with the king unto the banquet. And the thing pleased Haman; and he caused the gallows to be made" (ver. 14).

Fifty cubits would be about eighty feet: rather unduly high, one would think, for one insignificant, undersized Jew to swing from; but Haman will publish his revenge abroad and thus give an object-lesson to any other who would dare defy the man of the hour.

And so our chapter closes, with the last nails being driven in the gallows in Haman's court, while Mordecai is all unaware of the fate which is purposed to be meted out to him on the morrow; and a score of hours have yet to run ere the queen will prefer her request before the king.

"Hath God forgotten to be gracious?"

# CHAPTER VI

## A SLEEPLESS NIGHT, AND ITS RESULTS

IT has been well said that "although the *name* of
God is not in this book, the *hand* of God is plainly
to be seen throughout." Nowhere is this more
clearly manifested than in the present chapter, every
verse of which attests His overruling providence
and His unfailing love and care for His people, in
a wrong place though they were. He is behind the
scenes, it is true; but, to use the expression of another, He moves all the scenes that He is behind.

It is not until the last night that He interferes:

> "God never is before His time,
> And never is behind."

To all appearances, Satan was to have everything
his own way, at least so far as Mordecai was concerned. In Haman's tessellated courtyard the now
completed gallows stands fifty cubits high. The
lofty Amalekite is already gloating over the death
of the unyielding descendant of Kish, and tosses
restlessly upon his couch as he waits for the first
glimmer of the morning for the execution of his
wrath. He is not, however, the only restless one,
for "on that night could not the king sleep."

In itself this was apparently a very trifling thing. How many a crowned head before and since has turned uneasily on its pillow and courted slumber in vain! But in this case, how much that sleepless night was to mean to Mordecai, and all his con- demned brethren!

In his insomnia, the king, at last despairing of natural rest, called for "the strangest soporific ever sought." "He commanded to bring the book of records of the chronicles; and they were read before the king" (ver. 1). Surely in those bloodstained annals there was enough to have driven away sleep forever. But One is overruling all, and the august Iranian emperor is but as a chess-king in His hand to be moved by Him at will.

As the records of his reign are read aloud in his hearing, "it was found written that Mordecai had told of Bigthana and Teresh, two of the king's chamberlains, the keepers of the door, who sought to lay hands on Ahasuerus" (ver. 2). How well had all been timed! He who knows the end from the beginning had caused this service to be here re- corded. He had also so ordered it that, at the time it was rendered, the preoccupied monarch should overlook entirely the one to whose faithfulness he owed his life. To Mordecai this may have seemed at the time like base ingratitude, though we read of no word of complaint. Possibly he had learned to "endure as seeing Him who is invisible." At any rate it was now made manifest that there was a divine reason for the king's forgetfulness. God had timed everything well, and He "makes everything beautiful in its season."

Do these pages meet the eyes of some tried and discouraged saint? Have you been overwhelmed at times by a nameless dread as though God had utterly forgotten you, and you were cast off forever? Have you wearied yourself devising one human expedient after another, in the vain hope of averting threatened disaster by the arm of flesh? Learn, then, from God's dealings with His servant of old that His heart and hand are for you still. And "if God be for us, who can be against us?" He has heard every sigh; noted, and stored in His bottle, every tear; taken account of every cry of anguish; heard every confiding prayer. His arm is in nowise shortened; His ear is in no sense deaf to your cry. At the appointed time He will awake in your behalf, and you shall know that it is "the God of all grace" with whom you have to do. Only look up: be not cast down, for you are ever on His heart; and if you just leave all with Him, He will make your affairs His care. "Casting all your care upon Him, for He careth for you." How sweet the words! **He** careth. He, the most high God: yea, the God and Father of our Lord Jesus Christ **careth**. He is no indifferent spectator—no callous, unconcerned looker-on; but, as no one else can, He careth for **you**. Assured of this, may not the reader and the writer well cry, "I will trust, and not be afraid"?

The hitherto neglectful king is at once aroused as his memory is refreshed in regard to Mordecai's service in days gone by. "And the king said, What honor and dignity hath been done to Mordecai for this? Then said the king's servants that ministered unto him, There is nothing done for him" (ver. 3). He had shown himself to be a loyal and faithful subject, despite the fact that he was of the children of the captivity; but though the king had profited by his devotion, he allowed him to go utterly unrewarded, while bestowing favors with lavish hand on so worthless a character as the selfish and despicable Haman. Such is the favor of princes. "Cursed is the man that trusteth in man, and maketh flesh his arm, and whose heart departeth from the Lord. For he shall be like the heath in the desert, and *shall not see when good cometh;* but shall inhabit the parched places in the wilderness, in a salt land, and not inhabited. Blessed is the man that trusteth in the Lord, and whose hope the Lord is. For he shall be as a tree planted by the waters, and that spreadeth out her roots by the river, and shall not see when heat cometh, but her leaf shall be green, and *shall not be careful in time of drought,* neither shall cease from yielding fruit" (Jer. xvii. 5-8). How sharp the contrast between the time-

serving man of the flesh, whose eyes are fixed
on man for his reward—doomed ever to disappointment—and the God-fearing man of faith,
who rises above all creature-help to the Most High
Himself! Mordecai has left all in His hands. He
is now about to make his way prosperous.

And yet even at the last moment how active
is Satan in his efforts to thwart God's purpose
of grace! At this moment a step is heard in the
outer court of the royal sleeping apartment. "And
the king said, Who is in the court? Now Haman
was come into the outward court of the king's
house, to speak unto the king to hang Mordecai
on the gallows that he had prepared for him. And
the king's servants said unto him, Behold, Haman
standeth in the court. And the king said, Let
him come in" (vers. 4, 5).

If God is at work, so is the great adversary.
Haman, still burning with wounded vanity, is early
on the scene. He would forestall all further
slights from Mordecai by getting the easily-influ-
enced and luxurious despot to sign the order for
the Jew's execution as soon as he shall rise. Then,
the hated object out of the way, he will be in
good humor for the festal board. He is, however,
but to learn that "those who walk in pride, God
is able to abase." He has reached the highest pin-
nacle of earthly glory to which he can lawfully

aspire. He is about to be hurled into the lowest depths of shame and ignominy.

The king's first words fairly cause his head to swim with wild exultation, and seem to point to the early fulfilment of his most cherished dreams. "What," asks his royal master, "shall be done unto the man whom the king delighteth to honor?" It is hardly to be wondered at that the vainglorious prince whose only concern was the advancement of his own interests "thought in his heart, To whom would the king delight to do honor more than to MYSELF?" What a place that same "myself" had in this conceited, wretched man's mind! And what a snare is self-occupation, in any form, to the saint of God! Pride is distinctly said to be the cause of Satan's fall. "Thy heart was lifted up because of thy beauty; thou hast corrupted thy wisdom by reason of thy brightness: I will cast thee to the ground" (Ezek. xxviii. 17). And when giving instruction concerning overseers in the house of God, in the New Testament, the Holy Ghost says, "Not a novice, lest being lifted up with pride he fall into the condemnation of the devil" (1 Tim. iii. 6).

When we see pride in another, how hateful a thing it is! Haman is the very incarnation of it; and how we loathe so despicable a character! Yet, alas, how readily we tolerate in ourselves what is so detestable in others. "The proud He knoweth afar off," but "the meek will He guide in judgment; the meek will He teach His way."

Filled with a sense of his own self-importance, Haman replies to the king's question in the boldest manner. He would have the man whom the king delights to honor appear before men as king himself in all but name. That, too, might come later if the populace but grew used to him appearing in royal garb, and the king's most noble princes were made to have a due sense of his power and ability. How plainly the Amalekite shows himself! The hand which of old was upon the throne of Jah is now stretched out to grasp the throne of the world! "And Haman answered the king, For the man whom the king delighteth to honor, let the royal apparel be brought which the king useth to wear, and the horse that the king rideth upon, and the crown royal which is set upon his head: and let this apparel and horse be delivered to the hand of one of the king's most noble princes, that they may array the man withal whom the king delighteth to honor, and bring him on horseback through the street of the city, and proclaim before him, Thus shall it be done to the man whom the king delighteth to honor" (vers. 7-9). Could human pretension and ingenuity go farther? Intending all this for himself, can there be any doubt regarding his desire to have the people behold him in all the outward trappings of royalty, in order to accustom their minds to a future usurpation of imperial power?

Did the king begin to see beneath the surface? Did he already commence to mistrust his favorite? Or is it only in our imagination that we see a touch of genuine irony, meant to cut to the very quick, in the brief and pithy command, "Make haste, and take the apparel and the horse, as thou hast said, and do even so to Mordecai the Jew that sitteth at the king's gate: let nothing fail of all that thou hast spoken." Did the royal eye detect the way the color came and went in Haman's face? Did it note the downcast countenance and the disappointment too deep for words that marked him as he turned away without reply? We do not know. But the readiness with which the erstwhile favorite is given up to a richly deserved judgment later in the day, would imply a lack of confidence already cherished in his heart.

"Then took Haman the apparel and the horse, and arrayed Mordecai, and brought him on horseback through the street of the city, and proclaimed before him, Thus shall it be done unto the man whom the king delighteth to honor" (ver. 11). A terrible come-down, surely, and a remarkable turn of events! No wonder that we read, "And Mordecai came again to the king's gate. But Haman hasted to his house mourning, and having his head covered" (ver. 12). Did Mordecai see in this sudden transition from ignominy to honor the pledge of his deliverance from condemnation? It would seem so, for he made no effort to resist the changing of his attire on this occasion. Haman too reads a lesson in it all, and in shame and confusion of face hurries from the public gaze to the seclusion of his own house. He knows it is in vain now for him to seek permission to hang Mordecai. The gallows stand like a monument to folly and vanity, still towering up to heaven, casting a shadow that speaks of approaching disaster.

"And Haman told Zeresh his wife and all his friends everything that had befallen him. Then said his wise men and Zeresh his wife unto him, If Mordecai be of the seed of the Jews, before whom thou hast begun to fall, thou shalt not prevail against him, but shall surely fall before him" (ver. 13). Little comfort indeed does he find in this, which is all too true, as the sequel shows.

"And while they were yet talking with him, came the king's chamberlains, and hasted to bring Haman unto the banquet that Esther had prepared." His enthusiasm is greatly dampened. He would, without question, prefer retirement until he has regained his accustomed poise and self-confidence, but the king's command must be obeyed. Yesterday he would have needed no chamberlains to summon him. To-day all is changed. Already he has been greatly humbled. Ere the remaining hours of light pass he shall have more crushing experiences still, and shall prove to the full the truth of the ominous prophecy of his wife and friends.

# CHAPTER VII

## THE SECOND BANQUET AND THE AMALEKITE'S END

IT is hardly to be supposed that the remarkable happenings of the forenoon had all taken place without Esther's knowledge. We know that she was in daily communication, through her chamberlains, with her aged cousin; and there can scarcely be any question as to her having been made familiar with his sudden elevation to the imperial favor. This would account for the lack of hesitancy and the implicit confidence with which she prefers her request when "the king and Haman came to banquet with Esther the queen" (ver. 1).

The feast was not yet concluded when the king said, "What is thy petition, queen Esther? and it shall be granted thee: and what is thy request? and it shall be performed, even to the half of the kingdom" (ver. 2). It is the same invitation to ask largely with the same assurance, as on the previous occasion, that all shall be given. "In the word of a king there is power." How much more to be relied on is the word of "God that cannot lie," who has said, "Everyone that asketh, receiveth;" and who invites implicit confidence, on

the part of His own blood-washed and redeemed
saints, in His faithful promises.

"Then Esther the queen answered and said,
If I have found favor in thy sight, O king, and
if it please the king, let my life be given me at
my petition, and my people at my request: for
we are sold, I and my people, to be destroyed,
to be slain, and to perish. But if we had been
sold for bondmen and bondwomen, I had held my
tongue, although the enemy could not countervail
the king's damage" (vers. 3, 4). Knowing that her
lord's favor is toward her, she pleads both her own
cause, and her people's. She petitions him to
spare their and her life.

How surprised must the king have been to hear
her so speak. Who would dare seek the life of
his beloved queen? And who could her people be
who were thus placed in jeopardy of their lives?
It is to be remembered that Esther's kindred had
not yet been made known to the king. He was in
ignorance of the fact that she was a Jewess.

Her words must have deeply agitated the already
toppling son of Hammedatha. Was there not even
a designed coincidence on her part between the
decree drawn up by Haman and the queen's words
as she said, "We are sold, I and my people, *to be
destroyed, to be slain, and to perish?*" How could
he forget that such had been the language he had
caused the king's scribes to write? What an appall-

ing discovery to learn that he had included the wife of Ahasuerus in his bold scheme of bloodshed and revenge! How earnestly he would listen for the king's reply.

"Then the king Ahasuerus answered and said unto Esther the queen, Who is he, and where is he, that durst presume in his heart to do so?" (ver. 5). He at once makes her enemy his; and demands the name of the infamous wretch who could dare conceive so fearful a plot. The guilty conspirator reclines but a few feet from him. His sin is to find him out at last!

"And Esther said, The adversary and enemy is this wicked Haman. Then Haman was afraid before the king and queen" (ver. 6). He is manifested now in his true character. The fawning and politic courtier appears as the deep-dyed villain whose perfidy is almost too great to be believed. Satan has again been foiled in his attempt to destroy the line of promise, and God has once more vindicated His Word.

It is easy to cherish a feeling of contempt and disgust for so low and vile a character as Haman. But it is well to remember, that in every man's heart is found the same evil thing, which when brought to its full fruition, appears so abominable in the ungodly Agagite. "The heart is deceitful above all things, and desperately wicked," and God asks the question, "Who can know it?"

He solemnly answers Himself: "I the Lord search the heart, I try the reins, even to give every man according to his ways, and according to the fruit of his doings" (Jer. xvii. 9, 10). It is "out of the heart," says the Lord Jesus, that all kinds of evil things proceed, and He names "evil thoughts, murders, adulteries, fornications, thefts, false witness, blasphemies" (Matt. xv. 19). "These are the things which defile a man," He adds; and we desire affectionately to remind the reader, lest any should be in danger of forgetting it, that it is the grace of God alone which makes one man to differ from another.

No amount of education or culture, nay, nor self-restraint or religiousness, will eradicate the evil. It is the *nature* that is wholly and utterly corrupt and pernicious. Therefore before one can please God there must be a new nature imparted, and this is the result of new birth. "That which is born of the flesh is flesh, and that which is born of the Spirit is spirit." Nothing but this second birth, through receiving the word of God, will avail to place any natural man on a different footing before the throne of the Majesty on high, than that occupied by the Hamans, the Pharaohs, and the Herods of the Bible. "There is no difference, for all have sinned and come short of the glory of God."

People often consider it a mark of superior

virtue to be shocked and horrified by the crimes of others whom they imagine to be worse than themselves. It is well to realize that the worst acts of the worst men all spring from a nature identical with that of all other sons and daughters of Adam. It is because of this humbling fact our Lord had to tell a religious doctor that "except a man be born again he cannot see the kingdom of God," and again, "Marvel not that I say unto thee, Ye must be born again."

Is my reader certain that he or she is the subject of this great change? Have you truly turned to the Lord for yourself, and from the heart believed the gospel-message which declares that "Christ Jesus came into the world to save sinners?" If not, I beseech you, read no further, but stop right here and consider, until you have, as a guilty, helpless sinner, cast yourself unreservedly upon that blessed One, "who died for all, that they which live should not henceforth live unto themselves, but unto Him which died for them and rose again" (2 Cor. v. 15).

If truly a Christian, turn with us once more to our narrative. The poor discovered wretch trembles before the king and the queen; as some day men will tremble before the Omnipotent Judge when all their secret guilt shall be made known before an assembled universe and it will be too late to seek a hiding-place.

It would seem that Ahasuerus is dazed for the moment, as he begins to realize what Haman had obtained his royal consent for. He is, in a very grave sense, a party to the proposed indiscriminate slaughter of the Hebrews, which would include his beloved spouse. We are told that "the king arising from the banquet of wine went into the palace garden: and Haman stood up to make request for his life to Esther the queen; for he saw that there was evil determined against him by the king" (ver. 7). The man who without a twinge of remorse could devote a nation to destruction, is in dire distress at the thought of himself losing life or liberty. He takes the place of suppliant at the feet of the now triumphant Esther, cousin to the unbending old man he had led through the streets in the morning. One is reminded of the word to Philadelphia, "I will make them to come and worship before thy feet, and to know that I have loved thee" (Rev. iii. 9, last clause).

In his desperation Haman oversteps the bounds of both court etiquette and ordinary decency, by throwing himself upon the divan where the queen was reclining. At this juncture "the king returned out of the palace garden into the place of the banquet of wine; and Haman was fallen upon the bed where Esther was. Then said the king, Will he force the queen also before me in the house? As the words went out of the king's mouth they covered Haman's face" (ver. 8). His very importunity, unwise in the extreme, is the means of his complete undoing. At a signal from the outraged monarch his face is covered—token of his condemnation to death. Hope is gone. He shall never see the king's face again; nor shall he be troubled by Mordecai's uplifted form evermore. "It is a righteous thing with God to recompense tribulation to them that trouble you" (2 Thess. i. 6). The ungodly may now be supreme, while to the righteous "waters of a full cup" are wrung out; "but the triumphing of the wicked is short." God is still the moral Governor of the world, to whom all men must give an account. He will manifest His power eventually when "all the proud, yea, and all that do wickedly, shall be stubble: and the day that cometh shall burn them up, saith the Lord of hosts, that it shall leave them neither root nor branch" (Mal. iv. 1). This passage has no reference to judgment after death. It is not the unsaved dead being cast into the lake of fire. It refers solely and simply to God's judgments which will be meted out to the oppressors of His people at the end of this age. Of this Haman's case gives us a hint.

The chamberlains, quick to discern the mind of the king, waste no sympathy on the fallen premier. "Harbonah, one of the chamberlains, said before the king, Behold, also, the gallows fifty cubits high, which Haman made for Mordecai, who had spoken good for the king, standeth in the house of Haman. Then the king said, Hang him thereon" (ver. 9). So certain had the now friendless wretch been in the morning of his having no difficulty about getting the king's permission to hang the refractory Jew, that he appears to have made no secret of his intention. It is evident that Harbonah was quite familiar with it, and as it is very unlikely that such information had been vouchsafed after the procession through the street in the forenoon, it would seem that Haman had but added to his own discomfiture by explaining the purpose of his early visit to some of the chamberlains before being summoned to the royal presence. The attendant mentions now the fact of the gallows having been erected, and the reason for it. Mordecai would have been strung up there had not Providence interfered. The king, hearing of it, utters but three words, "Hang him thereon," and the Amalekite's doom is sealed.

It is not the only time in Scripture history that in God's governmental dealings such a thing has occurred. Daniel furnishes us with a similar instance. Saved himself by Almighty power from the lions' jaws, his accusers are cast into the den and destroyed. David wrote of the wicked; "Behold he travaileth with iniquity, and hath conceived mischief, and brought forth falsehood. He made a pit and digged it, and is fallen into the ditch which he made. His mischief shall return upon his own head, and his violent dealing shall come down upon his own pate" (Ps. vii. 14-16). So shall it be with the personal Antichrist, "the Jews' enemy" of the future, of whom Haman, if not a type, is at least an illustration. At the moment when his power shall seem to be supreme, and all hope for deliverance for the Remnant of Israel, who in that dark day shall cleave to the Lord, will have practically fled away, the warrior of the 19th of Revelation shall descend and hurl the impious usurper alive into the lake that burneth with fire and brimstone.

"So they hanged Haman on the gallows that he had prepared for Mordecai. Then was the king's wrath pacified" (ver. 10). The sentence, as soon as uttered, is carried out. Haman is hanged as one "accursed of God." Thus "the righteous is delivered out of trouble, and the wicked cometh in his stead" (Prov. xi. 8). "Riches profit not in the day of wrath;" his wealth and power availed him nothing. In one moment all is manifested as being altogether lighter than vanity. He has gone out into eternity naked and alone; and as a later revelation tells us, "It is appointed unto men once to die, and after this the judgment" (Heb. ix, 27). That stark, cold body suspended to the gallows preaches loudly, to all who will give heed, of the evanescent character of all earth's baubles, and the importance of living for eternity.

"I have seen the wicked in great power, and spreading himself like a green bay tree. Yet he passed away, and, lo, he was not: yea, I sought him, but he could not be found" (Ps. xxxvii. 35, 36.)

# CHAPTER VIII

## THE DESPISED MAN EXALTED AND THE DECREE OF GRACE

IT was not enough that Haman should be put to death. Some means must be devised whereby the people of the Jews could be saved and yet the unalterable laws of the Persians and the Medes remain unviolated. Of this the present chapter treats.

"On that day did the king Ahasuerus give the house of Haman, the Jews' enemy, unto Esther the queen. And Mordecai came before the king, for Esther had told what he was to her. And the king took off his ring, which he had taken from Haman, and gave it unto Mordecai. And Esther set Mordecai over the house of Haman" (vers. 1, 2).

The power of the enemy is overthrown. Haman's house is presented to Esther and she appoints Mordecai over it. She tells at last what relation he bore to her, and there is nothing more to hide.

Her discipline, and his too, had been severe, but at last both reach a place where they can be used in blessing to their people. There must

ever be a divine schooling ere there can be use-
fulness and enlargement.    But although the circumstances are so remarkably altered, the decree con-
demning "all Jews, both young and old, little
children and women," to be slain on the thirteenth
day of the twelfth month still stands unrevoked.
Nor can it be revoked—for the laws of the kingdom
once made were unchangeable.    But strong in faith
that some means would be found whereby the evil
might be averted, and yet the dignity of the laws remain untouched, we are told that "Esther spake
yet again before the king and fell down at his
feet, and besought him with tears to put away
the mischief of Haman the Agagite, and his device
that he had devised against the Jews" (ver. 3).
The position of her people was strikingly analogous
to that of unsaved men and women in general;
conscious of having richly deserved the judgment
of God, the curse of the broken law hanging over
their heads: "Cursed is every one that continueth
not in all things which are written in the book of
the law to do them" (Gal. iii. 10; Deut. xxvii. 26).
So runs the unchangeable decree of a holy God.
All are worthy of death; for all have sinned.    None
have continued in obedience to all the commandments of God.    Therefore all are under the curse.
It will not do to plead ignorance of the law, or
sorrow for having failed.    "The soul that sinneth
*it shall die.*"    The law knows no mercy for the

violator of it. Neither will it do to promise to do better in days to come; to endeavor to obey the Word in the future. A better future, if that were to be, could not change the past—and "God requireth that which is past" (Eccl. iii. 15).

If saved at all, it cannot be at the expense of God's character or by the violation of His word in any manner whatsoever.

But it is right here that the gospel comes in. God can say, "Deliver him from going down to the pit: I have found a ransom" (Job xxxiii. 24). The Lord Jesus has borne the sinner's judgment. Yea, "God hath made Him to be sin for us, who knew no sin; that we might be made the righteousness of God in Him" (2 Cor. v. 21). He, ever spotless and undefiled, was not under the curse. The sentence of condemnation did not hang over Him. But in infinite love and mercy He stooped vicariously beneath our load, and "bare our sins in His own body on the tree" (1 Pet. ii. 24). "He was wounded for our transgressions; He was bruised for our iniquities: the chastisement of our peace was upon Him; and with His stripes we are healed" (Isa. liii 5). A righteous basis has now been laid, upon which God can act according to the love of His heart, and yet in perfect holiness. A second decree goes forth, not contradicting or annulling the former one; but which, while in perfect harmony with it, will provide a means whereby all

can be saved who avail themselves thereof.
So we read, "Christ hath redeemed us from the curse
of the law, being made a curse for us: for it is
written, Cursed is every one that hangeth on a
tree" (Gal. iii. 13). The work that saves is finished.
All can find deliverance from the judgment of God
who in simple faith receive and act upon the message
of grace.

And so, returning to our chapter, it is beautifully in keeping with this that "the king held out
the golden sceptre toward Esther." Grace is
reigning and upon that ground alone can there be
deliverance for her people. "So Esther arose, and
stood before the king, and said, If it please the king,
and if I have found favor in his sight, and the thing
seem right before the king, and I be pleasing in
his eyes, let it be written to reverse the letters devised
by Haman the son of Hammedatha the Agagite,
which he wrote to destroy the Jews which are in
all the king's provinces: for how can I endure to see
the evil that shall come unto my people? or how
can I endure to see the destruction of my kindred?"
(vers. 4-6.)

It is a touching plea that she gives utterance
to. It hangs on this, "If the thing seem right
before the king, and I be pleasing in his sight."
She does not attempt to plead the good works,
the benevolence, or the loyalty of the Jews. She
would have him deal with them according to his

estimate of her. Like the great apostle of the
Gentiles who, when entreating Philemon in behalf
of Onesimus writes, "If thou count me therefore
a partner receive him as myself" (Phile. 17).
And surely we have more than a hint, both there
and here, of the great and wondrous truth expressed in the blessed words of inspiration, "He
hath made us accepted in the Beloved."    Esther had
risked her life for her people and would now have
them dealt with according to the king's thoughts
of herself.    The Lord Jesus Christ gave His life
a ransom for lost, guilty sinners, and now all who
trust in Him are dealt with by God according to
His thoughts of His Son.    How tenderly this
precious truth is expressed in the Lord's great inter-
cessory prayer!    He says, "I in them, and Thou
in Me, that they may be made perfect in one; and
that the world may know that Thou hast sent Me,
and *hast loved them even as Thou hast loved
Me*" (John xvii. 23).

Esther's touching plea avails, and "the king
Ahasuerus said unto Esther the queen, and Mordecai the Jew, Behold, I have given Esther the
house of Haman, and him they have hanged upon
the gallows, because he laid his hand upon the
Jews.    Write ye also for the Jews as it liketh you,
in the king's name, and seal it with the king's
ring: for the writing which is written in the king's
name, and sealed with the king's ring, may no man

reverse" (vers. 7, 8). He who "had the power of death" has been destroyed. The message of grace can now be sent out "to deliver those who through fear of death" had been subjected to so cruel a bondage.

"Then were the king's scribes called at that time, in the third month, that is the month Sivan, on the three and twentieth day thereof; and it was written according to all that Mordecai commanded unto the Jews, and to the lieutenants, and the deputies and rulers of the provinces which are from India unto Ethiopia, a hundred twenty and seven provinces, unto every province according to the writing thereof, and unto every people after their language, and to the Jews according to their writing and according to their language" (ver. 9). Less than nine months remained ere the decree of Haman was due to be put into execution. Short enough time if the message of grace was to reach the farthest limits of the kingdom ere the day of slaughter appointed! The proclamation is as universal as the previous one, and is written in every language of the known world. Its text is given in the verses that follow.

"And he wrote in the king Ahasuerus' name, and sealed it with the king's ring, and sent letters by post on horseback, and riders on mules, camels, and young dromedaries: wherein the king granted the Jews which were in every city to gather themselves together, and to stand for their life, to destroy, to slay, and to cause to perish, all the power of the people and province that would assault them, both little ones and women, and to take the spoil of them for prey, upon one day in all the provinces of king Ahasuerus, namely, upon the thirteenth day of the twelfth month which is the month Adar" (vers. 10-12). It will be seen that this proclamation in no sense contradicted the one that had gone before. The other gave the people command to destroy the Jews. This one gave to the afflicted nation the privilege of defending themselves. In other words it provided a means of salvation which they could accept or reject as they chose. It is not otherwise with the glad tidings proclaimed in the gospel. A Saviour is provided. All who avail themselves of God's gracious interference are saved. All who reject the means of His providing, do so at their own peril.

No time is lost in sending out the joyful tidings. Would that Christians were as much in earnest in making known to all people, far and near, the good news of eternal salvation through a crucified and risen Saviour! "The copy of the writing for a commandment to be given in every province was published unto all people, and that the Jews should be ready against that day to avenge themselves on their enemies. So the posts that rode upon mules and camels went out, being hastened and pressed on by the king's commandment. And the decree was given in Shushan the palace" (vers. 13, 14). To every corner of the habitable earth, the messengers go forth "being hastened" by the monarch's word, reminding us forcibly of another commission given by a greater than Ahasuerus: "And Jesus came and spake unto them, saying, All power is given unto Me in heaven and in earth. Go ye therefore, and teach (Gk., "disciple") all nations, baptizing them in the name of the Father, and of the Son, and of the Holy Ghost: teaching them to observe all things whatsoever I have commanded you: and, lo, I am with you alway even unto the end of the world. Amen" (Matt. xxviii. 18-20). His commandment was urgent. Men were in danger of something far worse than temporal destruction—in danger of the eternal judgment of God against sin. Nothing was to hinder. "Go ye," He says. And, commissioned by the Lord Himself, they went forth to make known to Jew and Gentile the exceeding riches of His grace.

But what lethargy has come in since those early days of devotion to His name! What millions of heathen are unevangelized in this vaunted century of progress and enlightenment. Solemn indeed must be the reckoning with those by and by who are so indifferent to "the King's commandment." What would have been thought of one of the couriers of Ahasuerus who, forgetting the urgency and importance of his message, loitered among the leafy bowers of the wayside khans, or amused himself with the sights of the way; losing valuable time; forgetting that hundreds of lives depended upon his errand being fulfilled ere the thirteenth day of the month Adar. Would such an one not have justly deserved the severest censure, if not death itself? And what is to be thought of Christians who have heard the charge of the Lord Jesus, "Go ye into all the world and preach the gospel to every creature" (Mark xvi. 15), but who, paying no attention to the appalling condition of lost souls on every side of them, think only of their own pleasure and comfort? "If thou forbear to deliver them that are drawn unto death, and those that are ready to be slain, if thou sayest, Behold we knew it not; doth not He that pondereth the heart consider it? And He that keepeth thy soul, doth He not know it? And shall not He render to every man according to his works?" (Prov. xxiv. 11, 12). These are unspeakably solemn words and worthy of being carefully pondered in the presence of God by every converted reader of these lines. May grace be given to each one to weigh well their solemn import, and to seek day by day to faithfully make known the only message which can deliver from the second death.

"And Mordecai went out from the presence of the king in royal apparel of blue and white, and with a great crown of gold, and with a garment of fine linen and purple; and the city of Shushan rejoiced and was glad" (ver. 15). The condemnation past, Mordecai puts off the sackcloth, to be worn no more. Robed now as befits his exalted position he goes into the king's presence. His clothing of blue and white and purple may surely have a meaning for our hearts to enter into. Blue is the color of the heavens, and ever seems to speak, in Scripture, of that heavenly character which should be manifested by the redeemed soul. White is righteousness, and put on as a habit tells of the practical righteousness that should adorn the child of God. Of this too the fine linen reminds us for "the fine linen is the righteousness of saints" (Rev. xix. 8). The purple is the color of royalty; while the "great crown of gold" would tell of the divine glory, in harmony with which Mordecai has now been raised from the depths of woe to the heights of power and blessing: blessing not for himself alone, but for all who harken to his word. And so, from time to time, even in the broken condition of things in which we see the professing Church to-day, does God raise up men who will honor Him in honoring His Word, and who are thus made a means of untold blessing to others.

The king's message *believed* brought joy and gladness; even as the gospel, believed, brings the same to-day. "The Jews had light, and gladness, and joy, and honor. And in every province, and in every city, whithersoever the king's commandment and his decree came, the Jews had joy and gladness, a feast and a good day. And many of the people of the land became Jews; for the fear of the Jews fell upon them" (vers. 16, 17). It is important to notice that it was the word of the king which brought all the grief and anguish of heart described in chapter four. The king had spoken. They believed his decree, and they were miserable. Now it is his word that gives them peace and happiness, and drives away their sorrow. Even so, God's word as to man's lost estate and the judgment hanging over him brings the soul to cry, "The pains of hell gat hold upon me: I found trouble and sorrow" (Psa. cxvi. 3). But by the message of grace and truth which has come by Jesus Christ, truly believed, the gloom is banished, and the exultant heart cries with joy, "Thou hast delivered my soul from death, mine eyes from tears, and my feet from falling" (Psa. cxvi. 8). It is in neither case a question of experience or wrought-up feelings, but of *faith in the message proclaimed*.

And so God had turned the mourning of His people into rejoicing, and the result was that the fear of them fell upon the people of the provinces, many of whom sought the God of Israel and became proselytes, taking their places as members of the chosen nation. There is nothing that so appeals to the world as a happy, holy company of saints, whose spirits have been refreshed by the goodness of the Lord.

# CHAPTER IX 1–19

## THE DELIVERANCE

IT was faith in the written word of the king that gave the Jews joy and gladness, even though the formerly dreaded thirteenth of Adar had not yet come. So does faith in the written word of God give boldness and confidence though the day of doom once feared has not yet arrived. The revelation of His grace and "perfect love" as revealed in the cross "casteth out all fear," for "faith is the substance" (or confidence) "of things hoped for, the evidence" (or conviction) "of things not seen" (Heb. xi. 1). "We walk by faith, not by sight," for "what a man seeth, why doth he yet hope for? But if we hope for that we see not, then do we with patience wait for it" (Rom. viii. 24, 25). It was not an inward emotion or a passing feeling that gave to the people of Esther and Mordecai the assurance that they would not be destroyed, as originally intended by Haman. They had something far better than that. Their tears were dried, their sorrow assuaged in resting upon the word alone.

This cannot be insisted on too strongly. There

are many to-day seeking peace in an utterly wrong way. Some hope, because of a restful feeling within, that they have at last been accepted of God, and are now on the way to heaven. Others trust in the fact that they pray and attend to various religious duties; while many more are without any confidence at all, but hope at last to have an inward sense of pardon ere they die. To all of these classes we would say, Do not rest in anything short of the revealed word of God. That Word *believed*, joy and peace must follow; but it is faith first, peace afterwards.

To go direct to Scripture is the only safe way for every soul. For instance: I am a sinner; my awakened conscience troubles me about many things I had formerly treated as matters of indifference; an awful sense of condemnation and wrath hangs over me; I long for deliverance. I pray, and groan, and weep. Still there is no peace. I try to change my ways; break loose from old habits; forsake evil companions,—I am miserable even then. I perhaps go to church; submit to baptism; partake of the Lord's Supper; give of my means to assist the cause of Christ. But alas, alas, all is in vain! I am only more and more aware of my true state since so great changes seem to be necessary to fit me for God's presence. I have no assurance that my sins are forgiven: and it is this I must know if I would be at peace. At last, wearied and almost hopeless, I come to the Word itself. Perhaps such a passage as Acts xiii. 38, 39 meets my eye: "Be it *known* unto you." Ah yes, that is it! I want to KNOW. This awful uncertainty is what is harassing me and taking from me all rest, and plunging me into deepest anxiety. What is it that can be "known" in this verse? "Be it known unto you that through *this Man*"—that is, through Jesus—not through my prayers, my devotions, my benevolences, or my changed manner of life! Nor yet through the church, her services, her ministers or her ordinances. No! blessed be God, I am turned from all these things—good as they may be in their place; I am turned to "this Man," to Jesus—the Man of Calvary—the Man who is now in the glory. "Through this Man is preached unto *you*,"— how intensely personal it is: "known unto you;" "preached unto you;"—surely, then I cannot be mistaken in appropriating it to myself. "Preached unto you the *forgiveness of sins!*" Ah! That is what I want so earnestly. This is what I can never be happy without. How, then, is this preached forgiveness to be really mine,—known and enjoyed as mine? Here is the answer: "By Him *all* that *believe are justified* from all things, from which ye could not be justified by the law of Moses." Here, then, is the peace-giving testimony of God's infallible Word. I can rest on that. I believe in the Lord Jesus. He died for me. I trust in Him alone.

God declares all who so believe are "justified from all things." I can trust His declaration. I have sure and perfect peace. "Being justified by faith, we have peace with God, through our Lord Jesus Christ: by whom also we have access by faith into this grace wherein we stand, and rejoice in hope of the glory of God" (Rom. v. 1, 2).

Resting on the word of the king, the Jews found peace. Now we are to learn how the word of the king is actually fulfilled. "Now in the twelfth month, that is, the month Adar, on the thirteenth day of the same, when the king's commandment and his decree drew near to be put into execution, in the day that the enemies of the Jews hoped to have power over them, (though it was turned to the contrary, that the Jews had rule over them that hated them,) the Jews gathered themselves together in their cities throughout all the provinces of the king Ahasuerus, to lay hand on such as sought their hurt: and no man could withstand them; for the fear of them fell upon all people" (vers. 1, 2). The day that had been so dreaded, ere the posts brought the message of grace, is now awaited with eager anticipation. It is to be a day of triumph and rejoicing to the Jews, and a day of overthrowing the power of their enemies. The government is for, not against, them. This is the reason of their gladness. "And all the rulers of the provinces, and the lieutenants, and the deputies, and officers of the king, helped the Jews; because the fear of Mordecai fell upon them. For Mordecai was great in the king's house, and his fame went out throughout all the provinces: for this man Mordecai waxed greater and greater" (vers. 3, 4).

How truly had the word been fulfilled which says, "Them that honor Me, I will honor; and they that despise Me shall be lightly esteemed"! It will be remembered that in the beginning, when Mordecai sided with God, and refused to bow to the haughty enemy of Jehovah, that the king's servants wondered "whether Mordecai's matters would *stand*." How has the Lord vindicated His servant now! Not only have his matters stood, but the despised man who acted for God—although that meant at the time to be misunderstood by almost every one else—is now waxing greater and greater. And so will it ever be that he who sides with God will be triumphant at last. It is not to be expected that natural men, or carnal Christians, will understand a man who takes this ground. "He that is spiritual discerneth all things; yet he himself is discerned of no man" (1 Cor. ii. 15—literal rendering). Such an one must ever be an enigma to men who reason from a human standpoint, and who have not the mind of Christ. But God will vindicate His servant in His own way and time, if all is humbly left in His hands. Of the greatest of all servants it is written that "when He was reviled,

He reviled not again; when He suffered, He threatened not; but committed Himself to Him that judgeth righteously" (1 Pet. ii. 23).    And how gloriously has He been vindicated and exalted! Blessed Lord, may we Thy servants walk in Thy path until we see Thy face!

"Thus the Jews smote all their enemies with the stroke of the sword, and slaughter, and destruction, and did what they would unto those that hated them.    And in Shushan the palace the Jews slew and destroyed five hundred men" (vers. 5, 6).    It was the overthrowing of the enemies—not of the Jews only, but of the Lord.    They impiously lifted their hands against the separated nation; and, however unfaithful they may have been, He made their troubles His own, and delivered their foes into their hands.

The Lord remembers, too, His word as to Amalek spoken in the wilderness so long ago: "I will utterly put out the remembrance of Amalek from under heaven."    Hence we read of the destruction of the last of the nation mentioned in Scripture. "And Parshandatha, and Dalphon, and Aspatha, and Poratha, and Adalia, and Aridatha, and Parmashta, and Arisai, and Aridai, and Vajezatha, the ten sons of Haman the son of Hammedatha, the enemy of the Jews, slew they; but *on the spoil laid they not their hand*" (vers. 7-10).    The last of this ungodly race have perished.    God's word, whether telling of grace or judgment, will be fulfilled to the letter.

As typifying the lusts of the flesh, what comfort there is for the Christian in the utter destruction of Amalek! The day is not far distant when the old nature that dwells in every believer, and is the cause of so much of our failure, and sins, and sorrow, will be completely removed; and with it all lust and pride: yea, everything that hinders spiritual enjoyment will be gone forever. This never occurs while we are in the body. The dream of the eradication of inbred sin, and of perfection in the flesh while in this life, is not founded on the word of God. As long as we are in this scene we have to "mortify" our members which are upon the earth; but at "the coming of our Lord Jesus Christ, and our gathering together unto Him," we shall be fully delivered from our hated foe: "for our conversation is in heaven; from whence also we look for the Saviour, the Lord Jesus Christ; who shall change our vile body" (or, transform the body of our humiliation), "that it may be fashioned like unto the body of His glory" (literal rendering); "according to the working whereby He is able to subdue all things unto Himself" (Phil. iii. 20, 21). Then will the remembrance of the fleshly lusts that war against the soul, and now trouble us, be blotted out from under heaven.

A striking evidence of subjection to God is brought before us at the end of the verses noted above: "upon the spoil they laid not their hand." The king had granted "the spoil of them for a prey." But long before, God had said, when sending Saul to smite the Amalekites, that he should "utterly destroy all that they had." They were to take no spoil that day. Saul disobeyed the word and brought down Divine judgment upon himself and his house (1 Sam. xv, throughout). The scattered Jews of Esther's time manifest greater faithfulness. They abhor the spoil and refrain from touching it. As it was an Amalekite that had stirred up the enmity of the people against them, they class all morally in the same category. It is an example of disinterested obedience beautiful to notice. They overcome the world but do not seek to profit through it nor derive benefit by indifference to that which they see to be evil.

The news of the slaughter in the city of Shushan is reported to the king at the close of the day. "And the king said unto Esther the queen, The Jews have slain and destroyed five hundred men in Shushan the palace, and the ten sons of Haman; what have they done in the rest of the king's provinces? Now what is thy petition? and it shall be granted thee: or what is thy request further? and it shall be done" (ver. 12).

It would seem from Esther's reply that the day had closed in the midst of the conflict. There were still a large number of persons who were evil disposed toward the Jews. "Then said Esther, If it please the king, let it be granted to the Jews which

are in Shushan to do to-morrow also according unto
this day's decree, and let Haman's ten sons be
hanged upon the gallows" (ver. 13). It must be
borne in mind that the decree simply granted the
Jews the privilege of self-defense. It is no indiscriminate massacre that Esther desires, but another
day of opportunity in which to meet their foes if
they sought to rise against them. She also desires
the ten sons of Haman to be hung up before the
people as accursed according to Deut. xxi, 22, 23.
"And the king commanded it so to be done: and
the decree was given at Shushan, and they hanged
Haman's ten sons" (ver. 14).

On the fourteenth day of the month therefore
the Jews again met any who had the hardihood
to oppose them, and "slew three hundred men at
Shushan," over half the number of the previous
day. Again we are told that "on the prey they
laid not their hands" (ver. 15). They would
not be enriched at the expense of the enemies of
the Lord.

Throughout the rest of the empire they had
been equally victorious. We read not of the death
of even so much as one; but they "slew of their
foes seventy and five thousand, but they laid not
their hands on the prey" (ver. 16). Truly their
sorrow had been turned into rejoicing. "Weeping
may endure for a night but joy cometh in the
morning."

In the outside districts and distant provinces
the fourteenth day was devoted to feasting and
gladness, while in the palace-city the day following was so observed. It was a season of thanksgiving and congratulations one to another: gifts
and portions being exchanged. From our record
of it though, as described in vers. 17-19, it would
be impossible to prove that they remembered the
Lord in it all, and gave the glory to Him. This,
however, is but in keeping with the character of
the book. There can be no question as to their
hearts going out in gratitude to the God of their
fathers who had so mercifully interfered on their
behalf; but in describing their joy, as in making
known their former sorrow, His name is unmentioned in the record, because they are not where He
can publicly own them. How loudly does this very
silence speak to every opened ear! God could do
all we have been noting in our study of this book
for His people who refused to gather to the place
where He has set His name (and where a few
"afflicted and poor" ones were trying amidst many
discouragements to rebuild His ruined temple and
to order their ways according as "they found it
written"), but though He so graciously watches
over them in His providence, and loves them unto
the end, He nevertheless takes care that the inspired
record of it all shall not so much as mention His
name.

## CHAPTER IX 20–32

### THE INSTITUTION OF PURIM

**F**ROM this time, until he disappears from sacred history, Mordecai takes the place of a judge or a deliverer among his brethren. He has proven himself a faithful man in the main, whatever failures he may also have had. In a certain sense his position is very similar to that occupied by Joseph in Egypt. In position being next to the king, he has been the preserver of his people and is afterwards their protector.

He would have them never forget the great deliverance they had known, nor the means whereby it had been accomplished. From the twentieth verse, it has generally been concluded that he himself was the author of this book, and surely no person would be more likely to have been chosen for this service. He also, in conjunction with Esther the queen, established the feast of Purim, or "the lot," as a perpetual commemoration of the overthrowing of Haman's device.

"And Mordecai wrote these things, and sent letters unto all the Jews that were in all the provinces of the king Ahasuerus, both nigh and far, to establish

this among them, that they should keep the fourteenth day of the month Adar, and the fifteenth
day of the same, yearly, as the days wherein the
Jews rested from their enemies and the month which
was turned unto them from sorrow to joy, and from
mourning into a good day: that they should make
them days of feasting and joy, and of sending
portions one to another, and gifts to the poor"
(vers. 20-22). There is no reason to believe that
this was a divinely instituted festival, like the seven
feasts of Jehovah in Lev. xxiii. It was simply
the grateful remembrance of a rejoicing people
for signal mercy vouchsafed at a time of deepest
distress. Naturally the Jews in the land did not
as readily observe it as those scattered among the
heathen. History tells us that it was some years
ere it became a universal season of festivity among
the Hebrews, and many more elapsed before a dis-
tinctively religious character was given to it.

But, as commanded by Mordecai and Esther, all
was in perfect keeping with the times. In full
accord with their Lo-ammi condition, God's name
is in no wise connected with it. It has kept, however,
the record of their providential deliverance clearly
before their minds. The exact reason for the name
of the feast is given in the verses that follow: "And
the Jews undertook to do as they had begun, and
as Mordecai had written unto them; because Haman
the son of Hammedatha, the Agagite, the enemy

of all the Jews, had devised against the Jews to destroy them, and had cast Pur, that is, the lot, to consume them; but when Esther came before the king, he commanded by letters, that his wicked device, which he had devised against the Jews, should return upon his own head, and that he and his sons should be hanged upon the gallows. Wherefore they called these days Purim, after the name of Pur. Therefore for all the words of this letter, and of that which they had seen concerning this matter, and which had come unto them, the Jews ordained, and took upon them, and upon their seed, and upon all such as joined themselves unto them, so as it should not fail, that they would keep these two days according to their writing, and according to their appointed time every year; and that these days should be remembered and kept throughout every generation, every family, every province and every city; and that these days of Purim should not fail from among the Jews, nor the memorial of them perish from their seed" (vers. 23-28).

How truly had they been made to know that "the lot is cast into the lap; but the whole disposing thereof is of the Lord" (Prov. xvi. 33). No device of the wicked against the people of the Lord can ever be carried out unless He see fit to permit it. Hence the Christian can exultingly cry, "If God be for us, who can be against us?" (Rom. viii.

31). But, though His care is over all His saints, it will always be observed that there is not that same direct, manifest interference on their behalf when not walking according to His revealed will, as when they take the place of absolute dependence on Himself in subjection to His Word. Thus also in Christendom generally, it is more this distant Providential oversight that is known.

In an indefinite way saints learn to look for divine interposition for evidence of the Lord's concern. But it is only as one walks with God and trembles at His word, manifesting real heart for Himself, that the special supervision and intimate Fatherly care of which Scripture speaks is entered into and enjoyed. This may be seen by turning for a little to that exceedingly striking passage in 2 Cor. vi. 14-18. Believers are here counseled to avoid putting their necks into an unequal yoke with those who believe not. This would refer to every concern of life; whether it be in regard to business, marriage, or ecclesiastical associations. No child of God can be linked up with an unconverted man in a business partnership without violating this Scripture. Neither could one enter into an engagement or marriage with an unsaved person and enjoy the approbation of the Lord. An old Puritan once wrote, "If you marry a child of the devil you can expect to have trouble with your father-in-law." Alas, that so many, despising the Word of truth and the bitter experiences of thousands before them, should, with open eyes, yet venture on such a course, because through their affections they have been ensnared! How many Samsons have been thus shorn of their strength! And how many Solomons have thus had their hearts turned away!

But there are many who see the nature of the business yoke and the family yoke, who seem quite unconcerned as to the ecclesiastical association with the world. "What agreement hath the *temple of God* with idols? For ye are the temple of the living God." Believers, and believers alone, comprise this spiritual house. "Know ye not that ye are the temple of God, and that the Spirit of God dwelleth in you?" (1 Cor. iii. 16). Of no unregenerate soul could this be said. Of those only who are born again and sealed with the Holy Spirit can it be true. It is therefore of the greatest importance that Christians refuse all association with worldlings in spiritual things. This is beautifully set forth in the books of Ezra and Nehemiah, where the faithful remnant, having come up from Babylon and Persia, are found not only separate from the nations, but, when gathered at the place where Jehovah's name had been set of old, they indignantly refuse the help of the uncircumcised in building the house of God or the walls of the city. For them, despite the fact that the Lo-Ammi sentence remained unrepealed, God could act in a more open and manifest way than when He interfered for the scattered ones of the provinces who separated not from the nations when they had the opportunity presented to them in the imperial decree. For this remnant, He raised up suited ministry. Haggai and Zechariah were able to give with no uncertainty "the Lord's message." When failure came in, they were in the place where all could be dealt with according to the Book; while teachers of the Law, like Ezra and the Levites, were given to them to instruct them in what was there written.

And so in the passage we have under consideration, God says to those who "come out from among them," and who "touch not the unclean thing," that He will receive them; and He adds, "I will be a Father *unto you,* and ye shall be My sons and daughters, saith the Lord Almighty." This is unspeakably precious. God is the Father of all who are born again. All such have life eternal—divine life, and can say by the Spirit, "Abba Father;" but though He is the Father *of* all, He is not able always to act as a Father *unto* all.

It is the obedient who know His gracious and special care spoken of in this sense. Leaving all else for Him, they find Him to be more than all else to them, even in regard to temporal matters.

"He knows, and loves, and cares ;
  Nothing this truth can dim:
He gives the very best to those
  Who leave the choice to Him."

Separated to Himself, dependent alone upon
His omnipotent power, they are given to see His
hand and to discern His actings in grace as others
cannot who "follow afar off," and fear to leave
all that is contrary to His mind, as revealed in
His Word.

How blessed is it, on the other hand, that even
where there is not this devotion to Himself that
should characterize those redeemed at such cost,
yet He never forgets His own, nor does He ever
neglect them.   But it is more in the manner of His
actings in the days of Esther that He watches over
and cares for them—often unseen and unacknowl-
edged.   "His mercy endureth forever," and He who
walked with His unbelieving people for forty years
in the wilderness never ceases to care for His
children now, however little they may realize it.
"Having loved His own which were in the world,
He loved them unto the end" (John xiii. 1).

The feast of Purim, then, witnesses the nation's
gratitude, however feebly it may set forth their
recognition that it was God Himself who had so
wondrously made their affliction the occasion for
His acting in grace.

"Then Esther the queen, the daughter of Abihail" (Father of strength), "and Mordecai the Jew, wrote with all authority to confirm this second letter of Purim. And he sent the letters unto all the Jews, to the hundred twenty and seven provinces of the kingdom of Ahasuerus, with *words of peace and truth,* to confirm these days of Purim in their times appointed, according as Mordecai the Jew and Esther the queen had enjoined them, and as they had decreed for themselves and for their seed the matters of the fastings and their cry" (vers. 29-31). It is not likely that the name of God was left unmentioned in the publications they thus put forth, for "words of peace and truth" clearly connected the humiliation of the people and their fasting, with the deliverance God gave them at the end. "Their cry" is also mentioned. To whom could it be but to God? Were this narration of it then written by mere man, how natural would it have been to have added the words "to God" or "to the Lord." But the pen of inspiration never errs. The One whose ways are perfect, is the real author of the book, whether Mordecai or some unknown one was the writer.

"And the decree of Esther confirmed these matters of Purim; and it was written in the book" (ver. 32). To the present day, and for ages past, it has been the custom of the Hebrews to read this book at the annual observance of the feast; and whenever the name of Haman is uttered, the orthodox Jews hiss, and stamp, and curse his memory.

In the days when our Lord was upon earth, the canon of Old Testament Scripture, as we now know it, had been long since completed, and was composed of "the law, the prophets, and the Psalms." Esther was always included in the latter division, called in the Greek version "the Hagiographa." Jesus spoke of all as Scripture. Therefore we cannot question the full inspiration of this book, as He set His seal upon it. And yet we shall look in vain to find any quotation from or reference to it in the New Testament. It is the unique evidence of God's unfailing care to a faithless people.

The feast of Purim is never referred to in the Gospels either. It did not properly belong to the people as in the land. While the yearly reminder of unchanging grace, it was also the evidence of their lack of heart for the One who had so acted towards them. At the present time it has degenerated into a season of godless merry-making, and is more patriotic than devotional in character.

# CHAPTER X

THE story of Satan's effort to destroy the nation of promise, together with the manner in which he was thwarted, having been so minutely told, there remains nothing more than to picture the changed conditions resultant upon the destruction of Haman and his house, and the advancement of Mordecai. The far-reaching rule of the Persian monarch is first shown in the statement that "the king Ahasuerus laid a tribute upon the land and upon the isles of the sea" (ver. 1). All nations had to know and own his power, as soon they shall own the sway of God's chosen King. How blessed the day when

> "Jesus shall reign where'er the sun
> Doth his successive journeys run:
> His kingdom spread from shore to shore,
> Till moons shall wax and wane no more."

"The powers that be are ordained of God;" but all are merely provisional during the present period of the true King's rejection. Soon shall this groaning scene be changed to one of unmingled joy and gladness for the delivered nations when there shall be revealed from heaven "a righteous ruler over men, a ruler in the fear of God!" This, Ahasuerus was not. Consequently his world-wide domination soon passed to other hands; but when God's Anointed reigns, His kingdom will never be superseded.

Let the reader not fall into a mistake very commonly made to-day. The Kingdom is not the Church. The latter is the body of Christ, composed of all who, in this dispensation, are called out from Jew and Gentile, and baptized in the power of the Holy Spirit. During the period in which God is doing this special work of His grace, the Kingdom, properly speaking, is in abeyance. It is true the principles of the Kingdom are spreading through the world, and all who are born again are, even now, in, and morally of it.

But for all that the reigning time has not yet come. It is still "the kingdom and patience of Jesus Christ." When the Lord returns from heaven He will descend "with a shout" into the upper air, accompanied by "the voice of the archangel and the trump of God." The Church will then be complete and her period of testimony and rejection on earth will be accomplished. Therefore "the dead in Christ shall rise first: then we which are alive and remain shall be caught up together with them in the clouds, to meet the Lord in the air: and so shall we be forever with the Lord" (1 Thess. iv. 16, 17; see also 1 Cor. xv. 51-56).

This will be the end of the Christian dispensation, but *not* the end of the world. There are other periods to follow. The first will be very brief, and is commonly referred to in Scripture as "the great tribulation," "the hour of trial," and "the time of Jacob's trouble." In this season (with which a great part of the Scripture is occupied, notably Matt. xxiv, and the bulk of the Revelation—chaps. iv-xix inclusive), the Jewish nation will once more be taken up by God. A remnant of them in their unprecedented tribulation will turn to His Word and will there see that, on account of their rejection of Messiah, they had been given up to partial blindness "until the fulness of the Gentiles be come in." That time having been reached at the rapture of the Church, God will then open their eyes to their great sin. They will acknowledge the Crucified as the Anointed of Jehovah, and will separate themselves from the ungodly mass to wait for His appearing as their deliverer. In the land of Palestine one will arise of whom Haman is a fit type—the personal Antichrist, referred to in Scripture under various titles, as "the king" of Dan. xi. 36, who "shall do according to his own will;" "the idol shepherd" of Zech. xi. 15-17; one who "shall come in his own name" in John v. 43; "the wicked" or "lawless one" of 2 Thess. ii, "whose coming is after the working of Satan with all power and signs and lying wonders;" and the two-horned beast of Rev. xiii, who has the appearance of a lamb, to simulate the Lamb of God, but is betrayed by his speech, which is that of a dragon. This fearful character will be the bitter persecutor of the faithful Jews for a short period, but as in the matter of Haman and Mordecai, when all seems darkest, the Lord shall appear for the destruction of the power of evil and the salvation of His people. Then follows the establishment of the kingdom which is never to be given to another, when for one thousand years the Lord Jesus shall reign over all the earth.

Whenever world-wide dominion has been entrusted to man, he has, as in all else, utterly failed. But when "He shall come whose right it is," He will judge the nations in righteousness and manifest Jehovah's perfect rule on earth. This is the Kingdom which is the burden of the Old Testament prophecies and which is frequently referred to in the New Testament. One passage from this latter portion we shall here quote. "Having made known unto us the mystery of His will, according to His good pleasure which He hath purposed in Himself: that in the *dispensation of the fulness of times* He might gather together (or head up) in one all things in Christ, both which are in heaven and which are on earth; even in Him" (Eph. i. 10, 11). When that long-waited-for dispensation arrives, "the knowledge of the Lord shall cover the earth as the waters cover the sea." The heavenly saints will then be associated with their Lord in government, while saints on earth will, with rejoicing, own His beneficent sway.

Misrule and oppression will have ceased forever. Earth's long wail will have changed to a song of unending praise to the Lamb once slain.* We cannot forbear referring the reader to one beautiful passage, this time from the Psalms, ere leaving this intensely interesting subject. We refer to Psalm lxxii, where Messiah's kingdom is described most vividly. After telling how "He shall come down like rain upon the mown grass," bringing refreshment and blessing to this poor parched world, we read that "He shall have dominion also from sea to sea, and from the river unto the ends of the earth. They that dwell in the wilderness shall bow before Him; and His enemies shall lick the dust. The kings of Tarshish and of the isles shall bring presents: the kings of Sheba and Seba shall offer gifts. Yea, all kings shall fall down

---

*The attentive reader who may desire further light on the Kingdom and connected themes will find great help in "Plain Papers on Prophetic Subjects," by W. Trotter. $1.50. At the same publishers.

before Him: all nations shall serve Him" (vers. 8-11). No wonder that at the conclusion of the recital of His glories the inspired singer writes, "The prayers of David the son of Jesse are ended"! All will be then as it should be; for the whole earth will be full of His glory.

The evanescent character of human greatness and the crumbling kingdoms of earth as contrasted with the "stone kingdom" yet to come are well brought out in the second verse of our chapter in Esther. "And all the acts of his power and of his might, and the declaration of the greatness of Mordecai, whereunto the king advanced him, are they not written in the book of the chronicles of the kings of Media and Persia?" These books are probably lost beyond recall. God has, however, preserved His own record of the events of those days. Were it not for this, we should never have known from secular history of Mordecai and of God's intervention for the preservation of His people in the land of their exile.

Ahasuerus' power was of the fading glory of this world. He is gone, and his records have perished. Mordecai had the interests of Jehovah at heart, despite the peculiar circumstances in which he was placed. His faithfulness will be remembered forever. "For Mordecai the Jew was next unto king Ahasuerus, and great among the Jews, and accepted of the multitude of his brethren, seeking the wealth of his people, and speaking peace to all his seed" (ver. 3). He appears as a thoroughly disinterested, unselfish person, who, though honored by the proud conqueror, never acts now as of old, when he counseled Esther against revealing her kindred; but is a guileless man, known to all as a Jew, and using his power for the blessing of the once jeopardized nation.

That from time to time, even where there is much that is contrary to the mind of God, He manifests His unbounded grace by giving to His people such deliverers is evident both in Scripture and in the dark and sorrowful annals of the Church on earth. Let no one conclude from this fact that it is a matter of small moment to Him if His saints go on with that which is contrary to His revealed Word. It is one thing to know a Father's love and care, even though walking in self-chosen paths; it is another thing, like Enoch, to walk with God and have the testimony that one is pleasing Him.

As an evidence of how feebly man enters into Divine design in Scripture, I would draw attention, ere closing, to the well-known fact that in the Septuagint version of the Old Testament, and found in English in the Apocrypha, there are a number of additions to the book of Esther which are commonly supposed to be the work of pious Egyptian Jews who were troubled by the omission of all reference to God, and therefore supplemented

the book with productions of their own, in which
the glory would all be given to Him. These inter-
polations are rightly rejected in our version, as
they never formed part of the Hebrew text, and
were written after the voice of prophecy had ceased,
in the days of Malachi. In one of these added
portions, Haman is referred to as a Macedonian
whose desire it was to turn the kingdom to his
people. This would be quite in keeping with the
times in which they were written. The Persian
empire was overthrown, as we know, by Alexander
the Great, whose Macedonian troops so readily
routed the luxurious Iranian armies.

Man cannot tamper with God's word save to
his ruin, and to the marring of that which is absolutely perfect in itself. "All Scripture is given by
inspiration of God (literally, God-breathed), and
is profitable for doctrine, for reproof, for correction,
for instruction in righteousness: that the man of
God may be perfect, thoroughly furnished unto all
good works" (2 Tim. iii. 16, 17).

May writer and reader seek, ever more and more,
to walk as men of God; thus finding in every
portion of Holy Writ divine furnishing for our
path through this scene.